THE BIBLE IN THE AGE OF EMPIRE

THE BIBLE IN THE AGE OF EMPIRE
A CULTURAL HISTORY

Edited by Scott McLaren

LONDON • NEW YORK • OXFORD • NEW DELHI • SYDNEY

T&T CLARK
Bloomsbury Publishing Plc, 50 Bedford Square, London, WC1B 3DP, UK
Bloomsbury Publishing Inc, 1359 Broadway, New York, NY 10018, USA
Bloomsbury Publishing Ireland, 29 Earlsfort Terrace, Dublin 2, D02 AY28, Ireland

BLOOMSBURY, T&T CLARK and the T&T Clark logo are trademarks of Bloomsbury Publishing Plc

First published in Great Britain 2024
Paperback edition published in 2026

Copyright © Scott McLaren and contributors, 2024

Scott McLaren has asserted his right under the Copyright, Designs and Patents Act, 1988, to be identified as editor of this work.

Cover design by Jade Barnett
Cover image: 'The Secret of England's Greatness' by Thomas Jones Barker © Art Collection 2 / Alamy

All rights reserved. No part of this publication may be: i) reproduced or transmitted in any form, electronic or mechanical, including photocopying, recording or by means of any information storage or retrieval system without prior permission in writing from the publishers; or ii) used or reproduced in any way for the training, development or operation of artificial intelligence (AI) technologies, including generative AI technologies. The rights holders expressly reserve this publication from the text and data mining exception as per Article 4(3) of the Digital Single Market Directive (EU) 2019/790.

Bloomsbury Publishing Plc does not have any control over, or responsibility for, any third-party websites referred to or in this book. All internet addresses given in this book were correct at the time of going to press. The author and publisher regret any inconvenience caused if addresses have changed or sites have ceased to exist, but can accept no responsibility for any such changes.

A catalogue record for this book is available from the British Library.

Library of Congress Cataloging-in-Publication Data

Names: McLaren, Scott, 1970- editor.
Title: The Bible in the age of empire: a cultural history / editor, Scott McLaren.
Description: London; New York: Bloomsbury Publishing PLC, 2024. | Includes bibliographical references and index.
Identifiers: LCCN 2023030498 | ISBN 9781350087682 (hardback) | ISBN 9781350438545 (paperback) | ISBN 9780567714367 (pdf) | ISBN 9780567714374 (epub)
Subjects: LCSH: Bible–Criticism, interpretation, etc.–History–20th century. | Bible–Criticism, interpretation, etc.–History–21st century. | Christianity and culture.
Classification: LCC BS511.3 .B526 2024 | DDC 220.609/034–dc23/eng/20230906
LC record available at https://lccn.loc.gov/2023030498

ISBN: HB: 978-1-3500-8768-2
PB: 978-1-3504-3854-5
ePDF: 978-0-5677-1436-7
eBook: 978-0-5677-1437-4

Typeset by Deanta Global Publishing Services, Chennai, India

For product safety related questions contact productsafety@bloomsbury.com.

To find out more about our authors and books visit www.bloomsbury.com and sign up for our newsletters.

CONTENTS

LIST OF FIGURES		vi
Introduction *Scott McLaren, York University, Canada*		1
1	Theology and Interpretation *Joshua Bennett, Lincoln College, Oxford University, UK*	5
2	History and Politics *Todd Webb, Laurentian University, Canada*	23
3	Literature *Jessica Ann Hughes, George Fox University, United States*	43
4	Visual Culture *Sarah C. Schaefer, University of Wisconsin-Milwaukee, United States*	63
5	Faiths, Confessions and Denominations *Lydia Willsky-Ciollo, Fairfield University, United States*	91
6	Science *Matthew J. Kaufman, Congregation Kehillat Israel, United States*	109
7	Women, Gender and Sexuality *Amanda Paxton, Trent University, Canada*	129
8	Popular Culture *Scott McLaren, York University, Canada*	147
INDEX		167

FIGURES

3.1	*Christ in the House of His Parents*, by John Everett Millais, 1829–96	48
3.2	*Cleansing the Temple* by Doré, Gustave, 1883	50
3.3	*Jesus Teaches the People by the Sea*, by James Tissot, 1886–96	51
3.4	*Uhde Das Tischgebet anagoria*, by Fritz von Uhde, 1885	55
3.5	*The Last Supper*, by Nikolai Ge, 1863	56
3.6	Ivan Kramskoi *Christ in the Desert*, by Ivan Kramskoi 1872	56
3.7	*The Light of the World*, by William Holman Hunt, c. 1851–3	59
4.1	*Still Life with Bible*, by Vincent van Gogh, 1885	64
4.2	*Destruction of the Beast and the False Prophet*, by Benjamin West, 1804	66
4.3	*Job's Evil Dreams*, by William Blake, 1825	67
4.4	*The Fifth Plague of Egypt*, by Joseph Mallord William Turner, 1800	68
4.5	*The Dream of Eve*, by Henry Fuseli, 1804	70
4.6	*Entry of Christ in Jerusalem*, by Hippolyte Flandrin, 1843–6	71
4.7	*Shalumit and Mary*, by Franz Pforr, 1811	72
4.8	*The Pool of Bathesda* from *The Holy Land, Syria, Idumea, Arabia, Egypt and Nubia: From drawings made on the spot*, by David Roberts, 1842–9	74
4.9	*Jerusalem, Tomb of the Judges*, by Auguste Salzmann, 1854	75
4.10	*Moses Breaking the Tablets of the Law*, by Gustave Doré and Laurent Hotelin, 1865	77
4.11	*Moses Breaks the Commandment Tablets*, by Julius Schnorr von Carolsfeld, 1860	78
4.12	*The Crucifixion*, by Godefroy Durand, 1870, from Ernest Renan's *Vie de Jésus*	80
4.13	*What Our Lord Saw from the Cross*, by James Tissot, 1886–94	81
4.14	*A Chronological Chart of the Visions of Daniel and John*, 1843	83
4.15	*Vision of the Sermon (Jacob Wrestling the Angel)*, by Paul Gauguin, 1888	85
4.16	*Angels and Airplanes*, by Natalia Goncharova, 1914	87
4.17	*The Day of the Last Judgement*, by Vassily Kandinsky, 1912	88
6.1	*Duria Antiquior*, by Henry De la Beche, 1830	111
6.2	Memorial to Francis Henry Egerton	114
6.3	*On the Origin of Species by Means of Natural Selection*, by Charles Darwin	115
6.4	*A Venerable Orang-outang*, a caricature of Charles Darwin from *The Hornet* (1871)	118
6.5	Caricature of Charles Darwin from the *London Sketch-Book* (1874)	121
6.6	*Preadamites*, by Alexander Winchell	124
8.1	Jerusalem Exhibit, St. Louis World's Fair, 1904	149
8.2	Mother and Children Reading the Bible, Library of Congress, 1877	160
8.3	The Thomas Cook office in Jerusalem, c. 1890	162
8.4	*The Ten Commandments*, DeMille, 1923	164

Introduction

SCOTT McLAREN

In 1863, Thomas Jones Barker completed a remarkable painting of Queen Victoria, regally attired, handing an ornately bound Bible to a kneeling and anonymous African prince who, with outstretched arms, appears to reach up with gratitude towards the book. The Queen is attended by the most powerful people in the realm: Prince Albert, the husband she adored; Lord Palmerston, the prime minister; Lord John Russell, the foreign secretary; and, in the shadows and perhaps to balance the painting's composition with a second female figure, Elizabeth Hay, the Duchess of Wellington. There is a story behind this painting. Apparently, at least according to several Victorian periodicals, a mysterious ruler visiting from Africa was so astonished at the wealth and power of the British metropole that he fell to his knees in the Queen's presence and begged her to reveal to him the secret of England's greatness. Her response was to wordlessly hand him a Bible. Although the story is probably apocryphal, both the narrative and the painting succeed in conveying a clear message: 'The Secret of England's Greatness', as the painting was of course titled by Barker, is, and can only be, its unwavering commitment to the Bible. It is a commitment that one must make in an attitude of submission: note that while Victoria stands, the African figure kneels with his back bent, suggesting not only deference and submission to the Queen and her Empire but also to the Bible as a uniquely sacred text. Similarly, the prince's outstretched arms denote a pliant and eager willingness to embrace Christian values and teachings – a central aim in the wider Victorian project to 'civilize' the inhabitants of their colonial possessions (Procter 2020).

After it was completed, the painting went on tour throughout the British Isles. It carried an important lesson for all those who gazed upon it about just how the Empire domesticated its foreign subjects under the joint power of both monarchical and biblical authority (Munich 1996: 147). The painting was also self-congratulatory. In the middle decades of the nineteenth century, the British Empire was undergoing a major economic and social transformation as it shifted from being a willing participant in the transatlantic slave trade to becoming a global force in the fight against slavery. The British government had abolished the transatlantic slave trade in 1807 and subsequently passed the Slavery Abolition Act in 1833, which led to the eventual emancipation of enslaved people, or at least the children of enslaved people, throughout the British Empire. By the 1860s, the British Empire was actively involved in suppressing the slave trade as the Royal Navy's West Africa Squadron patrolled the Atlantic on a mission to intercept slave ships and enforce a ban on international slave trading. The British government also engaged in more polite diplomatic efforts to persuade other nations to abolish the slave trade. For those inclined to celebrate this tidy confluence of imperial and religious agendas in the wider promotion and even enforcement of abolitionist Christian values, Victoria's reign must have seemed a time of almost unlimited promise.

Undoubtedly, the nineteenth century was an era of tremendous innovation and change. Rapid advancements in technology, transportation and communication reshaped the world in profound ways, transforming whole societies and economies. The Industrial Revolution, which had begun in the late eighteenth century, reached new heights during the nineteenth, as mechanized production methods revolutionized industries, such as textile manufacturing, mining and agriculture. Steam engines, railways and the telegraph expanded connectivity and facilitated the exchange of goods, ideas and people across vast distances. And yet, while the Industrial Revolution brought about significant economic growth and improved standards of living for many, for members of the lower classes, rapid urbanization led to overcrowded cities with inadequate sanitation and housing conditions that gave rise to public health crises and widespread poverty. The exploitation of workers, including women and children, in factories demanding long hours, paying low wages and plagued by dangerous working conditions, became a pressing social issue. The environmental impact of increased industrial production and the use of fossil fuels also resulted in pollution, deforestation and other ecological problems. As conditions improved for some and worsened for others, Christian organizations like the British and Foreign Bible Society (BFBS) saw both a pressing need and a new opportunity to produce and distribute copies of the Bible on an unprecedented scale.

But not everyone believed that the Bible was the secret to England's greatness. Indeed, even though a wider reading audience than ever before found themselves suddenly with access to the Bible as a result of the steam press, stereotyping and philanthropic organizations like the BFBS, the Bible also witnessed an unprecedented rush of new challenges to its authority. The growing acceptance of higher criticism, at least in some circles, had a profound impact on the study and interpretation of the Bible. Higher criticism, also known as the historical-critical method, sought to understand the historical context, authorship and formation of biblical texts by analyzing their literary and historical features. Many saw this as nothing short of a brazen and daylight attack on the Bible's authority, arguing that the approach inevitably subverted orthodox beliefs about the divine inspiration, infallibility and inerrancy of Sacred Scripture. Theological debate and controversy raged within and without religious communities. As if this were not enough, Charles Darwin's work *On the Origin of Species*, published in 1859, presented a devastating challenge to the authority of the Bible on scientific grounds. Darwin's theory of evolution through natural selection provided a compelling explanation for the development and diversification of life on earth – all without reference to or respect for the biblical account of creation as described in the book of Genesis. While some Christians sought to reconcile their faith with Darwin's work by emphasizing a reading of the biblical creation account that was metaphorical or allegorical in nature, others insisted on defending a literal reading of the biblical narrative and vociferously rejected the theory of evolution out of hand.

And yet, despite the significant challenges the Bible faced on all these fronts, it would be hard to argue that the pervasive influence it exercised over literature, art, music, politics and even popular culture was much diminished as a result. The Bible continued to serve as a rich source of inspiration for artists, writers and composers who drew upon its themes, reinterpreted its narratives and reimagined its archetypes for their own creative ends. However contested its status as a historical record of human origins might be, the Bible remained a powerful and seemingly inexhaustible source for both mythmaking and moralizing. Examples abound, from the tropes of exile and redemption in Charlotte Bronte's *Jane Eyre*, to the themes of sacrifice and resurrection that pervade

Charles Dickens's *A Tale of Two Cities*. Similarly, John Everett Millais's painting *Christ in the House of His Parents*, though obviously inspired by the Bible, recreates a scene in Joseph's workshop that brilliantly foregrounds themes of suffering and sacrifice. Millais depicts a young Christ cradling his injured hand while both Mary and Joseph attempt to comfort him (Figure 3.1). In addition to foreshadowing the Crucifixion, the scene also invites the viewer to reflect on the universality of pain and compassion as elements central to human life. Despite the shifting intellectual landscape and the challenges posed by scientific discoveries and critical scholarship, then, the Bible's stubborn durability served as a testament not only to its own adaptability but also to the determination many Victorians evinced in finding new ways to ensure its continued relevance. Indeed, how else could the Bible have remained a perennial source of contested inspiration for the century's social reform movements, political leaders and cultural figures? The chapters in this book explore all these arenas of human endeavour – and more.

Perhaps the most significant constant or thread that runs through all these chapters is that the Bible – despite being a printed book that was regarded as sacred, inviolable, canonical and therefore forever fixed – was not a static object. In addition to being a sacred text, the Bible also served as a kind of arena in which Victorians contested ideas and reshaped their beliefs. Thus, though it would be difficult to exaggerate the degree to which the Bible affected and impinged upon every area of Victorian culture and life, it must not be forgotten that the Bible itself was also shaped by Victorian culture. The meanings it conveyed were dependent not only on the printed text but also on how that text was presented, framed, illustrated, distributed and commodified. The identities of the people reading it mattered. The circumstances under which it was read mattered, and so too did the purpose for which it was being read. Indeed, although the Bible played a significant role in various social movements in the nineteenth century, including abolition, women's rights and labor rights, its teachings were routinely cited both in support of and in opposition to these causes. For example, activists like Elizabeth Cady Stanton and Susan B. Anthony argued that the Bible's overarching message of love and equality provided a foundation for gender equality, while critics pointed to passages like 1 Tim. 2.12, which states, 'But I suffer not a woman to teach, nor to usurp authority over the man, but to be in silence', as evidence for a divinely ordained hierarchy between the sexes (Ginzberg 2010). Similarly, advocates of labor rights pointed to passages such as Lev. 19.13, which commands, 'Thou shalt not defraud thy neighbour, neither rob him: the wages of him that is hired shall not abide with thee all night until the morning', as biblical support for fair wages and treatment of workers. Conversely, critics of labor reform argued that the Bible upheld the authority of employers and the importance of maintaining social order, citing passages such as Rom. 13.1-2, which reads, 'Let every soul be subject to the higher powers. For there is no power but of God: the powers that be are ordained of God. Whosoever therefore resisteth the power, resisteth the ordinance of God: and they that resist shall receive to themselves damnation'. Thus any attempt to challenge the existing social order, including advocating for workers' rights, was tantamount to defying God's will.

In a way, this ambiguity takes us back to Thomas Jones Barker's painting, *The Secret of England's Success*. We have already seen how the painting could be read differently by those who brought to it different subjectivities and different agendas. Similarly, the titanic efforts of the BFBS to distribute bibles around the globe have often been interpreted as a powerful example of cultural imperialism because the Bible itself contributed to the erosion of the values and beliefs of indigenous peoples. Indeed, the distribution of the

Bible was often closely linked to the broader project of colonial expansion since the spread of Christianity was used to justify and legitimize the colonization of foreign lands. And yet, as recent scholars have argued, the Bible could also act as a powerful anti-colonial force, subverting the colonial project by furnishing indigenous populations with a means for communicating with one another in written form in their own languages (Howsam and McLaren 2015). Indigenous communities, in their struggle against colonialism, also reinterpreted biblical narratives in such a way as to foreground messages of resistance and hope that reflected their own experiences. By doing so, they were able to reclaim the Bible from the colonizers and refashion it to suit their own ends. Thus, despite its longstanding association with colonialism, the Bible also holds a significant place in the history of anti-colonialist movements and the struggles of indigenous peoples.

As the world urgently grapples with some of these same issues today, the stubborn elusiveness of the Bible in the nineteenth century might strike some as unsatisfying or even dishonest. But the Bible has always been an elusive text, particularly in times of great social and economic change. Is it any wonder that in the Victorian period – a period that experienced an unprecedented and bewildering tumult of technological, cultural, religious and political change – the Bible's elusiveness only intensified? New readers, of whom there were many in the nineteenth century, inevitably meant new interpretative approaches, new emphases and new applications. Far from being unsatisfying, this is the very thing that makes a book about the Bible in Victorian culture – this book – worth reading.

REFERENCES

Ginzberg, L. (2010), *Elizabeth Cady Stanton: An American Life*, New York: Farrar, Straus, and Giroux.

Howsam, L. and S. McLaren (2015), 'Producing the Text: Production and Distribution of Popular Editions of the Bible', in *New Cambridge History of the Bible: Modernity, Colonialism, and Their Successors*, Vol. IV, ed. John Riches, 49–82, Cambridge: Cambridge University Press, 2015.

Munich, A. (1996), *Queen Victoria's Secret*, New York: Columbia University Press.

Procter, A. (2020), *The Whole Picture: The Colonial Story of the Art in Our Museums & Why We Need to Talk About it*, London: Cassell.

CHAPTER 1

Theology and Interpretation

JOSHUA BENNETT

INTRODUCTION

The Bible declares, and its Christian readers have always believed, that history has a divine beginning, salvific purpose and ultimate end. The interpretation of the Bible and the attempt to derive theologies from it have therefore always possessed a historical dimension. The first shoots of something approximating to biblical 'criticism' in the period of the Renaissance, moreover, meant that, by 1820, attempts had already been made for upwards of three centuries to establish the authentic text of Scripture; to determine the biblical chronology; and to account for apparent disparities between the state of the churches and religion as Scripture presented it (Cameron 2016). Before the age of historicism began in earnest, therefore, Western critics had long known that the biblical history was a complex subject, in which it could be difficult to disentangle the respective provinces of divine and human agency. The period from 1820 to 1920 nevertheless stands out in the history of biblical interpretation for the way in which newly differentiated and developmental understandings of history came to possess intellectual primacy, and argumentative intensity, among students of the biblical text. The history of interpretation in the century can thus be written as the story of the encounter between the Bible and the historical consciousness. This chapter, accordingly, considers the emergence and history of successive attempts, written from different starting points, to situate the Bible in relation to wider conceptions of historical development. It concludes with an examination of the critical and cultural forces which tended to prise understandings of biblical faith and historical evolution apart once again in the early years of the twentieth century.

The story of the role of historicism in transforming the biblical understanding is not a new one. Hans Frei, in his brilliant 1973 study, *The Eclipse of Biblical Narrative*, offered a highly influential statement of the classical and still standard view that, from the eighteenth to the nineteenth centuries, interpretation more and more became 'a matter of fitting the biblical story into another world with another story rather than incorporating that world into the biblical story' (Frei 1973: 130). While this statement contains a large grain of truth, this chapter proposes an alternative reading of the case. Frei's account, written from within the discipline of theology, privileged a tradition of critical exegesis transplanted from English deism to German universities. A cultural history of interpretation must recognize, however, that the nineteenth-century influence of religious revival ensured that, for a greater number of contemporaries, the 'biblical story' remained the paramount mode of understanding history, even if what that story was understood to involve underwent considerable modification. At the same time as advanced-biblical criticism issued profound shocks to contemporary religious culture, more conservative understandings of the Bible themselves showed a striking degree of cultural dynamism.

Both impetuses drew energy from the prevailing historicist atmosphere. The chapter considers interrelated liberal and conservative trajectories in, first, the historicizing of the Bible itself; and, second, in the interpretation of the Bible as a model, or symbol, for the historical process as a whole. Within the history of exegesis in the narrower sense, upon which Frei focused and where his case has the greatest purchase, the study of the Bible led the text increasingly to be treated as a phenomenon within, rather than outside, the history of the ancient world. This could lead the Bible to be regarded as a local or transient by-product of the ancient Levant; but – especially owing to the growth of what today would be regarded as uncritical ideas of biblical geography and archaeology – it was not always so. The rise of historicism also intersected with the age's insatiable appetite for biblical study in a second, much more unremarked way. This was the tendency for biblical interpretation to become the key to understanding historical development as a whole. At the same time as advanced intellectuals sought to marginalize the biblical narrative, or to make it a proxy for an exclusively human history, religious thinkers tried inventively to rescue the primacy of biblical faith for the interpretation of history more generally. Radically Idealist interpretations of the Bible, which made it a central stage in the outworking of the universal human spirit, competed for attention with prophetic and Johannine ideas of history, which insisted that human history should still be contained and understood within schemes derived from the biblical revelation. Thus the Bible offered innovative theologies of history to nineteenth-century theologians, precisely at the same time as its authority became superseded in other quarters. The radical and more conservative approaches to biblical interpretation, as they developed in the high nineteenth century, thus mirrored one another, in the sense that they both sought to tie the Bible into different kinds of world-historical synthesis. The crumbling of such attempts to unify faith and history in the years around 1900, partly owing to developments in biblical study itself, became part of the wider fading of far-reaching syntheses, and the crisis of historicism, which marked the age. The biblical narrative did not so much experience a nineteenth-century eclipse, as collide with the nineteenth century's swirling historicist atmosphere. The varied hues of the resulting aurora spread widely, before dwindling as the conditions which had once given rise to them passed away.

THE BIBLE AND REVIVAL

The evangelical revival that coursed through and transformed the world's rapidly expanding Protestant denominations prided itself on its rediscovery and elevation of the Bible as the rule of faith. 'Let us never forget in all our studies, that there is but one book of supreme, and paramount, and incalculable value – the WORD OF GOD – A book to be constantly studied by all ranks and by all classes', the evangelical Anglican leader, Edward Bickersteth, advised Christian students in an internationally popular advice manual of 1827 (Bickersteth 1829: 57–8). Such absolute views of biblical authority involved a correspondingly stringent view of scriptural inspiration. Nineteenth-century evangelicals inherited and usually reiterated the belief in the verbal inerrancy of Scripture which had solidified among orthodox Protestants during the post-Reformation period. Anglophone evangelicals often admired the Geneva theologian Louis Gaussen's insistence that every word of the biblical text was inspired, including in its minutest historical details, as expounded in his 1841 treatise, *Theopneustia*. He understood this Pauline term to denote God's dictation of an inerrant text, through the apostles, which was thus blessed with plenary inspiration (Gaussen 1841: 311). Commentators who argued in this way typically adopted a highly dualistic view of the relationship between biblical revelation and the human reason that required its instruction. Divine revelation was 'not only possible and probable, but NECESSARY', because of 'the utter inability of mere human reason to attain any certain knowledge of the will or law of God, of the true happiness of man, or of a future state', argued Thomas Hartwell Horne, a London-based Methodist and later Anglican biblical commentator, in his 1827 *Compendious Introduction to the Study of the Bible* (Horne 1827: 2).

A relatively ahistorical mode of interpreting Scripture followed from these positions. Because evangelicals regarded each part of the Bible as equally true, and as having arisen from miraculous divine intervention rather than through the cooperation of reasonable human agency, evangelicals approached the text as the source of a unitary body of teachings. These could be abstracted by means of proof texts. The American Presbyterian leader, Lyman Beecher, argued in a sermon of 1817 that Scripture's 'system of Divine Laws' consisted essentially of 'the doctrines of the Trinity and the atonement, the entire unholiness of the human heart, the necessity of a moral change by the special agency of the Holy Spirit' (Beecher 1828: 160). The Bible was an epistemic unity to be quarried for vindications of these doctrines, rather than an evolving historical life which presented a salvation-historical narrative within which the present-day believer could situate himself. Horne's *Introduction* took the form of a series of theses, counter-arguments, and replies to counter-arguments, with proof texts from across Scripture deployed in support of his exegetical positions.

The proof-text method of scriptural interpretation particularly assumed the integrated meaning and authority of the Old and New Testaments, where later liberals, attached to developmental ideas of history, tended more and more to separate out and demote the old dispensation. On such readings, the Old Testament, though its law had been superseded by that of the New, everywhere prefigured Christ's completion of God's purposes. The preeminent biblical commentators in earlier-nineteenth-century German Pietist circles, Heinrich and Wilhelm Richter, defended the Old Testament historical books as the record of God's covenanted transactions with Israel in the face of enlightened disparagement. They interpreted its prophecies as clearly anticipating Trinitarian Christology, more than as expressing the particular concerns and aspirations of the ancient Jews (Richter and Richter 1834–40: II, 1–3; IV, 38). More Catholic manifestations of the revival also shared aspects of this approach. Edward Bouverie Pusey, Oxford University's Regius Professor of Hebrew from 1828 to 1882 and a leader of the Catholicizing 'high church' Oxford Movement within the Church of England, emphasized the unity and inerrancy of Scripture. It was fatal to Christianity, he argued, to deny that the Hebrew prophets foresaw, in a detailed and miraculous way, Christ's 'Birth of a Virgin, Birthplace, Character, Offices, Life, Death, Divinity, Atonement, Sufferings, rejection by His own, acceptance by us Gentiles, Glory', and everlasting reign (Pusey 1864: 246–7).

A distinctively evangelical manifestation of this commitment to the dual authority of the Old and New Testaments lay in evangelicals' newly enthusiastic rediscovery of scriptural prophecy as the key to world history. Eighteenth-century writers had tended to adopt a postmillennialist conception of prophecy, which posited that Christ would return at the end of the age of the world's conversion to the gospel which contemporaries believed to be unfolding around them. After the French Revolution, at which a vast historical rupture appeared to have ushered in a tide of unbelief, revival mixed headily with a growing and more general Romantic appetite for vivid historical narrative and learning the secrets of human origins and destiny. This made a different mode of prophetic interpretation, historicist premillennialism, fashionable in evangelical circles between approximately 1820 and 1860. This school of thought, especially prominent among Anglicans and Presbyterians, posited that Christ's return was imminent, following the completion of a timetable of events recorded in Scripture. This chronology was intelligible according to various applications of the 'year-day' theory, an idea with a lineage stretching back to the Middle Ages, which assumed that a day mentioned in prophetic passages referred to a year of secular time (Spence 2015: 48). Edward Bishop Elliott, a former fellow of Trinity College, Cambridge, powerfully influenced contemporary evangelical Anglican opinion with his 1844 *Horae Apocalypticae*, a four-volume treatise which projected Old and New Testament prophecy, in a concretely detailed way, onto the later sequence of history. Elliott applied the year-day theory with the aid of modern and sometimes surprisingly infidel historians, such as Edward Gibbon (Elliott 1847). Premillennialists' attempts to use biblical history as the inerrant guide to subsequent world history, not just in principle but in application to specifiable temporal events and processes, were influential conservative expressions of the wider appetite to synthesize biblical ideas with increasingly complex understandings of historical movement more generally. More liberal minds were beginning to find more immanent and self-consciously reasonable ways in which to effect the same integration.

THE GERMAN EPICENTRE

Exegetes who thought in dualistic and literalist ways about Scripture found it ever more difficult to ignore the critical advances and philosophical revolutions in biblical study which had started to emanate from the universities of Protestant Germany during the Enlightenment. Anglo-American biblical scholars of the earlier nineteenth century, writing either alongside their practical work as ministers or in seminaries and ancient universities, were not the credulous bumpkins of liberal caricature. In accordance with their strong emphasis on the dangers of the unaided intellect, they nevertheless tended to regard their intellectual or academic labor as representing a kind of custody for a sacred tradition. In the later eighteenth and earlier part of the nineteenth century, German universities developed a wholly different and, in the end, globally normative model for higher learning. It idealized individual originality, published research and transformative discovery in place of the multifariously erudite or safely orthodox standards of the early modern period (Clark 2006). In biblical as well as in other fields of inquiry, Germany became the intellectual workshop of the world. Theology faculties justified their place in Germany's post-Napoleonic and state-supported universities by defining themselves as belonging, quite as much as other disciplines, to post-Kantian *Wissenschaft*'s pursuit of unified knowledge through criticism (Howard 2006). The new ethic often (though not always) induced scholars to approach the Bible less as the rule of faith, than as a network of labyrinths through which the scholar navigated his way for the sake of his vocation and its concomitant plaudits in the public arena. Scholarly apprenticeships and intense learning bore fruit in arresting displays of critical deconstruction and synthetic reconstruction, upon which promotion, even celebrity, depended.

Post-Kantian reason thus penetrated into biblical interpretation, in ways that fundamentally reshaped the conceptualization of biblical time and its relationship to human development. German theology tended to divide itself into systematic or dogmatic theology; biblical exegesis; practical theology; and church history; but *Wissenschaft*'s holism encouraged each to inform the rest, and to draw upon the developing permutations of Idealist philosophy. Under the impact of Kantian philosophy at the end of the eighteenth century, which encouraged critics to reflect on the difference and the distance between the knowing subject and the object of knowledge, Enlightenment-era 'neology', or the application of reason and historical criticism to the biblical record, had splintered into a series of more self-consciously differentiated analytical positions. 'Rationalists' tended to regard the New Testament as a republication of natural reason, and excluded supernatural agency from it. 'Supernaturalists', on the other hand, argued from the inherent limitation of human reason to the necessity, and admissibility, of just such a revelation (Stephan and Schmidt 1973: [11]–81). Both schools of thought lingered long into the first half of the nineteenth century, but were overtaken, however, by the development of post-Kantian idealism (Rasmussen et al. 2017). Friedrich Schleiermacher, a leading light of the foundation of the pioneering theology faculty at the University of Berlin in 1810, started from Kant's demolition of speculative metaphysics, and the grounding of religious truth within the knowing subject's practical reason, to reconstruct theology on the basis of consciousness and feeling. Georg Wilhelm Friedrich Hegel, building on Friedrich Wilhelm Joseph Schelling's turn to developing history as the space within which subject and object might be reintegrated, conceptualized history as the process by which absolute spirit manifested itself in human consciousness through the rational dialectic of negation, preservation and supersession. These philosophical dynamics soon inflected and often transformed biblical interpretation.

It was some years, nevertheless, before Idealist philosophy began to work its way into the presuppositions which underlay the varieties of biblical criticism which, germinating during the Renaissance and maturing during the Enlightenment, continued to develop amid the thickening historical atmosphere of the earlier part of the nineteenth century. Philology constituted an especially fertile source of biblical criticism. Its first major effects arose within the Old Testament study. Drawing on the antecedent development of comparative philology, Wilhelm Gesenius, a professor in Halle's theology faculty from 1810, compared Hebrew with other Semitic languages to argue that Hebrew's written form could not have arisen earlier than the time of David and Solomon, and that the language had continued to develop over the period of the Old Testament's composition (Schorch and Waschke 2013). The idea that the Old Testament was a developing text, shaped by processes of linguistic change and priestly redaction, challenged static conceptions of biblical revelation. But a distinctive area of philological interest, myth, proved to be much more inherently subversive. Originating in eighteenth-century classical scholarship, where myth had come to be treated as the mode of expression particular to the childhood of the race, Wilhelm Martin Leberecht de Wette, successively professor at Heidelberg, Berlin and Basel, from 1807 until his death in 1849, effected the radical importation of mythological analysis into the study of the Old Testament (Hartlich and Sachs 1952). De Wette argued that the Pentateuch could not have been written by Moses, but that it in fact reflected the religious conditions of centuries later, when the Israelites returned from Babylonian captivity. It should therefore be read, not as a record of historical transactions, but as philosophical mythology through which the Jews sought to make sense of their condition at the time of writing. It was, in this sense, 'the epic of the Hebrew theocracy' (de Wette 1806–7: II, 31). For all his radicalism, de Wette believed that his work served a fundamentally constructive religious purpose. A colleague of Schleiermacher at Berlin, and an admirer of the post-Kantian philosopher, Jakob Friedrich Fries, de Wette supposed that religion did not rely on a record of historic events, but on the intuition of eternal truths symbolized in myth and poetry. Myth did not belong to the childhood of the race, which it was the duty of Enlightenment to educate into full reason but rather to the eternal conditions of human sensibility (Rogerson 1984: 38–9).

It is striking that the pioneers of philological and mythological criticism of the sacred volume first broke their ground in the sphere of the Old, rather than the New Testament. The Old Testament was a text which liberal Protestant writers could, and increasingly did, relegate to a remote, oriental past. While this critical process distanced it from traditionally Christian appropriations of its meaning, it still offered safer ground for performative criticism to state-remunerated scholars than the founding documents of the Christian religion itself. The theologian who first applied radical mythical theory to the New Testament, and paid the price for his political incorrectness, was David Friedrich Strauss. A scholar at the Protestant Tübingen Stift, who had heard Hegel's lectures at Berlin in 1831 shortly before the sage's death, Strauss published a two-volume *Leben Jesu* between 1835 and 1836.

Strauss's *Leben Jesu* sought simultaneously to apply de Wette's mythical theory to explain the New Testament, and to use speculative philosophy to determine where such a critical process left Christian belief. Strauss argued that the gospel narratives reflected Jewish messianic expectations. History disclosed enough of Jesus to permit critical posterity to know that he understood himself to be the promised Messiah, proclaiming the imminent arrival of a millennial age of justice and righteousness, but his death marked the failure of his mission. Old Testament predictions, nevertheless, soon overlaid his followers' memory of a great man, and acquired a dogmatic life of their own as the church grew. The narrators of his life, in a mythopoeic process, attributed to Jesus the miraculous powers appropriate to the Savior of Israel (Strauss 1835–6). Having taken away, as he frankly stated, 'everything which the Christian believes about his Jesus', at the conclusion of his work Strauss set out to 're-establish dogmatically that which criticism has destroyed' (Strauss 1835–6: II, 686). Strauss argued, in Hegelian terms, that his own dissipation of the *Vorstellungen*, or representations, denoted by the myths attached to Christ, must be succeeded by purer apprehension of the *Begriff*, or concept, of Christology. The conceptual truth underlying the mythic representations, Strauss concluded, was that the idea of the God-man, which the church laid on Jesus as an individual, was growing in the consciousness of the race as a whole. Thus the infinite idea was incrementally realizing itself in the finite; God was becoming man (Strauss 1835–6: II, 729–44; Hodgson 2015). This process would become complete in no one individual but in the common life of humanity.

Strauss's emphatic rejection of historical Christianity, and the republican tendency to which it seemed to be allied, saw him removed from his teaching position in 1835 and constrained thereafter to a life of personal strain and flickering literary brilliance outside the universities. The influence of Hegelian metaphysics on radical biblical criticism nevertheless continued to manifest itself in the 'Tübingen School' under the leadership of Strauss's former teacher, Ferdinand Christian Baur. Baur united private sympathy for his pupil, underpinned by his shared confidence that Hegelianism represented the highest expression of dogmatic development yet attained by the church, with a more sustained enthusiasm for the textual reconstruction of historical individualities. For Baur, history was a developing unity, intelligible to reason, but that unity had to be discovered through the historical materials through which it was constituted, and so with greater empirical rigor than he felt that Strauss – or Hegel – had displayed (Wendte 2014). Baur's crucial insight was that early Christianity was not a unity, but a site of conflict. He accordingly wrote the history of the New Testament writings, and of the canon which sealed their authority, as the story of the process by which particularist Judaisers played out a dialectical conflict with Paul's more universally-minded followers. The ultimate result was Catholic Christianity. Where the Synoptic Gospels had presented a Jewish and human Jesus, John's Gospel – composed not by the apostle but towards the end of the second century – made him the incarnate *logos*, or Word. In the Fourth Gospel, 'Christianity is established as a principle of general salvation, and all the oppositions which it was wont to preserve from Jewish particularism are here taken up into Christian universalism' (Baur 1863: 172).

In positing a process of radical development between the composition of the Synoptic Gospels and that of John, Baur reversed the older view that John's Gospel presented the fullest account of the life of Jesus, and moved the question of the status of John to the centre of interpretative debate. Unlike Strauss, however, Baur still regarded Christianity as the 'absolute religion' (Baur 1863: 16). Historical criticism, on Baur's reading, stood at the far end of an ages-long process by which Christianity developed into the full self-consciousness of its own idea. He emphasized the importance of the person of Christ in manifesting the unity of divine and human wills which he made the normative religious type for after ages. History revealed that the most important element of the Christian consciousness, made originally evident in Christ himself, was the moral principle, proceeding from the unity of divine and human wills in Jesus which effected reconciliation with God (Baur 1864: 45–121). The elevating effects of Christ's moral type upon the religious consciousness of believers, an interest disclosing Baur's contact with Schleiermacher, recorded the outward realization of the inner truth of the Sermon on the Mount within the historical process (Baur 1863: [472]–527).

As Johannes Zachhuber has observed, Baur's commitment to 'presuppositionless' history existed in an unstable synthesis with his belief that history confirmed a rationalized version of the faith whose temporal manifestations he analysed (Zachhuber 2013). Though Strauss removed himself more acidly from church tradition, both he and Baur can be seen as having responded to the impact of history on the Bible by making the Bible central to the self-development of absolute spirit in history. But they left themselves open to the charge that they had turned the biblical revelation from the ruler into the result of human time: a stance which Strauss avowedly embraced. Whether historical criticism really did demote the authority of the biblical history and whether a more orthodox understanding of that history might be made an alternative ground for world-historical synthesis were questions that animated many of the Tübingen critics' mid-century opponents.

MEDIATION AND CONTAINMENT, 1830–60

Many Anglophone exegetes, more so than in German-speaking Europe, carried on writing and preaching as though the post-Kantian blaze through historical and theological brushwood had never erupted. But among intellectually engaged religious writers in the Protestant and Catholic worlds, two modes of biblical interpretation became popular among opponents of the increasingly unavoidable Tübingen tendency. The first lay in the remarkable growth of biblical geography and archaeology in the period: subjects which typically came as a pair. The second was the rise of *Vermittlungstheologie*, or 'mediating theology', an originally German exegetical tradition which became, for a time, wildly popular far beyond Germany itself. Where radical German critics undermined the historicity of biblical orthodoxy, a panoply of more conservative scholars, subsequently deemed uncritical and so largely forgotten within the discipline of theology, drew on a range of modern cultural resources in order to shore it up again.

From the later eighteenth century onwards, religious revival and the decline of Ottoman power encouraged a growing stream of foreign ministers to pour into the Eastern Mediterranean and the Holy Land to visualize the world of the Bible, and to define its relations to the growing fields of Egyptology and ancient philology (Gange and Ledger-Lomas 2013). Edward Robinson, a Congregationalist professor at Union Theological Seminary in New York, and his American missionary guide to the Levant, Eli Smith, went on the trail of Moses and his successors, launching biblical archaeology into the Anglophone world with their resulting 1841 *Biblical Researches* (Robinson and Smith 1841). Robinson wrote up the pair's experience of picturesque scenes, hillside paths and ancient ruins, for the purpose of verifying and vivifying the biblical narratives. From a premillennialist point of view, Alexander Keith, a Church of Scotland and then Free Church minister, continuously updated his study of the *Evidence of the Truth of the Christian Religion Derived from the Literal Fulfilment of Prophecy*, first published in 1823, to take account of the emerging evidence of biblical geography. He was particularly gratified that the advance of photography enabled him to disprove rationalistic cavils against the truth of prophecy all the more dramatically. With the aid of daguerreotypes of the ruins of the cities against which the prophets had pronounced doom, Keith was confident that 'the rays of the sun would thus depict what the prophets saw' (Keith 1873: vii, 533–42, [563]–612).

The fashion for biblical antiquities also touched the Catholic world. In 1877, a priest at the notably scholarly Sulpician seminary in Paris, Fulcran Vigouroux, published a four-volume study titled *La Bible et les découvertes modernes*. Setting his face against 'les excès de l'extrême gauche Hégélienne', which was the child of Luther, Vigouroux collated different kinds of ethnographic and archaeological evidence about the Holy Land and its environs, from Theban inscriptions to correspondences between biblical dress and contemporary Arab fashions, for the purpose of confounding 'le plus grande nombre des libre-penseurs' (Vigouroux 1889: I, 66–72, 97). Pope Leo XIII approved of Vigouroux's *tour de force*, and, through his secretary, graced subsequent editions with his complimentary testimonial (Vigouroux 1889: I, [i]–iii).

Where archaeological and geographical surveys furnished the biblical accounts with a local color suited to the tastes of the Romantic era, *Vermittlungstheologie* gave biblical theology a corresponding inwardness and psychological depth. The term broadly referred to German Protestant theologians' attempts, especially effulgent during the 1830s and 1840s, to integrate modern theological *Wissenschaft* with a continuing commitment to supernatural biblical revelation. Mediating theologians typically built on Schleiermacher's liberation of the autonomy of the subjective religious consciousness by affixing it to a more emphatic emphasis on the reality of objective scriptural revelation than Schleiermacher himself had displayed. They possessed their own journal, the *Theologische Studien und Kritiken*, and showed varying degrees of conservatism towards the biblical text. August Neander, a Jewish convert and professor of ecclesiastical history at Berlin from 1813 until his death in 1850, may be taken as representative. On the basis of one of Christ's parables in Matthew's Gospel, Neander's great work, his *General History of the Christian Religion and Church*, conceived of Christianity as a heaven-sent leaven which silently entered into and progressively transformed the Jewish, Hellenistic and barbarian forms of religious consciousness into which it entered (Neander 1825–52; Bennett 2020). Making a supernatural conception of the biblical revelation the kernel of modern progress, Neander's *History* offered an orthodox yet comparably synthetic alternative to the Tübingen argument which made the Bible significant for the way in which it witnessed to the unfolding of absolute spirit. His anti-Straussian *Leben Jesu* of 1837 was soon translated into English, and his home became a pilgrimage destination for scores of Protestant scholars (Neander 1848). Edward Robinson made use of Neander's library as he was completing his *Biblical Researches* (Robinson and Smith 1841: I, xiii–xiv).

Despite these vigorous and popular attempts to stem the tide of criticism, however, the years around 1860 marked a noted acceleration in the proliferation and respectability of attacks on received understandings of biblical orthodoxy across the Western world. Romanticism and religious revival encouraged a culture of sincerity, which encouraged critics to state their doubts publicly where once it would have seemed dangerous or silly, to do so. In Britain, *Essays and Reviews*, written by a group of Oxford dons and clerics dissatisfied with the doctrinal conservatism both of their university and of the wider Church of England, caused a storm upon its publication in 1860 for its plea that the Bible should be scrutinized using the same critical and historical methods which would be applied to other texts (Shea and Whitla 2000). A lapsed seminarian of Saint-Sulpice, Ernest Renan scandalized readers in France and worldwide with his 1863 *Vie de Jésus*. Renan examined the gospel records and found a Jesus who was a charming, charismatic, but fundamentally deluded Palestinian peasant; his story, and the religion he founded, were to be valued for the way in which they expressed values and experiences to which all humanity could relate (Renan 1863). Nor was Scandinavia, not normally drawn into surveys of nineteenth-century biblical criticism, immune. The previous year, the radical journalist and author, Viktor Rydberg, had disturbed ecclesiastical authorities in Sweden with his *Bibelns lära om Kristus*. Denying Christ's divinity, the text conceived of him as the ideal man, a kind of visitor from Plato's world of forms (Rydberg 1862). Though writing, he alleged, to halt the spread of atheistic materialism, Rydberg's interest in German mediating theologians led him, as those theologians would not themselves exactly have wished, to separate the moral value of Jesus's teaching and personality from the supernatural clothing in which official formularies had imprisoned it (Warburg 1900: I, 224–52, [509]–54). What is striking about all three cases is that, for all the outrage the books caused, none really sought to lessen the Bible's centrality as a source of cultural norms, but rather to re-establish it on what these authors regarded as more historically-grounded footings. Although radical critics prised history away from supernatural understandings of biblical authority, they insisted that they did so in order to reaffirm the centrality of the truths which the Bible contained to cultural and historical experience.

THEMES IN INTERPRETATION, 1860–1900

The need to secure biblical authority from increasingly public forms of dissent from it, and the independently-originating but overlapping inclination to blend biblical interpretation with immanentist notions of historical progress, incentivized the reconstruction of biblical orthodoxy across the Protestant world. (As will be seen, Roman Catholic engagement with this process came somewhat later.) In these years, an ethic of active biblical inquiry, though still apologetic in purpose, came to supersede the awestruck reserve and protective cautiousness characteristic of an earlier phase of biblical scholarship among orthodox Protestants. This trend itself drew energy from a changing historical sensibility. As Protestants came to recognize that their own religious traditions emerged not immediately from the Bible but from the ways in which the Bible had been interpreted in history, the importance of re-examining biblical religion afresh became newly important (Bennett 2019: [150]–98). To do so offered a means of securing biblical fundamentals at the expense of more untenable outward accretions. Biblical scholars, it could appear, followed in the paths first broken by the reformers in liberating the Bible from traditionalist accretions. For the controversially critical Free Church of Scotland Hebraist, William Robertson Smith, 'the first business of the Reformation theologian' was 'not to crystallise Bible truths into doctrines, but to follow, in all its phases, the manifold inner history of the religious life which the Bible unfolds' (Smith 1881: 15–16).

The primary task of biblical scholarship, in the new climate, was to vindicate the historicity of the Gospels, so as to prevent them from evaporating into mere expressions of mythic consciousness. An apologetic enterprise which began in Germany during the 1830s soon became a widespread industry across the Protestant world. Of particular importance was a Cambridge-centred triumvirate of Anglican clerics and New Testament scholars, active from the 1850s until approximately the final decade of the century. Brooke Foss Westcott, Fenton John Anthony Hort, and Joseph Barber Lightfoot worked intensively to sift patristic evidence, and details of manuscript transmission, to establish earlier dates for the original composition of the canonical writings than Tübingen scholars allowed. Paying close attention to the philological and cultural contexts for New Testament ideas and expressions, they concluded that the New Testament teachings were, in many respects, so innovative that they could not be accounted for on the hypothesis that they expressed pre-existing Jewish or oriental traditions. The only historically satisfying account of the texts must, in their view, proceed from the supposition of a divine revelation through Christ. Lightfoot, for instance, sought to vindicate the authenticity of the writings of Polycarp, a pupil of St John, as well as that of the seven first-century Ignatian epistles. He argued against Baur, on the basis of this evidence, that there was no real antagonism between the Johannine and Pauline tendencies in the post-apostolic period (Lightfoot 1889: 59–141). Much of Baur's case for a late dating of John's Gospel thus fell away. The post-apostolic fathers, Lightfoot connectedly maintained, were in fact already acquainted with the four canonical Gospels (Lightfoot 1889: [142]–216). The status of John's Gospel, especially, was becoming one of the most important questions in biblical criticism. Westcott's edition of the text insisted that it was historically implausible to ascribe the idea of the *logos* either to borrowing from a Greek source, or to a Jewish development: it was a fulfilment of Christ's own teaching (Westcott 1882). One of F. J. A. Hort's *Two Dissertations* was dedicated to vindicating Christ's divine uniqueness as stated in John's prologue (Hort 1876).

The enthusiasm for John, and for the essential value of the *logos* idea, overlapped with the rising fashion for emphasizing that Christianity was the religion of the incarnation. Although the doctrine of Christ's expiatory atonement for sin remained dynamic in this period, the incarnation offered a way of emphasizing Christianity's humane and communal dimensions. The idea that Jesus had unveiled a supremely attractive ideal of humanity often survived the rejection of its supernatural clothing, in a culture where the moral consequences of rejecting religion altogether seemed unknown and fearful. Baur and Renan, in their different ways, had demonstrated as much. So too had the proliferation of rationalistic lives of Christ after 1860, which tidied away the miraculous and mythical from the Gospels, to leave behind, as it was hoped, the more rationally relatable figure of a conscientious and self-sacrificing moral reformer (Hesketh 2017; Pals 1982). But an emphasis on Christ's earthly works, the emulation of which could build the kingdom of God in human time, equally characterized the writings of orthodox Trinitarians. The latter often made particular use of John's idea of the divine becoming human in order to advance their case. John Williamson Nevin, a leader of the mediating 'Mercersburg theology' which the German Reformed Church's Pennsylvania seminary broadcast into American Protestantism, considered that in the words of John's prologue, '*The word became flesh!*', 'we have the whole gospel comprehended in a word' (Nevin 1867: [199]). Charles Gore, a high church Anglican and leading light of Britain's Christian Social Union, held similar sentiments. 'We are sure that Jesus Christ is still and will continue to be the "Light of the World"', he explained in his preface to the essay collection, *Lux Mundi*, a work that sought to commend a cautious type of biblical criticism to a doctrinally conservative, Anglo-Catholic audience (Gore 1904: [vii]).

This rediscovery of the incarnation, and the enthusiasm for John's Gospel with which it was often connected, drew energy from yet another permutation of the wider nineteenth-century attempt to use biblical truth to interpret the tangible movements of human time. Especially after 1850, Johannine enthusiasm infused a distinctive kind of historical metaphysics. Mid-century mediating theologians had often understood the *logos* as the divine reason which connected the incarnation in Christ to the completion of God's work in history through the Holy Spirit, the Comforter, of which John also wrote. Neander, mixing admiration of the thirteenth-century mystic, Joachim of Fiore, with Schelling's historical philosophy, had expressed sympathy for the idea that a Johannine age would unfold at the last stage of history. This period would see the inner revelation of the spirit succeed external authority in the consciousness of believers (Neander 1825–52: V, 440–5). Neander's Swiss-German pupil, Philip Schaff, a colleague of Nevin's at Mercersburg, and later a professor at Union Theological Seminary, understood his own work in transplanting German religious historicism to the United States in the same, prophetic terms (Schaff 1890: 416–29). The development of modern thought, it appeared to such writers, harmonized more and more with the divine immanence distilled in the *logos*. J. R. Illingworth, another contributor to *Lux Mundi*, argued that 'our Christian creed, that all things were made by the Eternal Reason' harmonized wondrously with the modern knowledge that the world was 'an organism, a system in which, while the parts contribute to the growth of the whole, the whole also reacts upon the development of the parts' (Illingworth 1904: 139).

As New Testament exegesis became more personally and philosophically Christocentric in the years after 1860, the interpretation of the Old Testament became notably less so. A text in which early-nineteenth-century revivalists had seen the prefiguration of Christ and Christian doctrine everywhere, became, at least among scholars, more and more particular to the world of the ancient Jews. Though anticipated in some respects by earlier critics, Julius Wellhausen published a *History of Israel* in 1878 which made an epoch in Hebrew scholarship (Wellhausen 1878). Wellhausen, a professor at Greifswald, proceeded on the basis of the so-called 'documentary hypothesis', according to which the Pentateuch had emerged from a process of the combination and redaction of originally independent texts. The intelligibly composite literary structure of the Pentateuch, he argued, expressed the development of Israel's *cultus*, or religious practice, from a relatively eclectic nomadic stage, through the prophets' declamation against idolatry, to the consolidation of a centralized cult governed by religious law. Where orthodox and sceptics alike had once wondered why the Israelites had so often relapsed into idolatry after the delivery of the Mosaic law, Wellhausen showed that the law was not really Mosaic at all. Rather, it had only become fixed after the Exile, following the period in which the prophets, reflecting on a syncretic primitive situation, had sought to free Israel's cult from foreign admixtures. Wellhausen's researches inspired a number of studies of the prophets which treated them as sources for the growth of Israel's religion, rather than as messianic forecasts. Foreign critics, such as S. R. Driver, Pusey's successor as Regius Professor of Hebrew at Oxford from 1883, soon embraced his conclusions (Rogerson 1984: 247–72).

Ancient Israel's rising historical autonomy exercised ambivalent effects upon wider understanding of the religious significance of the Old Testament. In one vein of treatment, the identification of the Hebrew Scriptures with the world of the ancient orient amounted to a further increment in the demotion of its status, which had started to enter into Christian thought since the Enlightenment. 'The Old Testament, great as it is, is not so Divine as the New', declared the liberal Anglican, Arthur Penrhyn Stanley, in an essay on the results and conditions of biblical and religious inquiry, which he published for a North American audience in 1883 (Stanley 1883: 84–5). In Lutheran circles, the Hebrew scholarship of the period often radicalized the old *evangelisch* opposition between the Christian religion of the spirit and the Jewish religion of the law. The liberal Lutheran, Otto Pfleiderer, writing before Wellhausen, attacked the Mosaic institutes in a series of addresses, which he delivered on the history of religion while serving as a lecturer at Tübingen during the 1860s. Seeking, with so many post-Idealist German theologians, to integrate scholarly advances in the historical study of religion with a self-unfolding idea of the development of religion as such, Pfleiderer praised the Mosaic dispensation's integration of religion with the feeling of a nation. It constituted nevertheless not a *Kindes* – but a *Knechtsverhältnis*, a serfdom rather than religion's loving childhood, which Jesus would entirely dissolve (Pfleiderer 1869: II, 281–3, 416). Anti-Judaic disparagement was not, however, the only possible consequence of the application of more thoroughgoing historicism to the Old Testament, especially among doctrinal conservatives. William Robertson Smith antagonized many in his traditionally Calvinist denomination with his acceptance that much of the Old Testament was in fact post-Exilic, and that much of what his coreligionists had once thought infallibly to belong to sacred chronology was, in truth, lost to history. But for Smith, each stage in the mind of Israel – and the very distillation and redaction of its sacred books, emerging from the refreshment of its religious life – represented a scene of fellowship with God, and a preparation for the coming of the Gospel (Smith 1881).

After so much churning over of the biblical text, leaving its history ever more closely tied to the evolving needs and variations of human societies, what was left of the old, post-Reformation doctrine of biblical inspiration? The most advanced critics answered: very little. The Bible, they averred, could only be said to have been inspired in the same sense as a great work of literature might be. Ralph Waldo Emerson regarded the Psalms as akin to the Iliad, and Job as possessing the dignity of a Norse Edda (Zink 1935: 10). The liberal Anglican unbeliever, Matthew Arnold, sought to rescue the Bible from those who would dismiss it entirely by insisting 'that the Bible requires for its basis nothing but what they can verify', and that its language 'is not scientific, but *literary*' (Arnold 1970: 155). This kind of categorical redefinition encouraged Joseph Addison Alexander, professor of Hellenistic and New Testament literature at the conservatively Calvinist Princeton Theological Seminary, to insist upon 'the essential distinction between *literature* and *scripture'* in his commentary on Isaiah. A defender of plenary inspiration, Alexander affirmed that prophecy fulfilled a specific and predictive, not a literary and diagnostic function. He accordingly condemned those editors who arranged the prophet's words in verse rather than as prose (Alexander 1865: I, 23, 32–3, 43).

Among both evangelical and Catholic critics, nevertheless, writers who believed that the maintenance of intellectual authority required some appeal to modern standards of criticism became increasingly inclined to adopt a position between Arnold's and Alexander's criticism. Philip Schaff's *Religious Encyclopaedia*, published in 1888, contended that the sacred writers were inspired to the extent that they conveyed the Word of God. Geographical and historical detail mattered little in comparison to this (Schaff and Cremer 1888). The English Roman Catholic convert, John Henry Newman, worked out a similar position in his private papers on the subject. For Newman, inspiration did not amount to dictation. Pertaining to writers, more than to texts, inspiration admitted, at least in principle, of incidental errors in the sacred books, which the church had had the wisdom not to make integral to her faith (Newman 1979). Across the Western world, writers became ever more conscious that human historical subjectivity had shaped both the Bible's original composition and its later interpretation. Whether this awareness weakened or strengthened biblical authority was a question that admitted of a range of answers, but no exegete could ignore it.

THE SUBLATION OF HISTORICISM, 1890–1920

By the end of the nineteenth century, all aspects of human life had come to appear unintelligible except in relation to their courses of historical development. Precisely at the same time as history permeated Western thought most fully, nevertheless, doubts began to appear over whether historicism, as an intellectual attitude towards the human condition as such, could in and of itself provide the key to unlock the answers to the mysteries of human life. The tension between the continuing imperative to inquire historically, and the ultimate value of history as a way of knowing, expressed itself in biblical studies, no less than in other intellectual fields. The vigorous pursuit of the historical Bible continued, in ways that led to a more thorough reconstruction of its cultural and intellectual worlds. But the more that radical historicism tended to anchor the Bible in its Near Eastern context, the less obvious did it seem that the Bible, rightly understood, could act as a guide to the movements of human temporality as a whole. The historicizing of the Bible could not be undone. But the growing idea, nurtured in historical as also in systematic theology, that the Bible was, in fact, radically alien or opposed to the subsequent course of human development became an important starting point for twentieth-century exegesis.

The Göttingen theologian, Albrecht Ritschl, and the 'Ritschlian' theology he inspired, helped to propel biblical studies into this new era. In some respects sharing the wider Idealist movement's search for teleology and synthesis, Ritschl also turned biblical history against this impetus: tensions that pointed towards their impending disintegration. A former pupil of Baur at Tübingen, Ritschl firmly broke with his teacher's belief that faith was ultimately one and the same thing as the true understanding of history. He rediscovered Schleiermacher's conviction that religion existed in radical severance from reason and ethics, though it shaped the higher expressions of both; Christianity was properly social and experiential, not intellectual and dogmatic. To him the Bible was significant not as a text or as a source of doctrines but for its witness to the fact that Christ's mission had been to proclaim and practise the 'Kingdom of God', the reign of love and righteousness within a new community. Primitive Christianity was thus to be approached as a historical life, not a set of doctrines, as Lutheran and now Idealist theologians were wont to do. Though this life grew during subsequent epochs, the dogmatic forms into which the church had cast Christianity had prevented the theological apprehension of this truth, which historical criticism was now in a position to enable. Ritschl, whose thought expressed a wider neo-Kantian turn in German intellectual culture, thus continued to use history as the basis for a systematic philosophical theology, but he emphatically rejected the assumption that the Bible could be assimilated to the wider progressive unfolding of mind. Rather than supposing, with the Tübingen critics, that the history of theology had dialectically integrated the meaning of the Bible with the development of reflective consciousness, Ritschl believed that the latter had radically secularized the Bible's teaching (Ritschl 1870–4; Zachhuber 2013: [250]–96). Ritschl's ideas proved vastly influential. They helped to kindle into existence the 'History and Religion School' centred on Göttingen during the 1890s, which stressed that biblical teachings and practices acquired their meanings within the particular *cultus* within which their followers invoked them (Lehmkühler 1996). Ritschlianism also encouraged the church historian, Adolf von Harnack, to separate a moralized, neo-Kantian 'essence of Christianity' from the supernatural beliefs and Jewish national hopes of the New Testament, which now seemed radically alien to modern consciousness (Harnack 1900).

By 1900, therefore, German liberal Protestants were beginning to see a more acute tension between the religion which the Bible in fact proclaimed, and the religion which historical Christianity, with its lack of historical insight, had imagined that it had found within its pages. This disturbed those theologians who continued to interpret biblical doctrines within universal frameworks of historical evolution. Edward Caird, a British Idealist and defender of Hegelian metaphysics, criticized Harnack for treating Christianity as an 'eternal something' removed from the historical process (Jones and Muirhead 1921: 241–2). Writing in the liberal New England periodical, *The New World*, Caird argued that biblical criticism could never construct a picture of the original Jesus that would free the apprehension of Christ from the ways in which mind had, in its successive historical stages, conceptualized his work. Rather, it was both inevitable and right, that Christ's ideal had to be assimilated anew into the modes of thought particular to each successive historical era (Caird 1897). Alfred Loisy, a leader of the 'Catholic Modernism' which sought to apply the fruits of modern biblical criticism to eroding the hold of neo-Scholasticism over Roman Catholic theology, endorsed and adapted Caird's argument in his own reply to Harnack, *L'Évangile et l'église* (Loisy 1903). The essence of Christianity, Loisy argued, lay in the transmission of Christ's teaching in the life of the church. Critical study of the Gospels showed that Christ did not, with Ritschl or Harnack, view the kingdom of God as a kind of inner state which the community of believers actualized in time, but rather as a new creation that would arise on the far side of an impending apocalypse, which would totally transform the condition of human affairs. This transformation did not come about, however, in the near-term in which the first apostles expected it. The church responded by subjectively expanding the objective truths of the Gospels into a new kind of orthodoxy, as the conditions within which the Christian community expressed its faith changed radically (Loisy 1903: [ix]–x, [35]–46).

Loisy's book, swiftly condemned by the Roman Catholic Church, harked back in some respects to the Idealist quest for the unity of religious knowledge. In its recognition that Christ's teaching was primarily eschatological, however, it expressed a new and distinctive critical impetus which tended to separate biblical theology, as such, from what nineteenth-century divines had become accustomed to regard as the divine forces animating human time. The radical theologian, Albert Schweitzer, explained that the development of gospel criticism had prepared the ground for a paradigm shift in the understanding of Jesus's mission in his 1906 study, *Von Reimarus zu Wrede*, which was translated into English as *The Quest of the Historical Jesus*. Christ did not work to unveil an ethic of progressive improvement which confirmed the nineteenth century in its leading habits of mind, Schweitzer argued. Reflecting the growing priority which scholars now accorded to Mark's disruptively Messianic Jesus, where a previous generation of liberals had grown lyrical over John's lovingly philosophical portrait, Schweitzer insisted that Jesus had thrown down an apocalyptic challenge to the Jewish world of his day. He expected an imminent outpouring of the spirit, which would sweep away the priestly law and abolish all natural distinctions, through the creation of the kingdom of God. When the new dispensation did not materialize, Jesus accepted death, in the mistaken expectation that it would soon follow (Schweitzer 1911). Schweitzer's Anglican translator, Francis Crawford Burkitt, the Norrisian Professor of Divinity at Cambridge, came to very similar conclusions. Jesus was not, he argued, 'really and primarily an ethical teacher, or a social reformer', but a stormy Messiah, whom God made manifest in order to rule as his vicegerent on earth (Burkitt 1922: 51, 62–3).

The pivot towards eschatology in New Testament exegesis often took Ritschlianism's supposedly bourgeois and worldly conception of the coming kingdom as its straw man. But the two opposing *fin-de-siècle* fashions shared a fundamental discontent with Christendom's traditional Christology. This critical stance expressed their common scepticism as to whether post-apostolic history, which had given shape to that Christology and its interpretation, really did evince the providential or spiritual purposes which earlier scholars had so often made the Bible the key to interpretion; secular time increasingly appeared to be just that. It is a remarkable fact that conservative evangelicals, though oblivious or averse to the movements of advanced criticism, were simultaneously shifting from a historicist premillennialist to a futurist conception of scriptural prophecy. This anticipated that the fulfilment of prophecy would be narrowly concentrated around the end-times, rather than in the vale of tears which constituted the ordinary course of history, from which providential action now appeared to be more removed than it had once seemed (Bebbington 2005: 184–8).

The rising tensions between the perceived autonomy of the Bible, and the historical metaphysics into the service of which the Bible had so often been pressed, found particularly sharp and defiantly neoorthodox expression in the early writings of the Swiss reformed theologian, Karl Barth. Barth published a commentary on Paul's Epistle to the Romans in 1919 which offered a meditation on the interaction between divine sovereignty and human history. Barth accepted, as an uncontentious point of departure, that Paul had expressed himself to his contemporaries through the languages and ideas of his day. Even the most conservative kind of exegesis, at least if it laid claim to academic respectability, now recognized the Bible's historicity. Barth understood Paul's meaning, however, to make clear that the operation of God's grace, from Abraham down the generations, bound salvation history into the kingdom of God. The individualities, periods and temporal relations which pertained to human history were, in relation to this absolutely higher system of relations, merely the transient expressions of outward being. Thus Barth reached into Pauline theology in order to see beyond history, to apprehend the eternal opposition between God's sovereign revelation and the movements of sinful human time into which that revelation was delivered, but by which it was not constrained. Barth saved the Bible from history by defining its truth as a kind of anti-history (Barth 1985: 3–4, 135–45).

Barth, Calvinism's answer to Nietzsche, did not speak for all biblical interpreters. His work nevertheless represented a kind of mirror-image to Schweitzer's and Burkitt's radical liberal critiques, in that it insisted that the conventional apologetic modes of the nineteenth century simply did not recognize the profundity of the challenge which the Bible threw down to contemporary culture, and to the historical course through which that culture had evolved. In one sense, this rejection of nineteenth-century historicism, though not history *tout court*, helped believers to disentangle biblical authority from the souring of Western culture's idea of itself before and after the Great War. In another, not less consequential respect, it marked the acceleration of the eclipse of biblical narrative from the centre of that same culture as the twentieth century unfolded.

REFERENCES

Alexander, J. A. (1865), *Commentary on the Prophecies of Isaiah*, ed. John Eadie, 2 vols, Edinburgh: Andrew Elliot and James Thin.

Arnold, M. (1970), *God and the Bible*, ed. R. H. Super, Ann Arbor: University of Michigan Press, first edition 1884.

Barth, K. (1985), *Der Römerbrief (erste Fassung)*, ed. H. Schmidt, Zurich: Theologischer Verlag, first edition 1919.

Baur, F. C. (1863), *Kirchengeschichte der drei ersten Jahrhunderte*, 3rd edn, Tübingen: L. Fr. Frues, first edition 1853.

Baur, F. C. (1864), 'Die Lehre Jesu', in *Vorlesungen über neutestamentliche Theologie*, ed. F. F. Baur, [45]–121, Tübingen: Fues's Verlag (L. W. Reisland).

Bebbington, D. (2005), *The Dominance of Evangelicalism: The Age of Spurgeon and Moody*, Leicester: Inter-Varsity Press.

Beecher, L. (1828), 'The Bible a Code of Laws', in *Sermons Delivered on Various Occasions*, ed. Lyman Beecher, [138]–81, Boston: T.R. Marvin.

Bennett, J. (2019), *God and Progress: Religion and History in British Intellectual Culture, 1845–1914*, Oxford: Oxford University Press.

Bennett, J. (2020), 'August Neander and the Religion of History in the Nineteenth-Century "Priesthood of Letters"', *Historical Journal*, 63(3): 633–59.

Bickersteth, E. (1829), *The Christian Student, Designed to Assist Christians in General in Acquiring Religious Knowledge*, London: R. B. Seeley and W. Burnside.

Burkitt, F. C. (1922), *The Earliest Sources of the Life of Jesus*, new edn, London: Constable, first edition 1910.

Caird, E. (1897), 'Christianity and the Historical Christ', *The New World: A Quarterly Review of Religion, Ethics and Theology*, 6(21): 1–13.

Cameron, E. (2016), 'The Bible and the Early Modern Sense of History', in *The New Cambridge History of the Bible: Volume 3: From 1450 to 1750*, ed. Euan Cameron, 657–85, Cambridge: Cambridge University Press.

Clark, W. (2006), *Academic Charisma and the Origins of the Research University*, Chicago: University of Chicago Press.

de Wette, W. M. L. (1806–7), *Beiträge zur Einleitung in das Alte Testament*, 2 vols, Halle: Schimmelpfennig.

Elliott, E. (1847), *Horae Apocalypticae: Or, a Commentary on the Apocalypse, Critical and Historical*, 3rd edn, 4 vols, London: Seeley, Burnside, and Seeley, first edition 1844.

Frei, H. (1973), *The Eclipse of Biblical Narrative: A Study in Eighteenth and Nineteenth Century Hermeneutics*, New Haven and London: Yale University Press.
Gange, D. and M. Ledger-Lomas, eds. (2013), *Cities of God: The Bible and Archaeology in Nineteenth-Century Britain*, Cambridge: Cambridge University Press.
Gaussen, L. (1841), *Theopneustia: The Plenary Inspiration of the Holy Scriptures*, London: Samuel Bagster.
Gore, C. (1904), 'Preface', in *Lux Mundi: A Series of Studies in the Religion of the Incarnation*, 15th edn, ED. Charles Gore, [vii]–ix, London: John Murray; first edition 1889.
Harnack, A. (1900), *Das Wesen des Christentums*, Leipzig: Hinrichs.
Hartlich, C. and W. Sachs (1952), *Der Ursprung des Mythosbegriffes in der Modernen Bibelwissenschaften*, Tübingen: J. C. B. Mohr.
Hesketh, I. (2017), *Victorian Jesus*, Toronto, Buffalo and London: University of Toronto Press.
Hodgson, P. C. (2015), 'Idealist/Hegelian Readings of the Bible', in *The New Cambridge History of the Bible: Volume 4: From 1750 to the Present*, ED. John Riches, 197–207, Cambridge: Cambridge University Press.
Horne, T. H. (1827), *A Compendious Introduction to the Study of the Bible*, 2nd edn, London: T. Cadell.
Hort, F. J. A. (1876), *Two Dissertations*, Cambridge: Macmillan.
Howard, T. A. (2006), *Protestant Theology and the Making of the Modern German University*, Oxford: Oxford University Press.
Illingworth, J. R. (1904), 'The Incarnation in Relation to Development', in *Lux Mundi: A Series of Studies in the Religion of the Incarnation*, 15th edn, ed. Charles Gore, [132]–57, London: John Murray, first edition 1889.
Jones, H. and J. Muirhead, eds. (1921), *The Life and Philosophy of Edward Caird LLD, DCL, FBA*, Glasgow: Maclehose, Jackson and Co.
Keith, A. (1873), *Evidence of the Truth of the Christian Religion Derived from the Literal Fulfilment of Prophecy: Particularly as Illustrated by the History of the Jews and by the Discoveries of Recent Travellers*, 40th edn, London: T. Nelson, first edition 1823.
Lehmkühler, K. (1996), *Kultus und Theologie: Dogmatik und Exegese in der religionsgeschichtlichen Schule*, Göttingen: Vandenhoeck and Ruprecht.
Lightfoot, J. B. (1889), *Essays on the Work Entitled Supernatural Religion*, London.
Loisy, A. (1903), *L'Évangile et l'église*, 10th edn, Paris: Bellevue, first edition 1902.
Neander, J. A. W. (1825–52), *Allgemeine Geschichte der christlichen Religion und Kirche*, 6 vols, Hamburg: Friedrich Perthes.
Neander, J. A. W. (1848), *The Life of Jesus Christ in its Historical Connexion and Historical Development*, trans. J. M'Clintock and C. Blumenthal, New York: Harper and Brothers.
Nevin, J. W. (1867), *The Mystical Presence: A Vindication of the Reformed or Calvinistic Doctrine of the Holy Eucharist*, Philadelphia: S. R. Fisher.
Newman, J. H. (1979), 'The Inspiration of Scripture' (1861), in *The Theological Papers of John Henry Newman on Biblical Inspiration and Infallibility*, ed. J. Derek Holmes, 72–83, Oxford: Clarendon Press.
Pals, D. L. (1982), *The Victorian 'Lives' of Jesus*, San Antonio: Trinity University Press.
Pfleiderer, O. (1869), *Die Religion, ihr Wesen und ihre Geschichte, auf Grund des Gegenwärtigen Standes der philosophischen und der historischen Wissenschaft*, 2 vols, Leipzig: Fues's Verlag (R. Reisland).
Pusey, E. (1864), *Daniel the Prophet: Nine Lectures, Delivered in the Divinity School of the University of Oxford*, Oxford: John Henry and James Parker.

Rasmussen, J., J. Wolfe, and J. Zachhuber, eds. (2017), *The Oxford Handbook of Nineteenth-Century Christian Thought*, Oxford: Oxford University Press.

Renan, E. (1863), *Vie de Jésus*, Paris: Michel Lévy Fréres.

Richter, H. and W. Richter, eds. (1834–40), *Erklärter Haus-Bibel oder Auslegung der ganzen heiligen Schrift Alten und Neuen Testaments*, 6 vols, Barmen and Schwelm: Falkenberg'schen Buchhandlung.

Ritschl, A. (1870–4), *Die christliche Lehre von Rechtfertigung und Versöhnung*, 3 vols, Bonn: A. Marcus.

Robinson, E. and E. Smith (1841), *Biblical Researches in Palestine, Mount Sinai and Arabia Petraea: A Journal of Travels in the Year 1838*, 3 vols, London: John Murray.

Rogerson, J. (1984), *Old Testament Criticism in the Nineteenth Century: England and Germany*, London: SPCK.

Rydberg, V. (1862), *Bibelns lära om Kristus: Samvetsgrann undersökning*, Göteborg: Handelstidningen.

Schaff, D. S. and H. Cremer (1888), 'Inspiration', in *A Religious Encyclopaedia: Or Dictionary of Biblical, Historical, Doctrinal, and Practical Theology*, 3 vols, ii, ed. Philip Schaff, 1101–[6], New York: Christian Literature Co.

Schaff, P. (1890), *Literature and Poetry*, New York: Charles Scribner's Sons.

Schorch, S. and E.-J. Waschke, eds. (2013), *Biblische Exegese und hebräische Lexikographie: Das 'Hebräisch-deutsche Handwörterbuch' von Wilhelm Gesenius als Spiegel und Quelle alttestamentlicher und hebräischer Forschung, 200 Jahre nach seiner ersten Auflage*, Berlin: De Gruyter.

Schweitzer, A. (1911), *The Quest of the Historical Jesus*, trans. Francis Crawford Burkitt, London: Adam and Charles Black, first German edition 1906.

Shea, V. and W. Whitla, eds. (2000), *Essays and Reviews: The 1860 Text and its Reading*, Charlottesville and London: University Press of Virginia.

Smith, W. R. (1881), *The Old Testament in the Jewish Church: Twelve Lectures on Biblical Criticism*, Edinburgh: Adam and Charles Black.

Spence, M. (2015), *Heaven on Earth: Reimagining Time and Eternity in Nineteenth-Century British Evangelicalism*, Cambridge: James Clarke.

Stanley, A. P. (1883), *Addresses and Sermons Delivered during a Visit to the United States and Canada in 1878*, London: Macmillan.

Stephan, H. and M. Schmidt (1973), *Geschichte der evangelischen Theologie in Deutschland seit dem Idealismus*, 3rd edn, Berlin and New York: de Gruyter.

Strauss, D. F. (1835–6), *Das Leben Jesu, kritisch bearbeitet*, 2 vols, Tübingen: C. F. Osiander.

Vigouroux, F. (1889), *La Bible et les découvertes modernes en Palestine, en Égypte et en Assyrie*, 5th edn, 4 vols, Paris: Berche et Tralin, first edition 1877.

Warburg, K. (1900), *Viktor Rydberg: En lefnadsteckning*, 2 vols, Stockholm: Albert Bonnier.

Wellhausen, J. (1878), *Geschichte Israels*, Berlin: G. Reimer.

Wendte, M. (2014), 'Ferdinand Christian Baur: Ein historisch informierter Idealist eigener Art', in *Ferdinand Christian Baur und die Geschichte des Frühen Christentums*, ed. Martin Bauspiess, Christof Landmesser, and David Lincicum, [75]–88, Tübingen: Mohr Siebeck.

Westcott, B. F. (1882), *The Gospel According to St John: The Authorised Version with Introduction and Notes*, London: John Murray.

Zachhuber, J. (2013), *Theology as Science in Nineteenth-Century Germany: From F.C. Baur to Ernst Troeltsch*, Oxford: Oxford University Press.

Zink, H. (1935), *Emerson's Use of the Bible*, Lincoln: University of Nebraska.

CHAPTER 2

History and Politics

TODD WEBB

INTRODUCTION

It would be difficult to imagine an issue in nineteenth- and early-twentieth-century Europe and North America, or the wider imperial world, that was not influenced in some way by the Bible. The population of Victorian Britain, for example, was 'a people of one book', as historian Timothy Larsen (2011) has pointed out. Many of them were deeply concerned by what, at first glance, seems like the esoteric issue of the history of the Bible: that is, whether it should be treated as a divinely inspired text – and so above mere human criticism – or like any other historical document, shaped by the social and cultural conditions of its original writers and compilers, and so open to the most rigorous scholarly analysis. The place of the Bible in British society also influenced, and was influenced by, more strictly political issues. Some Britons turned to the Scriptures for guidance and inspiration as their already globe-spanning empire expanded and consolidated, while other erstwhile subjects of that empire used the Bible in their attempts to thwart or overthrow imperial rule. Closer to home, British Protestants battled Catholics over the role that the Bible should play in education. And, when Britain went to war in August 1914, there were many clergy and laity who turned to the Scriptures to explain and justify the titanic struggle with Germany and the Austro-Hungarian Empire. As we will see, these historiographical and political disputes, and a few others besides, were replicated in somewhat different forms across the nations of Europe and North America, and their colonial holdings between 1820 and 1920.

So pervasive was the influence of the Bible in the nineteenth and early-twentieth-century Western world that even quite specific topics like history and politics make up what the iconoclastic biographer Lytton Strachey (1986: 9) described as a vast sea of information. To get a sense of its unruly currents and darkest depths, we will have to adopt the same strategy that he used in his classic *Eminent Victorians* (1918). We are going to 'row over that great ocean of material, and lower down into it, here and there, a little bucket, which will bring up to the light of day some characteristic specimen . . . to be examined with a careful curiosity'. Like Strachey, who examined a churchman, a reformer, an educator and a colonial adventurer and general, we have to be selective in our subjects, yet with the hope of providing a sense of the wider events, contexts and developments of our period. Keeping that in mind, we will begin with the various approaches to the history of the Bible, and to the quest for the historical Jesus in particular, that took shape in Europe and North America. Then we will turn to the different reactions to those methodologies, stretching from revolution and schism in the early and mid-nineteenth century to wary acceptance by the late nineteenth and early twentieth centuries. In the second half of the chapter, we will examine the interface between the Bible and politics proper, concentrating on several of the most contentious and widely debated issues of the nineteenth and early twentieth centuries, including imperialism, education, slavery and war.

BIBLE AND HISTORY: APPROACHES

As the previous chapter demonstrated, the rise of historical or higher criticism in the early nineteenth century was one of the intellectual and religious watersheds of the period. It affected churches across the Western world, particularly among Protestants whose faith, since the Reformation, depended overwhelmingly on the printed word of God. In its most controversial form, biblical criticism focused on the vexed question of whether or not it was possible, or even really necessary, to understand the Jesus Christ of history – the 'real' man. That is the thread that we will try to follow through this complex story of interpretation, reinterpretation and debate.

Scholars often credit the German theologian and controversialist David Friedrich Strauss with inaugurating both modern biblical criticism and the quest for the historical Jesus, but as the historian John Barton (2019: 420–1) notes, there was another intellectual 'imp' who has an equally strong claim to that distinction. The deist Hermann Samuel Reimarus, writing in the mid-eighteenth century while a professor of oriental languages in the German city of Hamburg, prefigured some of the later arguments of Strauss and other biblical scholars. Reimarus emphasized the eschatological and revolutionary content in the teachings of Jesus Christ. As James Carleton Paget (2001: 142) puts it:

> For Reimarus, Jesus was a Jew in essential continuity with his culture. Central to his ministry was the preaching of the kingdom of God, a kingdom which, when viewed in its appropriate Jewish context, was to be seen in political terms. Jesus had messianic pretensions and saw himself as a future king of this new kingdom. His failure to bring this into being in a revolution led to his death, and it was only thanks to his disciples, who turned him into a universal saviour due to return in glory, that Christianity came into being.

Having staked out that revisionist position, Reimarus was bound to take an equally hard look at the miracles credited to Jesus in the Gospels. Not surprisingly, perhaps, he stated that many of Christ's miracles needed to be viewed not as the products of supernatural intervention but instead explained in terms of both the natural functioning of the universe and the all-too-human tendency towards wish-fulfilment. In the case of the resurrection, the most important miracle of them all, Barton (2019: 421) explains, Reimarus 'argued that the disciples had stolen Jesus' body to make it appear that he had risen. Then the later evangelists invented predictions of the resurrection, which they placed on Jesus' lips.' That Reimarus only shared such ideas in manuscript form, circulated anonymously among a group of acquaintances, suggests that he had the good sense to realize that this was explosive stuff. If his approach to the Bible was valid, it undermined much of the basis of Christian belief. Wisely, as it turned out, Reimarus's historical analysis was published only after 6 feet of German soil separated him from the outrage of his critics. David Friedrich Strauss was not so cautious.

Strauss's intervention in biblical scholarship began at the University of Tübingen. After attending that institution of higher learning as a student from 1825 to 1830, he briefly realized the dream of every graduate student since time immemorial, taking up a teaching position at his *alma mater* in 1832. While studying at Tübingen and completing his doctoral dissertation on *The Religious and Historical Development of the Dogma of the Return of All Things*, Strauss also fell under the intellectual sway of Georg Wilhelm Friedrich Hegel, one of the most complex and influential thinkers of the era. As a rebellious young theology student keen to shake up the status quo and make his mark in his chosen field, Strauss was particularly drawn to the possible implications of both Hegel's methodology and ideas for how people interpreted the Bible.

Georg Wilhelm Friedrich Hegel wrote about the importance of dialectical interactions in all aspects of human existence. For Hegel, history unfolded through a series of struggles between existing conditions (thesis) and challenges to the current order created by intellectual, economic, political or social forces (antithesis). This sometimes-violent conflict eventually resolved itself in a synthesis: that is, a compromise of sorts that led humanity to a higher state of being. And then the process would repeat itself, ending only when the human race attained a level of perfection. The revolutionary Karl Marx later adopted and adapted Hegel's dialect to explain the inevitable triumph of communism over capitalism. David Friedrich Strauss had an altogether different idea. Perhaps, he thought, Hegel's dialect could be applied to biblical analysis as a method to get at the core truth of Christianity: that it is God's will, the absolute spirit of the universe as Hegel put it, that ultimately drives history forward, though in the past, that awesome, otherworldly force had been misunderstood by less enlightened thinkers, like the men who wrote the Gospels, and personified it in the form of a living, suffering man – the carpenter and itinerant preacher from Nazareth, Jesus Christ.

It is no exaggeration to say that the first edition of David Friedrich Strauss's *Life of Jesus Critically Examined* (1835) is among the great scholarly and polemical works of the mid-nineteenth century. A later quester for the historical Jesus, Albert Schweitzer (2001: 74), went so far as to describe it as 'one of the most perfect things in the whole range of learned literature'. 'In over fourteen hundred pages', Schweitzer continued, Strauss 'has not a superfluous phrase; his analysis descends to the minutest details, but he does not lose his way among them; the style is simple and picturesque, sometimes ironical, but always dignified and distinguished'. Much of this praise was the result of Strauss's application of Hegel's dialect to the gospel stories of Jesus Christ. With all the fearlessness of an academic just embarking on his career, Strauss subjected each of those accounts to a rigorous three-part analysis. He began with what he saw as the thesis: those scholars who sought to harmonize the many contradictions among the gospel stories. Strauss then moved on to the antithesis: the rationalist critics of the Bible, like Reimarus, who tried to explain the miracles performed by Jesus in naturalistic terms. And, having demonstrated the problems, if not absurdities, of both of those approaches, Strauss presented his own radical synthesis. While there may have been an actual man named Jesus Christ, it was almost impossible, given the contradictory evidence of the Gospels, to say what relation, if any, he bore to the figure presented in the New Testament. Instead, Strauss's arguments on the various stories of Christ's life, ministry, death and resurrection made more sense once scholars realized that the gospel writers had projected the messianic prophecies of the Old Testament onto a man who may have briefly appeared among them. Fundamentally, the Jesus Christ of the Bible – Christ the Messiah – was a figure of myth. He was a projection of humanity's Hegelian quest for a higher order of existence. That mythical framework, Strauss stated, made sense of all the contradictions among the gospel stories and allowed Christians to look beyond them – or through them – to discover the mind and will of God.

As other German scholars rushed into print to support, oppose or extend David Friedrich Strauss's arguments, the influence of his *Life of Jesus Critically Examined* gradually spread. It sparked a variety of responses in England and across what the historian James Belich calls 'Anglo-World' (Belich 2009): the United Kingdom of England, Ireland, Scotland and Wales; its colonies of settlement, including Canada and the United States.

David Friedrich Strauss's magnum opus was translated into English and published in 1846, but in England itself, a variety of home-grown approaches to biblical criticism only made themselves felt in church, academia and beyond in the first half of the 1860s. In the beginning of that decade, in 1860, seven men, six of them well-known clergy in the country's legally-established Church of England (Anglican Church), published *Essays and Reviews* – a collection of individually authored pieces. 'While the essays ranged over a great many subjects, from the history of religious thought to contemporary education', the historian Ian Hesketh (2017: 15) points out, 'what was contentious was the apparent appropriation and defence of historical and biblical criticism that extended throughout the volume'. The clergyman Benjamin Jowett's argument that the Bible should be treated 'just like any other book' was especially upsetting to orthodox sensibilities. Even more shocking, however, was *The Pentateuch and Book of Joshua Critically Examined* (1862) by the Anglican bishop of Natal (South Africa), J. W. Colenso. Likely inspired by Strauss, as the title suggests, and certainly by *Essays and Reviews* – as well as by questions about the inconsistencies in the Old Testament raised by his Zulu charges – Colenso investigated the Mosaic epic in the hope of separating 'the historically possible elements of the narrative from the downright impossible' (Hesketh 2017: 20). The result was a hard-hitting study that drew on mathematics and demography to cast doubt on some of the most treasured stories of the Bible and that sold remarkably well in its intended market in England. But Colenso's sales figures were soon eclipsed by those of the anonymously published *Ecce Homo: A Survey in the Life and Work of Jesus Christ* (1865). It helped that its author, the historian J. R. Seeley, took a different route than previous biblical critics in England, eschewing the thesis of Strauss and that of Colenso. For Seeley, the Jesus Christ of the Gospels was not mythical nor was the Old Testament a farrago of nonsense. Instead, *Ecce Homo* tried to 'discern just what was eternal about what Christ thought and did' (Hesketh 2017: 53–4). For Seeley that came down to Jesus's attempt to unite the religious and the political in a harmonious whole, tied together by a universal 'love of man' (Hesketh 2017: 63).

A similar variety of approaches to biblical criticism took shape within two of the main dissenting denominations in Anglo-World: the Presbyterians and Methodists. Among Presbyterians, in the early 1830s, the study of the Bible itself was taken as proof of its divine origins and absolute authority, including on historical issues, but that position became increasingly difficult to maintain after Strauss's *Life of Jesus Critically Examined* appeared. Some Presbyterians in Scotland responded to the challenge of biblical criticism by refusing to engage with it altogether, ignoring the controversies rocking Anglicanism, such as Colenso's bombshell of a book. But ironically, given the bishop's own experience, this Presbyterian combination of orthodox certainty and wilful ignorance was shaken as the denomination's 'missionaries grappled with the problems associated with translating the Bible into the languages of indigenous societies' (Holmes 2018: 164). In response to that situation, some Presbyterians in Scotland and Ireland began to argue that the Bible was not in fact perfect, but rather a record of God's dealings with his people in a specific historical context. These ministers embraced what came to be known as 'believing criticism'. They continued to support the theological foundation of British Presbyterianism, the Westminster Confession of Faith, while also embracing the new ideas coming out of Germany. On the other side of the Atlantic, biblical criticism was also absorbed into the Presbyterian mainstream in Canada, though not without some controversy, by the late 1800s, while Wesleyan Methodists were divided between those who urged their church to include such new ideas in clerical education in order to keep abreast of the 'growth of our country in intelligence' and others who sought to 'restrict theological professors to a literal understanding of Scriptures' (Van Die 1989: 90). One of the leading reformers among Wesleyan Methodists in Canada, Nathaniel Burwash, argued that Jesus framed his message in the language of his time and that the Bible needed to be analysed with that truth in mind. The Scripture, Burwash stated pithily, was a 'heavenly treasure given to us in earthen vessels' (Van Die 1989: 103).

In making such arguments, Nathaniel Burwash was partly inspired by Wesleyan Methodists in Britain, who followed a similar path towards a watered-down version of biblical criticism during the same period, and by the thoughts of the much more radical American Unitarian Theodore Parker in the 1840s. In some ways, Parker was as thorough a critic of miracle stories of the Bible as David Friedrich Strauss, whose book he reviewed, though without fully endorsing Strauss's Hegelian approach. Parker's own work aimed to combine the rigorousness of German scholarship with the 'warm religious spirit' (Dorrien 2001: 82) that Strauss supposedly lacked. Picking and choosing from Strauss's ideas, Parker dismissed miracles as arguments that 'cannot be proven' and that 'prove nothing' (Dorrien 2001: 83), and as one would expect from a Unitarian, even the historical Jesus was dispensable for Parker. What mattered was 'the truth of the ideal' (Dorrien 2001: 87) that Christ represented. As the historian Gary Dorrien (2001: 87) explains, 'even if historical criticism were to prove that the Gospels are total fabrications and that Jesus never lived . . . the truth of Christianity would not be affected'. Parker himself put it this way: 'If Christianity is true at all, it would be just as true if Herod or Catiline had taught it' (Dorrien 2001: 98). That position troubled some American Unitarians who were keen to keep their denomination securely in the Protestant mainstream of the young American republic.

But, returning briefly to continental Europe, by the 1870s David Friedrich Strauss himself had gone on 'to lower things', as the intellectual historian J. W. Burrow (2000: 198) rather unkindly puts it. In his final barn-burning work, *The Old Belief and the New* (1872), Strauss finally came to the logical conclusion of his slashing Hegelian approach to the Bible and cut himself loose from his remaining connections with any sort of orthodox Christianity. Instead, he urged his readers to embrace the brutally unforgiving but efficient mechanism of natural selection as revealed by Charles Darwin and other modern scientists, which Strauss somehow managed to read as an expression of 'an all-pervasive spirit of love' (Burrow 2000: 198). This was too much for some otherwise sympathetic thinkers, including the up-and-coming philosopher Friedrich Nietzsche – himself no slouch when opportunities arose to undermine Christian orthodoxies. Strauss's latest book, Nietzsche declared, was the product of a mind 'smug, philistine and philosophically naïve' (Burrow 2000: 48). 'For the voice of Strauss, speaking of his new faith, is certainly not the voice of an evil genius', Nietzsche wrote in 1873 with crushing disdain:

> It is not the voice of a spirit at all, let alone that of an actual genius. It is the voice of those people whom Strauss introduces to us as his 'we' – they are, he says, 'scholars and artists, office workers and soldiers, tradesmen and land proprietors, in their thousands and by no means the worst in the land' – and who, when they tell us of their beliefs, bore us even more than when they tell us of their dreams. (Nietzsche 1997: 14–15)

Nietzsche was also angered by Strauss's late-in-life turn towards political conservatism. When France and Prussia went to war in 1870–1, Strauss came out publicly as a cheerleader for Prussian expansionism, brushing aside the plea of one of the leading French historical critics of the Bible, Ernest Renan, to unite with him in a 'cosmopolitan position above both sides' (Cromwell 1974: 135).

For his part, the Frenchman Renan came to the issue of the historical Jesus along a somewhat different route than Strauss. Renan was born in Brittany in 1823 and later entered the seminary of St Sulpice in Paris with every intention of becoming a Catholic priest. While a student, however, he began to read the work of German biblical critics and to question the truth of the Bible and of Christianity itself. Renan left the seminary in 1845 and took up teaching, like many young people at a loss for future employment. In 1860, Renan received a grant from Emperor Napoleon III to travel to the biblical lands in the Middle East. When he returned in 1862, Renan became a professor of Semitic Languages at the Collége de France. The next year, 1863, he published the book that made his name popular: *The Life of Jesus*.

As his *Life of Jesus* revealed, Renan was basically a sceptic with the heart and prose style of a Romantic. He took on many of the historical methods and insights of Strauss and his followers, but he made them somewhat more palatable to the majority of the reading public by sheer writerly zeal and imagination. For Renan 'the content of religious truth' was 'emphatically humanistic, a message of human brotherhood' (Burrow 2000: 200). Jesus Christ was at the centre of this faith – or, at least, the 'historically knowable, human Jesus' (Burrow 2000: 200). That flesh-and-blood Jesus was brought to life through Renan's combination of historical research and Romantic prose. One paragraph, describing the Crucifixion, gives a sense of the effect:

> Jesus tasted these horrors [of crucifixion] in all their atrocity. A burning thirst, one of the tortures of crucifixion, devoured him, and he asked to drink. There stood near, a cup of the ordinary drink of the Roman soldiers, a mixture of vinegar and water, called *posca*. The soldiers had to carry with them their *posca* on all their expeditions, of which an execution was considered one. A soldier dipped a sponge in this drink, put it at the end of a reed, and raised it to the lips of Jesus, who sucked it. The two robbers were crucified, one of each side. The executions, to whom were usually left the small effects ... of those executed, drew lots for his garments, and, seated at the foot of the cross, kept guard over him. According to one tradition, Jesus pronounced this sentence, which was in his heart if not upon his lips: 'Father, forgive them, for they know not what they do.' (Renan 1955: 364–5)

This was about as far away from the rigorous intellectualism of David Friedrich Strauss and some of the Anglo-World biblical critics as one could go.

One person who did not appreciate Ernest Renan's efforts was the last of the major questers for the historical Jesus in our period: Albert Schweitzer. As we saw earlier, Schweitzer admired David Friedrich Strauss's style and approach to the Christ of history, but Renan's *Life of Jesus* was '"Christian" art in the worst sense of the term – the art of the wax image'. 'The gentle Jesus, the beautiful Mary, the fair Galileans who formed the retinue of the "amiable carpenter"' Schweitzer continued, 'might have been taken over in a body from a shop-window of an ecclesiastical art emporium in the Place St. Sulpice' (Schweitzer 2001: 159–60). For Schweitzer, Renan, unlike Strauss, was a novelist more than a scholar, and Schweitzer situated himself solidly in the second camp. In his own research, however, Schweitzer went even further than his hero, Strauss. In his *Quest of the Historical Jesus* (1906), Schweitzer argued that Jesus Christ had, indeed, been a historical figure of the first century CE; he was not a figure of myth. But Schweitzer's historical Jesus bore little relation to the timeless and universal figure presented by Renan. Reaching back to an argument first made by the cautious Hermann Samuel Reimarus, Schweitzer situated Jesus Christ in a millenarian context. As James Carleton Paget (2001: 145) points out, *The Quest of the Historical Jesus* 'presented an alternative picture of Jesus the eschatological enthusiast and messianic pretender who died in dramatic fashion on the cross trying to force God to bring in his longed-for kingdom'. Such a view, as Schweitzer (2001: 478) admitted, meant that Christ 'will be to our time a stranger and an enigma'. That conclusion, J. W. Burrow (2000: 206) quite rightly notes, could be as troubling to the orthodox Christian faithful as anything that had been written by Strauss, Renan or their Anglo-World contemporaries over the previous seventy-one years:

> The more fully known the historical Jesus became, the more firmly historically located he became in the messianic, eschatological context of the first century. In doing so, he became more alien, more difficult, or even impossible, to identify with the Christ of modern faith.

The task of dealing with that potentially distressing possibility, however, was left to the next generation of biblical scholars.

BIBLE AND HISTORY: REACTIONS

In the meantime, the popular reaction to the various insights of the biblical critics set off a series of crises across the Western world. The key to the seriousness of those upheavals seems to have been the nature of connection between the affected church and the state. In other words, in several places in Europe and the Anglo-World, the reception of biblical criticism was itself a political issue, while elsewhere it affected, and was affected by, the internal politics of the churches themselves.

When David Friedrich Strauss first conceived the idea for his *Life of Jesus Critical Examined*, he knew that it might create controversy – that it might even be a 'dangerous' pursuit – but, he wrote to a friend, his argument 'had to come out' (Cromwell 1974: 48). As one of Strauss's biographers, Richard Cromwell (1974: 48), puts it, 'he could only hope that fate would favor him in the matter'. Fate was not so kind. Following the book's publication, in what would become an all-too-familiar event for biblical critics, Strauss's scandalized colleagues at Tübingen campaigned successfully to strip him of his tenured position. (It probably did not help that Strauss had taken to mimicking some of those professors' personal eccentricities during his lectures, much to the delight of an increasing number of jeering students.) This headlong fall from academic grace explains, at least in part, why Strauss made some major changes to his argument in the third edition of *The Life of Jesus*. As Cromwell (1974: 82) notes, Strauss 'dropped the leading idea . . . that the Christ of the Scriptures was an idealization of humanity', stating instead that 'Hegel's philosophy, rightly understood, called for the appearance of a real, historical, and ideal Christ'. These were serious concessions to Strauss's many critics, undermining, as they did, 'the inner unity of his book'. All of this intellectual back-peddling would be worth it, however, if it could resuscitate his prospects of university employment.

Just such a prospect emerged in 1839 at the University of Zurich in Switzerland, but David Friedrich Strauss encountered a problem there that later scholars of the Bible, particularly in England, would encounter: the close connection between church and state. In Zurich, a canton of Switzerland, church and state were allied; indeed, the constitution of the canton guaranteed the church's survival. That meant, of course, that any perceived attack on the church was not only a religious matter but also a political one. A majority of the canton's population saw Strauss's appointment to the faculty of theology at the University of Zurich as just such a religious-political assault. It was significant, in that respect, that the vote to offer Strauss the position carried by the slimmest of majorities: one vote. And even that hotly contested decision was a follow-up to a failed effort to appoint him to another position at the university three years earlier. When news of the 1839 appointment went public, it was greeted by a 'flood of pamphlets' (Lerner 2012: 225). Strauss's quickly-mobilizing opponents argued that he was a threat to the canton because he would be an atheistic cuckoo in Zurich's faculty of theology; as a professor, he would have a damaging, if not catastrophic, intellectual and moral influence on generations of future ministers, and his teachings – his questioning of the literal reading of the Bible – would cast doubt on the 'structure and basic principles of the constitutionally guaranteed state religion' (Lerner 2012: 227). Strauss and his fast-dwindling number of supporters fought back. They insisted that he was a believing, largely orthodox Protestant; that his argument that parts of the Gospels were mythical was meant to reveal, not undermine, the wider 'eternal truths' of the Bible (Lerner 2012: 227), and that, as a university professor, lecturing to a small number of students in any given academic term, he would have little real impact on the lives and souls of the canton's wider population. It was a valiant, if desperate, defensive effort, but events in Zurich were already spinning beyond the reach of rational thought.

By the early autumn of 1839, the canton of Zurich was split into religious and political factions over David Friedrich Strauss's appointment to the university's faculty of theology. Strauss's opponents saw the Bible itself as a record of historical truths; his supporters looked on the Bible as more of a poetic document that should be used to teach moral and ethical lessons. In making that case, Strauss's supporters convinced themselves that their appointee was a modern Ulrich Zwingli, buckling on his armor to do battle for a purer, reformed church; his opponents believed that the church was fine as it stood, and that Strauss's views on the Gospels revealed him to be more heretic than reformer. With such contradictory positions, and the close connection between religion and state, this debate quickly morphed into a larger dispute over which side truly represented the will of the canton's people. The opposition formed a Central Committee dedicated to making sure that 'Strauss may not and shall not come!' (Lerner 2012: 232). Its members demanded that his appointment should be withdrawn and that a more orthodox Protestant be brought in to replace him. Petitions making that case were popular, demonstrating that the Central Committee's propaganda effort had struck a chord among a largely rural and religiously conservative population worried about the impact that Strauss and his teachings would have on their church and on their immortal souls. The increasingly beleaguered government of the canton eventually gave in to the mounting popular pressure and decided to offer Strauss a retirement package before he had taught a single class. Strauss accepted, but even that concession could not save the government from the religious-political firestorm whipped up by the Central Committee. Its rural supporters marched on the city of Zurich and compelled the government to dissolve itself and to call for new elections. In the minds of the marchers, they had asserted their political sovereignty and saved their church. The road to heaven was once again open in the canton of Zurich.

That the route to the kingdom of God might not be so straight in the Anglo world is suggested by a brief afterword to the story of David Friedrich Strauss's *Life of Jesus Critically Examined*. In England, the Anglican Church's legally established position and the near-consistent support of its archbishops and bishops for the powers-that-be made it an obvious target for political reformers and radicals alike. Among the latter was Joseph Parkes, who first floated the idea of translating Strauss's book in the early 1840s. As the biographer Frederick Karl (1995: 74) notes, Parkes was 'not concerned with religious interpretation but with an undermining of belief itself'. After several false starts, Parkes and several of his fellow radicals hit on the best person for the job – Mary Ann Evans, who later wrote novels under the pen name George Eliot. Evans set about translating the over 1,500 pages of the fourth edition of Strauss's *Life of Jesus*. This was the most strident of the several versions of that study; having failed to gain a university post through compromise with his many critics in the third edition, Strauss came back at them with redoubled certainty in, and polemical zeal for, his original argument. While working day after day on translating, Evans herself 'did not lose her belief in the spiritual value of the Bible, but [rather] compared it to poetry and the arts in general' (Karl 1995: 78). That was a conclusion that would likely have pleased Strauss, who wrote a preface to Evans's translation praising its accuracy, but not the more atheistically inclined Joseph Parkes. When the translation appeared in print in 1846, it was received with a predictable combination of praise from the reform or radically inclined, and earnest hand-wringing among the orthodox faithful.

Those protectors of Anglican orthodoxy were even more alarmed when *Essays and Reviews* appeared in 1860. The essayists found themselves being denounced in the press as the 'seven against Christ' (Hesketh 2017: 15). In reality, however, they were representative of the Broad Church movement within the Church of England, whose supporters felt that room had to be made in the state-sponsored faith for the innovations of modern scholarship and science, including the evolutionary theories of Charles Darwin. This modernizing drive was opposed by two other groups inside the Church of England: High Anglicans, who aimed to bring their church closer to its Roman Catholic roots, and Low Anglicans, who embraced the evangelicalism of less socially respectable groups like the Methodists. Just as was the case in Zurich, the challenge to both high and low Anglican orthodoxy that *Essays and Reviews* seemed to pose produced a strong, if not alarmist, reaction. Two of the clerical essayists found themselves charged with, and tried for, heresy. As arms-length servants of the state, both were eventually cleared by the highest court in the British Empire, the Judicial Committee of the Privy Council, but the long-running trial process ironically kept *Essays and Reviews* in the public eye for much longer than the often-esoteric subjects covered in the book might otherwise have warranted. As the historian Owen Chadwick (1972: 88) notes, before it petered out in the late 1860s, this controversy had roused fears 'that the Church of England was near to schism'. 'If a division occurred', he adds, 'it would be fundamentally on the question whether modern biblical criticism was lawful for clergy of the Church of England'. And that, as the heresy trials of the two *Essays and Reviews* authors had demonstrated –

ending, as they did, in an appeal to a civil court – was bound to be both a religious and a political issue.

Just such an Anglican schism occurred not in Britain itself, but on the margins of its empire. As we have already seen, Bishop J. W. Colenso's book sold very well in England; the critical response, however, was predictably negative. From there, events developed along what was becoming the usual religious-political lines. Every Anglican bishop but one called on Colenso to resign his office, given that his book could not, in their view, be reconciled with orthodox Anglican beliefs. Like the anti-Strauss party in Zurich, the Anglican bishops saw Colenso as a heterodox cuckoo in the nest and so a threat to church and state alike. To deal with this growing problem, the bishop of Cape Town, Robert Gray, held a synod of South Africa's leading clergy in November 1863 and, a month later, deposed Colenso as bishop of Natal. In addition, Gray prohibited the rebel from performing the duties of an Anglican minister in the colony, while also giving him until April 1864 to recant his views on the accuracy of the biblical narrative and to return to the orthodox fold. Colenso responded by travelling to England and appealing the synod's ruling to the Judicial Committee of the Privy Council, like the *Essays and Reviews* heretics before him. Colenso's appeal was based more on civil than religious grounds: he was 'a citizen of the empire who had been wronged', as Owen Chadwick (1972: 93) puts it. Some of England's leading thinkers, including Charles Darwin, agreed, contributing to Colenso's legal expenses and hailing him as a symbol of intellectual liberty striving against orthodox conservatism. In 1865, the Judicial Committee of the Privy Council ruled in Colenso's favour, overturning the rule of Bishop Gray's synod. A triumphant Colenso returned to Natal, believing 'that for the sake of intelligent Englishmen he must prove it possible to hold his views and be a bishop' (Chadwick 1972: 93). Arriving in November 1865, Colenso called on the imperial parliament to use its power to open the way for modern intellectual and scientific thought in the Church of England. He also made a specifically political argument, stating that, in returning to a charge from which his fellow bishops had ejected him, he was acting as a loyal servant of the Queen. As the ruling of the Judicial Committee of the Privy Council had proven, at least to Colenso, it was Bishop Gray and his fellow South African clergy who were outside the law and so, in some ways, traitors. Gray responded to this wildly provocative statement by excommunicating Colenso in early 1866 and moving to appoint a new bishop of Natal to replace him. The result was schism in Natal and all the ill will and unedifying spectacle that always accompanied such episodes in the nineteenth century.

Bishop Colenso's troubles with his fellow clergy were the high point of the controversy around the historical interpretation of the Bible in nineteenth- and early-twentieth-century Britain and its empire. By comparison, the uproar about the historian J. R. Seeley's anonymous *Ecce Homo* was relatively tame. To be sure, Lord Shaftesbury, an ardently evangelical Anglican, denounced it as 'the most pestilential book ever vomited from the jaws of hell' (Hesketh 2017: 96), but that over-the-top statement was as frequently ridiculed as it was applauded in the British press. The sensation produced by *Ecce Homo*, as Ian Hesketh demonstrates, had as much to do with the public fascination with discovering the identity of its anonymous author as it did with the arguments that Seeley made. In the end, Seeley's analytical synthesis of academic rigor and respect for the tender consciences of the orthodox of the Church of England proved to be one that most middle-of-the-road Anglicans were willing to hear. *Ecce Homo*'s generally favourable reception among the great and good suggested that the long process of accepting the implications of modern historical criticism for the Bible was already underway in England, even as the storm over Bishop Colenso was still raging. Indeed, by the mid-1890s, most educated people in the metropole of the British Empire realized that they 'could no longer know the Bible by knowing only the Bible', as Owen Chadwick (1972: 109) writes.

Across the rest of the Anglosphere, the rise of biblical criticism was greeted with the same mixture of immediate alarm later tempering to sometimes grudging acceptance. At regular intervals, Unitarian, Presbyterian and Methodist churches brought charges of heresy against their own ministers who had embraced the methods of David Friedrich Strauss and his supporters. At one point in the early 1840s, the stormy petrel Theodore Parker found himself cut off from 'privileges of ministerial fellowship' (Dorrien 2001: 88) thanks to his views on miracles and the dispensability of the historical Jesus. When Parker persisted in those views, and expressed them eloquently and publicly, some of the more conservative of his fellow Unitarian clergy denounced him as a subversive, undermining Christendom. Others argued that Parker was no Christian at all. Those ministers pushed Parker to resign, but he refused. His colleagues eventually backed down, having brought their church to the verge of crisis. Forty years later, one less fortunate Scottish Presbyterian minister was forced out of his teaching position because of his dedication to biblical criticism. Across the Atlantic, in Canada, two Presbyterians were charged with heresy for the same reason in the final third of the nineteenth century, but in a suggestion of the way the wind was now blowing, one was acquitted and the church dropped the charges against the second before a hearing could even take place. The Canadian Methodist biblical critic George Workman was not as fortunate in the early 1890s: he was forced out of a teaching position at the denomination's leading college. But, within twenty years, the Methodists in Canada, like their fellow Protestants of most denominations, had made their peace with the modern historical approach to the Bible. In 1910 a majority of the Methodist ministry in Canada, following the lead of the reform-minded Nathaniel Burwash, voted that 'the new critical teaching' should remain on the syllabus for all future clerics (Van Die 1989: 90–1). It should be noted that, as heated as these debates over biblical criticism became, none of them affected politics beyond the denominations themselves. Neither Unitarianism, Presbyterianism nor Methodism was an established church in the same way as Anglicanism in England or the church in the canton of Zurich.

Finally, returning once again to continental Europe, the reaction to both Ernest Renan's *Life of Jesus* and Albert Schweitzer's *Quest of the Historical Jesus* demonstrated how different or changing national and intellectual contexts affected the reception of biblical criticism. The initial outrage among the faithful to Renan's *Life of Jesus* resulted, of course, in his removal from his professorship at the Collége de France. But, unlike the perpetually unfortunate David Friedrich Strauss, Renan was restored to his position when Napoleon III fell from power and was replaced by the more secular-minded Third Republic in 1871. By that point, Renan was not an orthodox believer in any recognizable sense of the word, but like many upwardly mobile Frenchmen of his day, he kept his political options open, supporting royalist, Bonapartist and republican causes in quick succession. Despite initial outrage in 1863, Renan quickly gathered supporters among France's liberal and secular newspapers and journals. That meant that, after 1871, he faced little danger in expressing his views since, though the Catholic Church remained France's legally recognized denomination until 1905, many of the liberal supporters of the Third Republic, Renan's people, were openly hostile to its place in public (and private) life. In short, the religious passions excited by Renan's *Life of Jesus* did not translate into a wider crisis, despite the often-feral political climate of mid-nineteenth-century

France. And when Albert Schweitzer's great study appeared in 1906 it was received with a mixture of respectful interest and debate in his native Germany. By then, the intellectual revolution that Strauss had inaugurated in the mid-1830s had triumphed, at least among the majority of that country's Protestant clergy and academics.

BIBLE AND POLITICS: NATION-BUILDING AND EMPIRE

Questing for the historical Jesus itself was often an overtly political exercise, but the Bible also played a role in the nineteenth- and early-twentieth-century politics beyond debates about the nature of the living Christ. It influenced politicians and political events, yet not always in ways or in places that we might initially expect. Leading statesmen lived in a world in which the Bible featured prominently, and its influence was critical in at least one instance of nineteenth-century empire building. Overall, however, the Bible's political impact was felt most significantly on the margins of society and, in particular, among those determined to resist the encroachment of the imperial or national centre on the periphery of Anglo-American and creole settlement.

Whether in its Catholic or Protestant form, Christianity had a pervasive impact on the thought and language of the politicians of Europe and the Anglosphere during the nineteenth and early twentieth centuries. It is nevertheless difficult to pinpoint examples of the Bible itself determining a specific policy or party platform. It is likely, in that respect, that the case of John Quincy Adams was typical of this period. He was an American diplomat, statesman and president who grew up and lived his life in a family and regional context imbued with biblical learning. The first-born son of John and Abigail Adams, arguably the first power-couple of the American republic, John Quincy took to the faith of his parents: regular study of, and reflection on, the Bible mixed with 'scientific curiosity, Scottish Common Sense philosophy, and Protestant piety' (Georgini 2019: 46). Following the lead of his imposing father and mother once again, Adams looked on the Scriptures as 'an ancient text capable of enduring myriad translations, which was clear proof of Christianity's robust nature' (Georgini 2019: 51). His eclectic approach to religion and his liberal reading of the Bible convinced Adams that the people of the United States, blessed by God, had been providentially granted the intellectual and moral tools necessary to construct a Christian republicanism that could, potentially, forge a great nation. At the same time, however, Adams was not willing to see the Bible as an infallible guide to human action, much less public policy. Though he served as the vice president of the American Bible Society beginning in 1818, Adams saw the Scriptures as simply one 'special book among many in the burgeoning religious press' (Georgini 2019: 53). Instead of turning to the Bible to guide his diplomatic and presidential actions, Adams and his long-suffering wife, Louisa Catherine Adams, relied on its lessons and their wider faith to overcome the routine disappointments of nineteenth-century life and to help them to raise their surviving children in the family's now-firmly established tradition of Christian republicanism and service to their country. Perhaps such an engagement with the Bible was good enough, politically speaking, given that the couple's children and grandchildren included distinguished diplomats, political advisors and possibly the greatest nineteenth-century historian of the early American republic, Henry Adams, whose own mature faith, however, was provisional at best.

The career of a near-contemporary politician, Samuel Leonard Tilley of the British North American colony of New Brunswick, was the rare exception that proved the rule of the Adams experience. As one of the architects of the confederation that formed the modern nation of Canada, Tilley was present at the intercolonial and imperial conferences that preceded the moment of creation on 1 July 1867. It was at the final of those meetings, held in London, England, that his daily reading from the Bible briefly but critically influenced the course of national politics. As the colonial statesmen gathered at the centre of the British Empire, they had several important decisions to make, including what their new country should be called. Some delegates pushed for the 'kingdom of Canada', but the grandees of the British imperial establishment would have none of that. They were keen to avoid any possible insult or provocation of the United States so soon after the triumphant conclusion of the Civil War. As the historian Donald Creighton (1964: 423) points out, the British ambassador in Washington, DC, 'had reported . . . that the title "Kingdom of Canada" had aroused "much remark of an unfriendly character in the United States"'. It was at this point that Tilley drew on his knowledge of the Bible to suggest an alternative, pointing to the seventy-second Psalm: 'He shall have dominion also from sea to sea and from the river unto the ends of the earth.' Impressed, perhaps, by the majestic cadence of the verse, the colonial delegates agreed to adopt the official name of the Dominion of Canada. Asked for her approval, Queen Victoria granted it, though she was not particularly amused with the compromise, suggesting that 'the style "Dominion" was not a very happy addition to the title' (Creighton 1964: 424). The British prime minister, the Tory Lord Derby, was both more cutting and outspoken than his monarch, declaring the use of the word 'dominion' 'rather absurd' (Hawkins 2008: 316). Still, with a fine scriptural flourish, Canada was launched upon its course.

Elsewhere across the transoceanic world, the relationship between the Bible and imperialism was more indirect, informal and complex than the naming of a predominantly white and Christian colony of settlement. Missions to the non-Christian people of the British Empire, for instance, often preceded official integration or conquest and necessarily involved the Scriptures. In order to spread the good word, and the civilizing influence of Christendom, the heathen had to be able to understand it first. Missionaries among the Yoruba and Kikuyu of north-western and eastern Africa, the Tswana of the Cape of Good Hope, the islanders of the Pacific, and the people of the Indian subcontinent, to give just a few examples, translated the Bible into multiple tongues. The challenge those earnest translators faced was often monumental. In the Pacific alone, as the historian Paul Landau (2005: 199) points out, they encountered 'hundreds of languages each with tiny numbers of speakers; vast and turbulent seas separating populations; [and] ritualized violence and hostility on individual islands'. Once a workable translation was achieved, the missionaries, their preaching, and their converts could open the door to imperial expansion, but things did not always work out quite so smoothly. Sometimes, as we saw in the cases of Bishop Colenso and the Scottish Presbyterians, the very act of explaining the Bible to colonial converts could have a transformative impact on metropolitan faith itself. And, on the imperial margins, a ministerial elite might try to control the interpretation of the Bible and Christianity more generally, but 'the Empire's peoples used their texts as they wished'. 'Even before missionaries lost their monopoly on the Empire's presses' to secular publishers and others, Landau (2005: 194) adds, '"print culture" had expanded beyond their reach'.

The most notable example of such a process of unexpected and, for metropolitan imperialists, unwelcomed consequences involved millenarian movements that arose across the Atlantic world during the nineteenth century and that mobilized indigenous and marginalized people to combat the spread of empire or the secular nation state. The fact that all of these movements were crushed, often through terrible violence, does nothing to diminish their cultural and political importance. The millenarianism of these movements drew on an often-heady combination of indigenous religious traditions and the more socially and politically radical parts of the Bible, including the book of Revelation, as interpreted by self-proclaimed prophets of the dispossessed.

Millennial prophets such as Louis Riel among the Metis people of western Canada and Antônio Conselheiro of the backlands population of north-western Brazil promised a world-shattering crisis that would see the enemy vanquished and the sufferers of this world granted victory by a righteous God. Riel had imbibed aspects of this apocalyptic message beginning in his youth, influenced by the Ultramontane clergy of French Canada, Catholic prophetic literature, and near-contemporary Protestant millenarian groups in the United States, including the Millerites. After suffering a series of mental collapses, Riel also turned to the Old Testament. He addressed his Metis followers, who had seen their lands and livelihoods threatened by encroaching eastern settlement in the years before the Northwest Rebellion of 1885, urging them to embrace parts of the Mosaic Law including 'polygamy, a married clergy, the Saturday Sabbath, and circumcision', as the political scientist Thomas Flanagan (1996: 203) notes. Riel also cast himself in the role of a biblical prophet, adopting the middle name 'David', and even of a Christ-figure: when he was executed for treason in November 1885, Riel promised an attending doctor that he would rise from the dead in three days. He did not, but Riel's millenarian imaginary nonetheless inspired his Metis followers to take on the government of Canada with its vastly superior forces, in terms of numbers, supplies and weapons. Similarly, Antônio Conselheiro positioned himself as a prophet who promised to combat the landlords of the Canudos region and the new, secular republic of Brazil that supported those men's hard-nosed policies towards their tenants and workers. Conselheiro declared that 'the backlands will become beaches and the beaches backlands', that 'there will be many hats but few heads' (Graziano 1999: 239), and in a somewhat less baffling paraphrase of St Matthew and St Luke, that 'there shall be a great rain of stars and that will mark the end of the world. God said in the Gospels: I have a flock which has strayed from the sheep fold and I must gather them because there is just one pastor and only one parishioner' (da Cunha 2010: 142). The rebels of Canudos, desiring 'miracles and messiahs', according to the historian Susanna Hecht (2013: 56), were inspired enough by such language to defeat three military expeditions that Brazil's new republican government sent to put them down, before succumbing to artillery bombardment, ferocious hand-to-hand combat and massacre in 1897. The rebels' tenacity in the face of overwhelming odds can only be explained, Hecht (2013: 77) suggests, by the fact that they 'were in a true end time', as the Bible predicted, and 'so perhaps they believed anything was possible', including the already-dead Conselheiro's return to life alongside 'battalions of angels'.

BIBLE AND POLITICS: EDUCATION, SLAVERY AND WAR

While the Bible was contributing to political upheaval around the margins of empire and nation, things were not much calmer at the centres of power and influence. During the mid-nineteenth century, British and American Protestants battled Catholics over the role that the Scriptures should play in education. At the same time, other Americans turned to the written word of God in debates over the nature and viability of slavery in their increasingly divided country. And then the Bible went into battle, with the supporters of the Union and the Confederacy using it to explain and justify their increasingly desperate and destructive efforts during the American Civil War and all sides claiming its sanction and God's support in the vast catastrophe of the First World War.

Given the central role that anti-Catholicism played in the cultural formation of Britain from the Reformation on, it is not surprising that questions about what made up a proper education for the young developed into political disputes or that the Bible was central to those frequently heated debates. In early 1820s Ireland, for example, campaigners for Catholic rights, such as the 'liberator' Daniel O'Connell, linked together the politically explosive issues of emancipation (Catholic enfranchisement on equal terms with Protestants), education, and the place of a version of the Bible approved by the country's Catholic bishops in schools and daily life. In the large part, this campaign was a reaction to the activities of various Protestant Bible societies in Ireland that aimed to woo the majority Catholic population away from their traditional faith by distributing copies of the Scriptures, usually the King James Version, free from any interpretive notes or comments. At least one Protestant minister foresaw that distributing such bibles 'might produce "less fruit than expected, [or] fruit in abundance of a poisonous quality"' (Whelan 2005: 131). That proved to be the case. The Irish Catholic bishops denounced the activities of the Protestant Bible societies and, with the support of O'Connell, made a case for seeing the 'Bible without note or comment' as 'a manifestation of Protestant culture and political supremacy and . . . as part of a scheme to undermine the authority of their Church' (Whelan 2005: 135). The resulting polarization over which Bible, Protestant or Catholic-approved, should be used in schools heightened the sectarian tension never far below the surface in the politics of Ireland and, by extension, Britain.

A similar course of events played out in the United States during the mid-1840s, where Protestantism and national identity were closely linked. There, as in Ireland, Protestants in northern states like New York and Pennsylvania were keen to ensure that their Bible, the King James or Authorized Version, was the only one used in the common school system. The battle lines were drawn when the combative Catholic bishop of New York, John Hughes, challenged Protestant control over the schools and tried to eliminate daily readings from what his loyal flock regarded as the very-much unauthorized version of the Scriptures. When the same issue came up in Pennsylvania, the resulting political conflagration was so heated that it led to church burnings in the city of Philadelphia. As the historian Richard Carwardine (1997: 83) points out, for torch-wielding American Protestants, 'to attack the Authorized Version [of the Bible] was to strike at the heart of America's religious values and civic order'. One political party, the Whigs, took up that message as a plank in its 1844 election platform, with its vice-presidential candidate publicly vowing to 'live by the Bible and TO DIE FOR THE BIBLE' (Carwardine 1997: 85). The Whigs lost that election, suggesting perhaps that, as in Ireland, such appeals to sectarianism could only take a cause so far in a country with a growing and politically motivated Catholic population determined to defend its version of the Scriptures and its wider culture.

By the 1850s, however, such political conflicts concerning the place of the Bible in American schools were overshadowed by the issue that threatened the unity of the United States itself: slavery. And here, too, the Scriptures became a source of, and a weapon in, the rhetorical and actual battles between opponents and supporters of what was euphemistically called America's 'peculiar institution'. While, in hindsight, those in favor of abolishing slavery clearly held the moral high ground, they had a much more difficult task making that case at the time, given that so much of the Bible was against them. Slavery's advocates could and did point to the fact that the Old Testament included many slave-owning patriarchs and that nowhere in the New Testament did Jesus Christ or his disciples denounce the practice. Beyond that, the supporters of slavery among the preachers of the southern states argued:

> That all humans were descendants of Adam and Eve and existed as a result of a single creation as described in the Bible. These ministers claimed that blacks were the descendants of Noah's son Ham and Noah's grandson Canaan. After the flood, according to the biblical story, Noah cursed Canaan, and the pro-slavery ministers claimed that the biblical 'curse of Canaan' was that Canaan and his descendants became black and were doomed forever to be 'servants' of their brethren. (Finkelman 2003: 26)

Of course, by 'servants' these southern clergymen meant slaves.

Such sophism angered the growing ranks of America's abolitionists, who were just as likely to turn to the Bible for ammunition in their battles to end slavery. Even a preacher not fully committed to the cause of ending slavery, such as the Methodist Peter Cartwright, was disgusted by the way that southerners drew on the Scriptures to support arguments in favour of their 'peculiar institution', remarking that some of his own brethren 'began to apologize' for slavery, 'then to justify it, on legal principles; then on Bible principles till lo and behold! it is not an evil, but a good! it is not a curse but a blessing' (Fox-Genovese and Genovese 2005: 476). Self-declared abolitionists went further, trying to combat their opponents' biblical-racialist points by drawing on the golden rule outlined in Mt. 7.12 – 'Therefore all things whatsoever ye would that men should do to you: do ye even so to them' – 'to make the persuasive point that slavery was antithetical to the spirit of Christianity' (Finkelman 2003: 27). Such appeals to a common humanity did nothing, however, to halt the consolidation of either slavery or the power of the slave owners in American politics. As a result, radical abolitionists turned to the Bible to help carry out and later justify more drastic measures. For instance, in the bloody struggle of the mid-1850s to determine whether Kansas would enter the union as a free or slave state, that most gleefully controversial of Unitarian ministers, Theodore Parker, shipped handguns and rifles to the enemies of slavery in 'boxes labeled "Bibles"' (Wineapple 2008: 87). Parker and five other leading abolitionists also secretly bankrolled the efforts of the most extreme of the crusaders against slavery: John Brown. Brown himself, who frequently looked, spoke and acted like a vengeful Old Testament prophet, drew on the Bible to vindicate his famously ineffective but politically divisive raid on a federal arsenal at Harpers Ferry, Virginia, in 1859. As he stated in a letter written while he awaited execution, quoting 2 Cor. 10.4, 'You know that Christ once armed Peter. So in my case, I think he put a sword in my hand . . . I bless God that it proves "mighty to the pulling down of strongholds"' (Earle 2008: 30–1). The supporters of slavery would have seen such opinions as heresy – the kind of thing that southern states would do well to avoid in the future, even if that meant secession.

When eleven southern states did secede from the United States over the winter of 1860–1, forming the Confederate States of America, the Bible went to war along with hundreds of thousands of soldiers. Supporters of both the Union and the Confederacy drew on the Scriptures to defend their increasingly blood-soaked causes. President Abraham Lincoln, for instance, 'treasured the Bible for its moral wisdom, and frequently peppered his political speeches with biblical quotes' (Scott 2011: 17), which his audience would have recognized at once. In the seceding states, educators encouraged school children 'to read the Bible as the inspired Word of God and to have daily devotions' (Stout 2006:

105) with the aim of instructing this future generation of southerners in the scriptural justification of slavery developed before the war. At the same time, in both the north and south, Bible societies did their best to make sure that soldiers marched into battle with the Scriptures in their pockets and packs, though southern groups had to contend with a crippling northern naval blockade and growing wartime shortages of paper. In the well-supplied northern armies, some 'battle-hardened veterans' grumbled that 'they would have preferred better food or extra socks' to a copy of the Bible (Rable 2010: 131), yet most troopers turned to the Scriptures to help ward off boredom, to maintain their morale, and for genuine religious uplift. The Bible could also save a soldier's life – literally. As historian George Rable (2010: 166) points out, 'tales of Bibles stopping bullets cropped up after nearly every major battle' in the Civil War, which tends to make most scholars suspect exaggeration, but we are told, 'pocket Testaments saved lives just often enough to make such stories believable' (Rable 2010: 166).

People on the home front of the American Civil War, both northern and southern, never seem to have tired of reading such tales, likely because they too increasingly turned to the Bible to explain the titanic struggle unfolding all around them. In the northern state of Illinois, for instance, the ardent unionist Mary Robinson, who had lost a son in battle, wrote a letter to another northern soldier in 1863, complaining about Confederate sympathizers in her neighborhood. As the historian Sean Scott (2011: 162–3) explains, 'like the Apostle Paul when opposed by the wicked schemes of Alexander the coppersmith as recorded in 2 Timothy 4:14, she could wait for the future judgment when "the lord will reward them according to their deed"'. Two years later, the Confederate diarist Mary Chesnut relied on the book of Job 'to make sense of the South's desperate situation' (Webb 2013: 11) as the war entered its dreadful, destructive endgame. If God allowed Satan to test Job's faith with a series of trials, Chesnut reasoned, perhaps He was doing the same thing to the Confederacy. Such examples of civilians grasping hold of biblical certainties in a time of political upheaval and collapse could be multiplied many times over.

The First World War was comparable to the American Civil War in a number of ways, including the manner in which the combatants, at all levels, turned to the Scriptures to explain and justify their role in the conflict. In the opening months of battle in 1914, the supporters of the Allied cause, particularly among the clergy, were quick to point to what they saw as one of the main causes of German militarism: the biblical criticism discussed at the beginning of this chapter. One American evangelical Protestant minister, the Baptist Cortland Myers, put it this way:

> The beer-soaked theologians of Germany have done more to preach Infidelity in the form of Higher Criticism into the world . . . than all other educators combined . . . The Abomination of abominations in the modern religious world is that ripe, rank, rampant, rotten new theology in Germany. (Sutton 2014: 62)

Biblical criticism, Myers continued, had unleashed a 'world-tidal wave of barbarism, savagery, and immorality' (Sutton 2014: 62). Other Allied clergy were less rabid in their denunciations, but as the historian Hew Strachan (2001: 1119) explains, they broadly agreed that German 'biblical scholarship had neglected faith in favour of research, religion in favour of rationality, and so removed the moral force from Christian teaching'. For French thinkers, this hollowing out of genuine Christianity in Germany was primarily the result of the influence of David Friedrich Strauss's main intellectual inspiration, the philosopher Georg Wilhelm Friedrich Hegel, whose teachings had encouraged 'materialist, militarist, and nationalist' (Strachan 2001: 1121) urges on the east side of the Rhine River, contributing to the warlike spirit that inspired the German invasion of Belgium and France in August 1914.

Rather surprisingly, this portrayal of the impact of biblical criticism on pre-war German thought and culture was not too far from the truth. 'For liberal Protestants' in Germany, as the historian Philip Jenkins (2015: 83) argues, 'the God presented in the Bible was only one limited perception of the deity, who became better understood through the progressive workings of history'. But, Jenkins adds, the result of such a liberal and open approach to the Scriptures was a 'lack of any external absolutes', which allowed Germany's Protestant churches to be 'swept along with contemporary political passions'. That explains, at least in part, why so many German churchmen sided enthusiastically with their country's war effort and turned to the Bible, in turn, to support what they saw as a crusade against the godlessness of the Allied powers.

The Bible played a different, less purely intellectual role among the soldiers who found themselves stationed along the Western Front and for the men and women they left behind on the home front. Faced with the almost unimaginable horrors of trench warfare, troops on both sides of the conflict turned to the Scriptures for comfort and inspiration. Many, according to Philip Jenkins (2015: 115), were particularly taken with the twenty-third Psalm with its evocation of 'those passing through the shadow of the valley of death', while they tended to avoid 'the Bible's harsh or military texts'. Soldiers also made use of the Bible and biblical language to make sense of the slaughter they were compelled to endure. 'Biblicizing', Jenkins (2015: 116) notes, 'gave a cosmic meaning, even a grandeur, to acts of extreme violence and mass killing.' Things were different on the home front, which was often far from the zone of combat. There, civilians could more readily take up the rhetoric of their bellicose preachers. In the summer of 1914, for instance, one German woman declared that the coming of the war had to be read in biblical terms to be understood fully. The end of days 'must come to pass', she stated, 'for it is foretold in the Bible; and we can only thank God if Satan's rule is soon to be destroyed. Then will come at last the true Empire of Peace, with our Lord Jesus Christ as ruler!' (Ferguson 1998: 210). It almost goes without saying that the First World War, like so many 'holy wars' before it, failed to deliver on the millennial expectations of its participants. Instead, all it produced was another, even more terrible world war, but one that falls outside the time frame of this chapter.

REFERENCES

Barton, J. (2019), *A History of the Bible: The Story of the World's Most Influential Book*, New York: Viking.

Belich, J. (2009), *Replenishing the Earth: The Settler Revolution and the Rise of the Anglo-World, 1783–1939*, Oxford: Oxford University Press.

Burrow, J. W. (2000), *The Crisis of Reason: European Thought, 1848–1914*, New Haven: Yale University Press.

Carwardine, R. J. (1997), *Evangelicals and Politics in Antebellum America*, Knoxville: University of Tennessee Press.

Chadwick, O. (1972), *The Victorian Church, Part Two: 1860–1901*, London: SCM Press.

Creighton, D. (1964), *The Road to Confederation: The Emergence of Canada, 1863–1867*, Toronto: Macmillan of Canada.

Cromwell, R. S. (1974), *David Friedrich Strauss and His Place in Modern Thought*, Fair Lawn: R.E. Burdick Inc.

da Cunha, E. (2010), *Backlands: The Canudos Campaign*, trans. Elizabeth Lowe, London: Penguin.

Dorrien, G. (2001), *The Making of American Liberal Theology: Imagining Progressive Religion, 1805–1900*, Louisville: Westminster John Knox Press.

Earle, J. (2008), *John Brown's Raid on Harpers Ferry: A Brief History with Documents*, Boston: Bedford / St. Martin's.

Ferguson, N. (1998), *The Pity of War: Explaining World War I*, New York: Basic Books.

Finkelman, P. (2003), *Defending Slavery: Proslavery Thought in the Old South: A Brief History with Documents*, Boston: Bedford / St. Martin's.

Flanagan, T. (1996), *Louis 'David' Riel: Prophet of the New World*, revised edn, Toronto: University of Toronto Press.

Fox-Genovese, E. and E. D. Genovese (2005), *The Mind of the Master Class: History and Faith in the Southern Slaveholders' Worldview*, Cambridge: Cambridge University Press.

Georgini, S. (2019), *Household Gods: The Religious Lives of the Adams Family*, Oxford: Oxford University Press.

Graziano, F. (1999), *The Millennial New World*, Oxford: Oxford University Press.

Hawkins, A. (2008), *The Forgotten Prime Minister: The 14th Earl of Derby: Achievement, 1851–1869*, Oxford: Oxford University Press.

Hecht, S. B. (2013), *The Scramble for the Amazon and the Lost Paradise of Euclides da Cunha*, Chicago: University of Chicago Press.

Hesketh, I. (2017), *Victorian Jesus: J.R. Seeley, Religion, and the Cultural Significance of Anonymity*, Toronto: University of Toronto Press.

Holmes, A. R. (2018), *The Irish Presbyterian Mind: Conservative Theology, Evangelical Experience, and Modern Criticism, 1830–1930*, Oxford: Oxford University Press.

Jenkins, P. (2015), *The Great and Holy War: How World War I became a Religious Crusade*, New York: Harper Collins.

Karl, F. R. (1995), *George Eliot: Voice of a Century*, New York: W.W. Norton and Company.

Landau, P. (2005), 'Language', in *Missions and Empire*, ed. Norman Etherington, 194–215, Oxford: Oxford University Press.

Larsen, T. (2011), *A People of One Book: The Bible and the Victorians*, Oxford: Oxford University Press.

Lerner, M. H. (2012), *A Laboratory of Liberty: The Transformation of Political Culture in Republican Switzerland, 1750–1848*, Leiden: Brill.

Nietzsche, F. (1997), *Untimely Meditations*, ed. Daniel Breazeale, Cambridge: Cambridge University Press.

Paget, J. C. (2001), 'Quests for the Historical Jesus', in *Cambridge Companion to Jesus*, ed. Markus Bockmuehl, 138–55, Cambridge: Cambridge University Press.

Rable, G. (2010), *God's Almost Chosen Peoples: A Religious History of the American Civil War*, Chapel Hill: University of North Carolina Press.

Renan, E. (1955), *The Life of Jesus*, New York: Modern Library.

Schweitzer, A. (2001), *The Quest of the Historical Jesus*, ed. John Bowden, Minneapolis: Fortress Press.

Scott, S. A. (2011), *A Visitation of God: Northern Civilians Interpret the Civil War*, Oxford: Oxford University Press.

Stout, H. S. (2006), *Upon the Altar of the Nation: A Moral History of the Civil War*, New York: Penguin.

Strachan, H. (2001), *The First World War: To Arms*, Oxford: Oxford University Press.
Strachey, L. (1986), *Eminent Victorians*, London: Penguin.
Sutton, M. A. (2014), *American Apocalypse: A History of Modern Evangelicalism*, Cambridge, MA: Harvard University Press.
Van Die, M. (1989), *An Evangelical Mind: Nathanael Burwash and the Methodist Tradition in Canada, 1839–1918*, Montreal and Kingston: McGill-Queen's University Press.
Webb, T. (2013), '"Calm Determination & Cool Brains": Mary Chesnut's God in the 1860s', *Historical Papers 2012: Canadian Society of Church History*, 5–19.
Whelan, I. (2005), *The Bible War in Ireland: The 'Second Reformation' and the Polarization of Protestant-Catholic Relations, 1800–1840*, Madison: University of Wisconsin Press.
Wineapple, B. (2008), *White Heat: The Friendship of Emily Dickinson and Thomas Wentworth Higginson*, New York: Alfred A. Knopf.

CHAPTER 3

Literature

JESSICA ANN HUGHES

In 1888, British parliamentary member William Gladstone denounced a popular work of fiction in a carefully argued 10,000-word review essay published in the popular press. Even by Victorian standards, such a lengthy engagement with popular culture was a notable distraction for someone of Gladstone's status. At the time, he was serving as the opposition leader in parliament and between his third and fourth term as prime minister. But the novel in question, *Robert Elsemere*, was a cultural phenomenon, provoking controversy across the English-speaking world as it became one of the most widely read novels of the Victorian era (Sutherland 1990: 125–7).

What made the novel so popular? The novel's interest lay in its lengthy discussions of the Bible's textual and mythological development being raised by German biblical criticism. So pressing was the issue of biblical reliability and authority that Gladstone himself felt the need to carefully parse the novel's arguments for the reading public. For Gladstone and his contemporaries in Europe and the Americas, the Bible was not just a guide for religious faith. It provided a common bank of stories, characters, images and languages, making it foundational for culture and particularly literature. In fact, in English-language literatures, one would be hard-pressed to find a literary work that does not allude to the Bible or make use of biblical languages and phrases in some way during the nineteenth century. But, while the Bible was everywhere, as *Robert Elsmere* demonstrates, it was hardly an uncontested text.

Throughout the period, the burgeoning disciplines of archaeology, textual criticism and modern science brought a new sort of scrutiny to the Bible that challenged the origin, historicity, traditional readings and cultural status of the text. For this reason, scholars of the period have often characterized the nineteenth century as an era of religious doubt, growing religious scepticism and secularization. To be fair, secularization certainly occurred during this period, particularly in terms of structural changes to European and American society that saw the state take increasing responsibility for things such as education, the registration of births, marriages and deaths, the operation of cemeteries and social services to support the poor. But, as Timothy Larsen has convincingly argued, the secularization thesis and growth of religious doubt presuppose a context of profound faith (Larsen 2006).

Nowhere is this context of faith more evident than in literature. Even when writers such as Dickens appear wholly to ignore religion, they inevitably allude to the Bible or play with its archetypes, at least in passing (Larson 1985). *Bildungsromane* and other narratives of vocation and conversion have their roots in biblical narratives of conversion, like that of Saul on the road to Damascus (McKeon 2002; Watt 2001; Hindmarsh 2005).

Reform novels from Russia to America appropriate some of the Bible's most radical social teachings as potential solutions to the plight of the poor and enslaved. In England, Elizabeth Gaskell, Charlotte Elizabeth Tonna, Benjamin Disraeli and Charles Kingsley all use the Bible to call for interclass compassion and improvement in working conditions. But such uses of the Bible were not limited to England. In America, abolitionist writers such as Harriet Beecher Stowe and William Lloyd Garrison used the Bible to denounce slavery. On the continent, Victor Hugo, Leo Tolstoy and Fyodor Dostoyevsky also turned to the Bible in their calls for social restructuring and class equality. Nationalistic poetry and prose adopt biblical tropes of evangelization to justify a variety of imperial projects (Colley 1992; Stanley 1990; Zemka 1995). And writers across the globe wrestle with the identity of Jesus and the tension between justice and mercy that shapes Christology. Given the ubiquity of the Bible in nineteenth-century literature, what exactly are writers doing with this text beyond using it as a common literary tradition? While it is easy to list examples of the Bible as a widely shared symbolic system and cultural context for literature, literary engagement with the Bible during the Victorian era is, broadly speaking, a project of appropriating and transforming the biblical text for an increasingly secularized and sceptical world. This project manifests itself in three modes of biblical engagement. First, typology provides a way of integrating biblical characters and narrative patterns into contemporary situations in order to reimagine the received tradition in light of rapidly changing societies. Second, rewritings of biblical stories – and particularly rewritings of the life of Jesus recorded in the Gospels – create space for writers to imagine Jesus's character in both historical and modern contexts, while wrestling with the reliability of the biblical text that originally represented him. Third, explicit and not-so-explicit literary explorations of biblical authority provide both a subject for literary reflection and a cypher for thinking about issues of textual authority, interpretation and the writing process more broadly.

BIBLICAL TYPOLOGY

Before exploring biblical typology in nineteenth-century literature, it is helpful to establish what exactly typology is. Within Christian tradition, typology is both a feature of a text and a way of reading a text. Essentially, the Old Testament provides a bank of characters and narrative forms, such as Adam and Eve, Abraham and Isaac, Moses and David. The New Testament draws on these characters and their stories, presenting figures such as Mary, Jesus and the apostles as new versions of older characters. For example, the Gospel of Matthew repeatedly presents Jesus as a new Moses. Such reworkings of a type are common across literary traditions the world over. What makes biblical typology unique within the Christian tradition is that the initial characters are not archetypes upon whom later characters are modeled. Rather, earlier characters are prototypes that find their fullest expression and ultimate fulfilment in later, New Testament characters. Thus, Moses is not the archetype for Jesus. Jesus is the fulfilment of a type first suggested by Moses. While New Testament writers use typology to mark characters as prophetic fulfilments of earlier Jewish types, Christian tradition also encourages the typological reading of Scripture, where readers continually read the New Testament back into the Old Testament's stories and characters while also reading both testaments forward into their own lives and times. As a result, Moses is a type of Jesus and Francis of Assisi is also a type of Jesus, with Jesus being the ultimate exemplary type to which all other types appeal. What distinguishes biblical typology from secular archetypes is the idea of fulfilment embedded within typology. When typology connects two discrete times, it also makes one of those times fulfil the other (Landow 1980: 109). In orthodox uses of typology, typological fulfillment is located in the story of Jesus and the church. Of course, not all writers use typology in an orthodox way. During the nineteenth century writers frequently secularize biblical typology, making the modern world the fulfilment of biblical ideals (Landow 1980; Bercovitch 1989).

In the nineteenth century, biblical typology frequently authorizes a particular social vision across both fictional and nonfictional literatures. Thomas Carlyle's *Sartar Resartus* (a foundational text for many later works in the nineteenth century), makes use of the biblical types of the Exodus, Israel's wanderings, the Promised Land and Christ's temptation to narrate Teufelsdröckh's conversion. Just as Israel was in slavery, found freedom from initial bondage, and then had to wander before coming to the Promised Land, the modern individual embodied in Teufelsdröckh must undergo a journey from socially constructed slavery to individual freedom that involves similar wandering, moments of freedom and finally an Everlasting Yea that marks intellectual salvation. Through such typology Carlyle connects the individual's journey to that of Israel and Jesus, albeit with highly self-aware irony that points to Carlyle's design to 'offer . . . a pattern in which other modern lives might participate' (Gibson and Larsen 2015: 196; Bossche 1991). Later writers including John Stuart Mill and John Henry Newman would use the same biblical typologies of slavery and the Exodus both to structure their autobiographies and to justify their conversions to art and Catholicism, respectively (Gibson and Larsen 2015). Similarly, John Ruskin and Edmund Gosse both draw on biblical typologies of conversion to narrate their conversions away from traditional religion to art. While Ruskin treats his conversion to art as a fulfilment of previous conversions to religious faith, biblical typology also shapes his understanding of artistic reality. As with new figures that fulfil the promise of older biblical types, art itself is 'completed only by reference to God', making art itself a typological representation of the divine (Landow 2014: 4). In all these autobiographical conversion narratives, biblical typology provides an authorized pattern for understanding the process of individual growth and self-realization. But using the biblical text for the modern, nonreligious individual also models the Bible's potential to serve as a culturally valued literary work separate from religious dogma. This nondogmatic use of biblical stories becomes a common way to approach the Christian Scriptures towards the end of the nineteenth century and in the early twentieth century.

Biblical typology also provides a particularly useful symbolic language for the literature of social reform by joining the cultural and religious authority of the Bible to the prophetic voice of the writer. For example, in British literature Florence Nightingale's *Cassandra* calls for social reform around the education and vocations of women by using Christ as a type representing the sufferings of Victorian women. Ultimately, Nightingale calls for a new vision of Christ, imagined as a woman instead of a man (Fraser and Burrows 2001; Jenkins 1995; Showalter 1981, 1991). In a similar vein, Josephine Butler adopts the typology of the Old Testament prophets to work as both a social reformer and biblical interpreter in her writings calling for women's rights and the better legal protection for children (Larsen 2012: 219–47; Benckhuysen 2007). In American literature biblical typology frequently shapes the works of abolitionist and anti-abolitionist writings. While Moses and the Exodus are well-recognized types in the writings of abolitionist literature (both to describe abolitionist leaders and as a way of narrating slave experience) other biblical types offer important claims to prophetic power for both Black writers and women. Applications of Balaam's donkey from Numbers 22–23 point to the culturally disruptive nature of both Black and women's voices within the public sphere, while also claiming the divinely authorized and empowered nature of their calls for freedom and equality (Bassard 2010: 19–22, 40–2). The figure of the Shulamite, the beloved woman in the *Song of Songs*, also becomes an important biblical type for Black writers. She is described as 'black but lovely', in the biblical text, a description used by Black writers to authorize their own representations of blackness as coexisting with goodness and beauty (Bassard 2010: 21). Both Black and white writers use the Old Testament judge, Deborah, as a type for considering women's leadership and governance, reimagining her character even as they lament the lack of attention she receives from male preachers (Stanton 1898: 18–22). In all these uses, biblical typology provides authorization for marginalized voices by drawing readers' attention to the way God speaks through marginalized characters within the Bible. The implicit argument of typology is that, if divine revelation has come through a donkey or a female military leader in the Bible, then divine truth regarding modern society might come from similarly marginalized and disempowered voices on the margins. As such, the very marginalized status of the voice becomes, through typology, a marker of divine (if not social) authority.

Just as nonfiction from 1820 to 1920 frequently uses biblical typology to authorize a prophetic vision for social reform and human progress, prose fiction and poetry make regular use of biblical typology to authorize a particular vision of human life, while reimagining the biblical text for the modern world. Harriet Beecher Stowe's *Uncle Tom's Cabin* uses the types of Moses and the Exodus along with Jesus himself to help readers imagine the sufferings of enslaved people and present a compelling vision for abolition. In fact, Eva's death in *Uncle Tom's Cabin* is, perhaps, the most well-known typological representation of Jesus in American literature. Less recognized is Stowe's use of typology in *The Minister's Wooing*, where 'earthly experience [is] a source of religious knowledge' and marriage, itself a biblical type for the relationship between God and humanity, becomes a means of dismantling the binaries of sacred and secular (Wilkes 2018: 438). Although deeply sceptical about the authority of the Bible, Herman Melville's *Moby Dick* still turns to the archetypes of the rejected son, Ishmael, and the worst of Israel's kings, Ahab. Through the types of Ishmael and Ahab, the novel reworks questions of birthright, pride and human overreach in light of America's nation-building project (Coleman 2018). Similarly, despite Mark Twain's heterodox approach to the Bible, typological appropriations of Adam, Eve, Noah, Joseph and the Prodigal Son recur throughout his work, as he explores the ideas of sin, expulsion, wandering and return in light of humanity's tendency towards self-destruction (Ensor 1969). Twain's 'diaries' of Adam and Eve, which began as Adam's diary in *The Niagara Book* and grew into book versions of *Adam's Diary* (1904) and *Eve's Diary* (1906) take a humorous approach to the biblical text, considering Adam and Eve in light of early twentieth-century feminism and women's suffrage, implicitly calling for social change. Likewise, Emily Dickinson's poetry frequently retells biblical stories and appropriates biblical tropes to challenge the paternalist and authoritative structures that shaped her religious context. Through her reworking of Jesus as the 'tender Pioneer' and a 'docile Gentleman', heaven as 'home', and God the Father as an elusive authority, her poetry explores the problematic nature of received religion and the tensions within trinitarian theology (Brown 1999: 29–65; Lundin 2014). Similarly, Nathanial Hawthorne's short stories and novels rework the characters of Adam and Eve, along with narratives of sin, exile and destruction from the Old Testament, to explore the failures of the American project and his disapproval of Transcendentalism (Courtmanche 2008). Hawthorne ironically appropriates biblical names like Hepzibah or Aminidab to draw attention to the gap between the future that typological thinking promises and the realities that humans actually create. Thus, Hepzibah Pyncheon is not the wife of a good king but a spinster who believes in her own grandeur. Yet, Hepzibah's delusions serve to rewrite the biblical Hepzibah, drawing attention to her role in raising Manasseh, a king who restored idol worship within Judah.

In Britain, biblical typology is particularly important in addressing 'the woman question' and reimagining the place of women in society. Even before 1820, novelists as different as Hannah More and Mary Shelley turned to the typology of Adam and Eve as models for marriage and the human struggle with the divine. In the 1830s, a new typological character became popular in British literature due to the Tractarian movement. The Tractarian, or Oxford, movement reintroduced Roman Catholic belief and practice to the English church, including an affirmation of apostolic succession as the basis for ecclesial authority, a more sacramental view of baptism and communion, liturgical practices such as altar candles and vestments during worship, and even convents. Not surprisingly, this transformation of the English church also drew increased attention to the Virgin Mary as a particularly potent type for writers exploring the nexus of gender, religion and social authority in England.

Treatments of the Virgin Mary in Victorian England ranged from a devoted, angelic virgin mother to a negligent, upbraiding and presumptuous mother. This latter image developed from polemical Protestant readings of Luke 2, in which Jesus's parents fail to notice his absence from the travelling party for an entire day, and Mary's presumption in John 4 that Jesus will turn water into wine (Herringer 2008). Among women writers, a more positive vision of the Virgin Mary offered a way to authorize women's voices and redeem women from social structures that frequently deemed women 'fallen' due to abuse and assault. For example, Elizabeth Barrett Browning appropriates the Virgin Mary through the character of Marian in *Aurora Leigh* (1856). After being deceived by the wealthy Lady Waldemar and sent to France, Marian is abandoned in a brothel where she is raped and becomes pregnant. Through aligning Marian's pregnancy with the Virgin Mary, her character becomes a comment on the power dynamics and lack of agency many Victorian women had, while calling attention to the intrinsically abusive nature of Victorian discourse around women and sexuality. Inverting the marriage plot through Aurora's care for Marian and her son, Barrett Browning imagines an alternative, exclusively female community of support constructed against the wealthy British man who marries the poor, often foreign woman of early nineteenth-century novels. Elizabeth Barrett Browning is not alone in her use of the Virgin Mary to call attention to the problematic nature of Victorian discourse around women. George Eliot, Margaret Fuller and Anna Jameson, all use the typology of the Virgin Mary as a way of imagining empowered, independent women within a Victorian construction of femininity that valued nurturing motherhood and self-sacrifice (Figure 3.1) (Adams 2001).

While the Virgin Mary offered a type of long-suffering, independent woman whose story could find a narrative fulfilment in the lives of Victorian women, the image of the Christ offered a more explicit narrative type of self-sacrifice. Characters defined by acts of life-giving self-sacrifice abound, ranging from Christina Rossetti's 'Goblin Market', Charlotte Yonge's Guy in *The Heir of Redclyffe,* and Helen Burns in *Jane Eyre,* to the less recognized (and more contested) Christ-figures of Dickens's *Dombey and Son*, Gaskell's *North and South*, Collins's *The Woman in White* and Eliot's *Danial Deronda*. Authors such as Eliot, Dickens, Nightingale and Carlyle use their Christ-figures as a way of demonstrating the modern individual's ability to fulfil ideals that, within the

FIGURE 3.1: *Christ in the House of His Parents* by John Everett Millais (1829–96). This painting reflects the typological approach to the Bible, where a rural, British carpentry shop and family become a representation of Jesus, Mary and Joseph. Photo by DeAgostini/Getty Images.

Christian tradition, were most fully imagined through the character of Jesus. As such, this replacement of a particular Jesus with numerous reiterations of self-giving sacrifice is a sign of human progress as we collectively and individually learn to fulfil the typology of the Christ-figure. As the ubiquitous nature of Christ-figures suggests, typology runs the risk of ultimately replicating the type unto meaninglessness. It is, perhaps, no surprise that by the end of the century the earnest Christ-figures of mid-century give way to problematic and even ironic figures in the works of Thomas Hardy, Joseph Conrad and James Joyce.

Perhaps nowhere is the ironic use of biblical typology more evident than in early Australian literature. Rather than calling for reform, Miles Franklin's *My Brilliant Career* (1901) uses typology to subvert organized religion, government and other cultural institutions while drawing attention to the isolation and abandonment that shape the Australian experience. The novel – which begins on an Edenic cattle station deep in the Australian bush, complete with a loving father and a threatening snake – quickly condemns the promises embedded in typological thinking when the father's foolish financial plans and alcoholism lead to the family being cast out of the garden to toil and starve. This Edenic expulsion serves as an indictment on the British government that has abandoned its citizens to Australia, but it is also an indictment on God himself, who appears to have forgotten that sunburnt country.

From 1820 to 1920 typology served as a primary means for engaging the narrative content of the biblical text in light of the modern world. Whether used to point to Jesus, argue that the modern world fulfills human promises, authorize a new vision for society, or call out the failures of institutions, biblical typology provided nineteenth-century authors a powerful symbolic structure that empowered new visions of society. But typological appropriations of the Bible assume, and even rely upon, the text's cultural authority. Because the Bible's place as a religiously and culturally authoritative document was increasingly insecure as the nineteenth century progressed, it is not surprising that biblical typology became a less significant means of biblical engagement towards the turn of the twentieth century.

REWRITING THE BIBLE

If typology is one primary way in which the Bible is appropriated by literature from 1820 to 1920, another significant form of biblical engagement is the rewriting of the Bible within poetry and prose. Rewriting the Bible differs from typology in that there is no sense of one time fulfilling another. Whereas in Carlyle or Nightingale the modern individual has the power to fulfil the potential of human life expressed in the story of Jesus, or in Yonge or Rossetti the modern individual's life can, like Christ, be an expression of divine love and sacrifice, biblical rewrites make no claims to progress or fulfilment. Instead rewritings of the Bible appropriate the characters, narrative outlines and even language of biblical stories, sometimes challenging and sometimes affirming traditional interpretations of characters and their stories in the process.

From 1820 to 1920, the most significant biblical rewriting in literature focused on the life of Jesus (Birney 1989). These representations took four major forms: the fictionalized biography, the historical Jesus novel, the imitation of Christ and the *Jesus redivivus* (Ziolkowski 1972). While fictionalized biographies of Jesus have existed since the early days of Christianity, the genre was particularly popular during the nineteenth century. Beyond the hundreds of retellings of Jesus's life that were published as part of Sunday school lessons, evangelistic tracts and devotional materials, literary lives of Jesus formed a significant genre from the 1830s to the end of the nineteenth century (Figure 3.2).

With the publication of Strauss's *Das Leben Jesu* (1835–6), writers began to treat the life of Jesus as more than a typology to be appropriated for self-sacrifice or as a model of death and rebirth. Instead, the historical, bodily life of Jesus itself became a source for artistic speculation and extrapolation. Earnest Renan's *Vie de Jésus* (1863) was by far the most popular and scandalous of these nineteenth-century texts. As Renan retells and expands the Gospel accounts of Jesus's life, he imagines Jesus's psychology in ways that contest traditional claims about Jesus's divinity and perfection. Although troubling to orthodox readers, *Vie de Jésus* took mid-nineteenth-century biblical scholarship seriously, popularizing an image of the historical Jesus as a man shaped by a particular geography, unique cultural practices and the practices of first-century Judaism. Granted, at times Renan's work conflates the Palestine of the first century with that of the nineteenth century, and he speculates wildly from time to time both about Jesus as a character and about first-century culture. But, on the whole, Renan provided readers with something approaching a novelistic reading experience of the Gospels, thereby bringing Jesus and the biblical text to life in the popular imagination.

Less well known than Renan's *Vie de Jésus* is the great Spanish writer Enrique Pérez Escrich's *El Mártir del Gólgota* published in Madrid in 1863. The work, which walks the fine line between history and fiction, examines the Roman world at the time of Jesus and reimagines Jesus's life and death, all the while intertwining fantasy and reality. Published serially at the same time Renan's work was sweeping Europe and England, this Spanish work highlights the common interest in the Bible's reliability and the historical Jesus across European literatures in the 1860s. While Renan's *Vie de Jésus* created more of

FIGURE 3.2: *Cleansing the Temple* by Doré, Gustave, 1883. Engraved by A Bertrand. The *cleansing of the Temple* was one narrative from the canonical Gospels that troubled the pious and scholars alike. The scourge in Jesus's hand was a feature Strauss particularly noted in Das Leben Jesu. Photo by Culture Club/Getty Images.

an international sensation than Escrich's *El Mártir*, clearly neither was unique in their shared concerns or approaches in bringing the Bible and the novel together. Nevertheless, thanks in large part to Renan's liberal imagination, *Vie de Jésus* sparked numerous similar projects and responses, including in Germany Franz Delitzsch's *Ein Tag in Kapernaum*

(1871), and in England John Seeley's *Ecce Homo* (1866), Joseph Parker's *Ecce Deus* (1867), F.W. Farrar's *The Life of Christ* (1874), Cunningham Geikie's *The Lives and Words of Christ* (1878), and Alfred Edersheim's *Life and Times of Jesus the Messiah* (1883) (Pals 1982). Each of these later works takes the material world of the Bible seriously, with religious and cultural practice providing a framework for better understanding of Jesus's life and teachings. As such, they reflect both the anthropological tendencies of the realist novel during the period, and the ongoing work of historical-critical scholarship that transformed people's understanding of the Bible, its origins and its consequent interpretations (Figure 3.3).

During the nineteenth century, leading literary figures also wrote fictional biographies or Fifth Gospels. Between 1846 and 1848, Charles Dickens wrote *The Life of Our Lord* for his children. While Dickens is pious in his treatment of Jesus and highly faithful to the language of the King James Version of the Bible, he systematically omits any passages in which Jesus appears at odds with his family, expresses negative emotions or in which his material body might come into focus. Dickens's tendency to treat Jesus in such a disembodied and idealized manner highlights just how transgressive works like Renan's were for the English-speaking world (Hughes 2015). Oscar Wilde, on the other hand, took a more complex approach to the character of Jesus as a misunderstood genius. As Jennifer Stevens has argued, Wilde was clearly influenced by Renan but also by numerous other French interpretations of Jesus's life, including Flaubert's *Trois Contes*, Catulle

FIGURE 3.3: *Jesus Teaches the People by the Sea* by James Tissot, 1886–96. This painting represents Jesus in history, emphasizing historical and geographical detail, much like the fictionalized biographies that made use of nineteenth-century biblical criticism, anthropology and travelogues. Photo by Ann Ronan Pictures/Print Collector/Getty Images.

Mendès's *Contes Évangéliques* and Anatole France's *Balthasar* (1889) and *L'Étui de Nacre*. In Wilde's poems 'Doer of Good' and 'The Master', along with *Le Chant du Cygne's* 'L'Evangile de Minuit' (which, while not written by Wilde, are attributed to him in their oral versions) and *De Profundis*, Wilde returns again and again to the life of Jesus both as a life to recreate in art and as a model for the suffering artist (Stevens 2010: 139–74).

Like fictional biographies, Jesus novels are set during the first century, but they focus on fictional characters or a minor biblical character's perspective of Jesus. In these novels, the biblical world, its customs and the narrative events of the Gospels form the context for the characters' lives and the larger historical plot in which they are entwined. While Jesus is not the protagonist in these works, he interacts with the fictional characters at key moments in their narratives. In fact, the presence of Jesus is so palpable in these novels that they really are about Jesus and the Bible, even though Jesus gets relatively little narrative attention. While Jesus is on the periphery, historical Jesus novels are clearly marked by the fictionalized biographies by writers such as Renan and Farrar. The most famous historical Jesus novel, Lee Wallace's *Ben-Hur: A Tale of the Christ* (1880), reflects Renan's emphasis on the historical Jesus in its ethnography and attention to cultural and religious practice, while sharing Farrar's piety towards Jesus. *Ben-Hur* was not the first Jesus novel; it was preceded by Harriet Martineau's *Traditions of Palestine* (1830) along with a handful of other novels set in the first century. These include Charles Beecher's *The Incarnation: or Pictures of the Virgin and her Son* (1849), and David Ingraham's *The Prince of the House of David* (1855), which was also translated into German. That said, *Ben-Hur* made the genre wildly popular, leading to works such as Marie Corelli's very popular *Barabbas: A Dream of the World's Tragedy* (1893), Joseph Jacobs's *As Others Saw Him* (1895) and George Moore's *The Book of Keith: A Syrian Story* (1916). Other titles of note include Archibald McCowan's *Christ the Socialist* (1894), Joseph Jacobs's *As Others Saw Him* (1895), William T. Stead's *If Christ came to Chicago* and Alphonse Louis Constant's *The Last Incarnation* (1912) (Gatrall 2014; Stevens 2010).

In both Britain and America, *Jesus redivivus* stories and imitations of Jesus form a primary way that writers engage the Bible across ideological lines. In the imitations narratives, a contemporary character attempts to imitate Jesus within his or her own context. In a *Jesus redivivus* Jesus himself appears within a contemporary context. In both these subgenres of Jesus novels, the canonical Gospels' portrayals of Jesus are of primary importance, with the new or revived Jesus-figures serving as exegetical commentary on the Bible. In Britain, Eliza Lynn Linton's *The True History of Joshua Davidson: Christian and Communist* (1872) lies somewhere between an imitation of Christ and a *Jesus redivivus* novel. Joshua, born to a poor Cornish carpenter and his wife, inadvertently reenacts key events in the life of Jesus throughout his childhood. As he learns about Jesus, his imitation becomes more conscious and revolutionary in its literalness. Joshua's reenactment of Jesus, which involves a deep compassion for prostitutes and involvement in the Paris Commune, ultimately leads to his death at the hands of Anglican clergymen. In the novel, the lines between Joshua as an imitator of Jesus and Joshua *as* Jesus frequently blur, which reveals the gap between Christian practice and Jesus's teachings. The novel's revolutionary representation of the Gospels, implicit challenge to the practicality of Jesus's teaching, and denouncement of Christian hypocrisy made it wildly popular. Charles Bradlaugh bought 1000 copies to give out because he believed the text served his atheistic campaign and by 1901 the work was in its eleventh edition (Anderson 1996: 126–7).

Somewhat less revolutionary but equally popular, Mary Augusta Ward's *Robert Elsmere* tells the story of its eponymous Jesus-imitator as he journeys from orthodox

Christianity to an understanding of Jesus in mythological terms (Sutherland 1990). In his long conversations with Squire Wendover, Robert explores the reliability of the biblical text as a historical document, wrestles with the impossibility of miracles, and ultimately must abandon his traditional view of the Bible in order to embrace the idea of Jesus. Through its focus on questions of historical reliability, textual transmission and moral practice, *Robert Elsmere* encapsulates late-Victorian anxieties about the status of the Bible and ultimately Jesus himself. By the end of the century, Victorian engagement with the biblical text had moved beyond Christological typology of self-sacrifice and presentations of the modern world as a fulfilment of biblical typology. Instead, the Bible itself was a highly contested text, making earnest uses of biblical typology problematic at best. Rather, the very nature of the Bible as a historical document and the applicability of its moral vision for modern life became the primary focus of literary engagements with the Bible.

The position of the biblical text in literature was much the same in America. Charles Monroe Sheldon's *In His Steps: What Would Jesus Do* (1896) created a sensation much like that of *Robert Elsmere* and *Joshua Davidson*. The novel imagines a community challenged to spend one year asking 'what would Jesus do' before taking action. Like *Joshua Davidson* and *Robert Elsmere*, reconsidering Jesus's life in a modern context inevitably leads to a deep engagement with the Bible, but the Bible is actually far less present than in *Robert Elsmere*. Whereas Robert and Wendover engage in lengthy conversations about primitive mythologizing, textual transmission and consequent historical reliability, Sheldon is much more focused on the moral vision represented by Jesus's narrative. As a result, although the division between the Bible and Jesus that Elsmere articulates is frequently implied by *In His Steps*, the Bible itself only makes a few appearances.

While British and American novelists favor Jesus imitators that at times begin to blur with *Jesus redivivus* stories, French and German writers wrestle with the Gospels through stories in which Jesus reappears as himself later in history, which is the classic hallmark of the *Jesus redivivus* tale. Honore de Balzac's *Jésus Christ en Flandre*, written in the early 1830s but published in 1846, tells the story of Jesus reappearing on a boat travelling from Flanders to Ostend. When a storm arises, those with faith follow Jesus and walk across the water to safety. Similarly, Jesus appears disguised as a leper in Flaubert's *La légende de Saint-Julien l'hospitalier*. In these *Jesus redivivus* stories, reenactments of gospel events are typically couched in oral tradition, mystery and ultimately dream, as in Balzac. These markers of symbolic deferral and unreliable narration point to the problematic nature of the Bible in nineteenth-century thought, particularly in light of higher criticism. The nature and meaning of the text seem only approachable when enshrouded in narratives that emphasize the mysterious, esoteric and ultimately unstable nature of the text.

Other French writers engage the Gospels through historical Jesus narratives, and in each, Jesus is an elusive figure. In Anatole France's *Balthasar* (1889), Balthasar's life is imagined before his famous trip to the nativity scene. In *Le Procureur de Judée,* published in 1892, Jesus is remembered only vaguely by Lamia and forgotten entirely by Pontius Pilate as they discuss life and politics over dinner. Eugène Sue's engagement with the Gospels is a bit more direct in *La Croix d'Argent*, with the Gallic slave, Genevieve, finding inspiration in Jesus's Marxist teachings. In all these works, the Bible is the background text from which Jesus's character and narrative are drawn. But the peripheral nature of Jesus himself points to the increasingly uncertain status of Jesus – and the Bible in which his life is first recorded – within late-nineteenth-century continental literature.

During the nineteenth century, Germany was the epicentre for the historical criticism that documented the historical process that led to the final text of the Bible. As part of this project, Jesus came to be viewed largely as a mythological figure, a man whose teachings are of great value, but whose life is better understood as a morality tale than as history. It is of little surprise, then, that German writers who engage the Bible frequently do so through *Jesus redivivus* tales that focus on biblical teachings rather than biblical history. Between 1890 and 1910 numerous stories of this sort were published, including Gerhart Hauptmann's play *Handles Himmerlfahrt* (1895), in which a rural school teacher becomes Jesus; Max Kretzer's *Das Gesicht Christi* (1897), where Jesus works among the poor in Berlin; and Betty Winter's *Unser Heiland ist arm geblieben* (1911), in which Jesus turns up at a party among the aristocracy of Vienna. Gerhart Hauptmann's novella *Der Apostel* (1890) and his longer *Der Narr in Christo Emanuel Quint*, published in 1910, both walk the fine line between a *Jesus redivivus* story and an imitation of Jesus (Figure 3.4).

In *Der Apostel*, a hiker considers his own potential greatness and, at the end, realizes that God the Father is speaking to him as his own son, reframing the story as a recapitulation of Christ's temptation. In *Narr in Christo Emanuel Quint*, a poor mystic reenacts the life of Jesus and is eventually murdered. Through this narrative, we again see the modern reenactment of Jesus's life and a re-enlivened Jesus blur together, allowing writers to rethink the ethics of Jesus's teachings and the biblical narratives that present those ethics, while appropriating the narrative power of biblical stories to serve a culture marked by deep religious scepticism. Such stories also illustrate that, even amid religious doubt and the Bible's shifting cultural status, the Bible remains inescapable for European literature.

In Russian literature rewritings of the Bible frequently rework the character of Jesus through secular and atheistic characters, reflecting both an apophatic theological tradition and the deeply contested nature of the biblical text during the nineteenth century. The most famous *Jesus redivivus* story from the nineteenth century takes place in the middle of Dostoyevsky's *The Brothers Karamazov* (1912). 'The Grand Inquisitor' that the atheist Ivan shares with his brother, Alyosha, is meant to be a disavowal of Christ, and yet Alyosha declares the story actually praises Jesus. Like many other *Jesus redivivus* stories, Ivan's tale highlights the impracticality of Jesus's teachings and points to the foolishness of Jesus himself. As John Givens points out, Alyosha's response to Ivan's story makes no sense, unless it is understood in terms of the apophatic tradition that shapes Russian literature's engagement with Jesus and, by extension, the Bible (Givens 2018: 52). By using the frame of apophatic theology, novels such as *The Idiot, Crime and Punishment* and *Anna Karenina* all point to the ridiculousness and beauty of the incarnation as the characters attempt to embody selfless love. But beauty is not the only response to the biblical representation of Jesus in the Russian literature. Rather, Jesus turns out to be quite disappointing in Ivan Turgenev's poem 'Christ'. In the poem, the speaker becomes disheartened upon realizing that Jesus was just like every other man. While the speaker's disappointment is grounded in the representation of Jesus in the Bible, the realization is presented as a profoundly negative experience. Such disappointment works to create space beyond received piety for readers to consider Christ for themselves (Figures 3.5 and 3.6).

Perhaps the most controversial Russian Jesus novel is Nicholas Notovitch's *La Vie Inconnue de Jesus Christ* (also known as *The Life of St Issa*). The novel purports to be a retelling of Jesus's years living and teaching in India, translated from a Sanskrit text by Notovitch during a time of convalesces in India. While even scholars at the time doubted the historical claims of the novel, the book created a great deal of controversy and was

FIGURE 3.4: *Uhde Das Tischgebet anagoria* by Fritz von Uhde (1885). This painting represents Jesus appearing in a late-nineteenth-century home, similar to *Jesus redivivus* narratives. But, unlike some literary *Jesus redivivus* stories, Jesus appears in historic attire. Photo: Fine Art Images/Heritage Images/Getty Images.

FIGURES 3.5 and 3.6: Ge's representation of Jesus at the Last Supper (1863, Photo: Alamy) – with downcast head and eyes, emphasizing Jesus's humanity and own disappointment – are made more explicit in the facial features of Kramskoi's Jesus (1872, Photo: Alamy). Both echo the speaker in Turgenev's Christ by depicting Jesus as 'Such an ordinary, ordinary man!'

translated into English, French, German and Italian. By capitalizing on the missing years of Jesus's life as recorded in the Gospels, the novel emphasizes the incomplete – and by extension unreliable – nature of the Bible. But by drawing attention to the unknown years that are still bounded by the biblical narrative, even this expected critique creates an opportunity for apophatic contemplation. Readers are not invited to imagine a Jesus of their own construction or outside history, but a Jesus whose beginning and ending are established by the boundaries of biblical history. Given the influence of Strauss and Renan in Russia, combined with the emphasis on apophatic theology within Orthodox Christianity, these apophatic representations of Jesus should not be surprising. This negative way of knowing provides a way 'to speak about Christ in an age of unbelief, but at the same time, to affirm him or his teachings through indirect, even negative, means' (Givens 2018: 6).

Poetry from 1820 to 1920 also wrestles with the character of Jesus, biblical narratives and ultimately the Bible itself. Appropriating the name of Rizpah, the mother of murdered sons in the Old Testament, Tennyson's late dramatic monologue 'Rizpah' denounces ineffective, well-intended Christian charity almost as forcefully as it denounces merciless justice and Calvinistic interpretations of the Bible. As Rizpah speaks to the visitor, the Bible's words expressing God's mercy are Rizpah's hope and also her weapon against the visiting woman. Charles Baudelaire's *Les Fleurs du Mal* (1857) takes on the narratives of Cain and Abel, Peter's denial of Christ and the character of Satan. While often aligned with anti-religious poetry, Baudelaire's poems frequently suggest the frustration of the Psalmist and even Job as they wrestle with boredom and dejection, not least when he directly engages the character of Satan (Avni 1973). Rainer Maria Rilke's poem, 'Visions of Christ' (1898) reimagines the relationship between Jesus and Mary Magdalene, in which Mary becomes the mother of Jesus's child. In England, Gerard Manley Hopkins's work is known for numerous hints and suggestions of Christ, as is the poetry of Christina Rossetti. That said, poetic retellings of biblical stories and the life of Jesus are far less popular in the period from 1820 to 1920 than prose engagements with the biblical text (Ludlow 2014; LaPorte 2011).

BIBLICAL AUTHORITY AND LITERATURE

Biblical typology and rewritings of biblical stories, particularly the story of Jesus, are two major ways the Bible is present in literature between 1820 and 1920. Equally important are direct engagements with the Bible as a cultural and religious authority, particularly in the Protestant literary traditions of the British Empire and America. One could say these literary traditions are haunted by the Bible – by questions of its literary legacy, its ongoing authority and the possibility of the written Word to ever achieve such cultural power again.

Matthew Arnold's *Literature and Dogma* explicitly questions the cultural authority of the Bible while suggesting that literature itself can replace the Bible as a source of culture-shaping narratives. Arnold positions the Bible as a great inspirer of moral conduct, reinterpreting both the Old and New Testaments in light of contentious action. Thus, 'Look up to God' becomes 'consult your conscience', 'the Eternal' is glossed as 'eternal righteousness' emphasizing human conduct, and 'trust in God is, in a deeply moved way of expression, the trust in the law of conduct' (Arnold 1968: 175, 83, 93). Such reworkings of biblical language provide a schema for redeeming the Bible as a purely ethical text within a pluralistic and scientific culture. Ironically, such rewordings also remove the very biblical language that had long been celebrated within English poetry and prose. Regardless of this move away from biblical phraseology, Arnold's hermeneutics and overall approach to the Bible influence much later work, most explicitly Mary Augusta Ward's *Robert Elsmere*.

One of Arnold's primary concerns is how the Bible might maintain its moral and cultural authority if its historical and miraculous claims are in doubt. But Arnold's anxiety about the Bible's cultural and moral authority is a recurring concern in the literatures of America and the British Empire long before Arnold's *Literature and Dogma*. In the 1840s, Grace Aguilar, well aware that the Authorized Version of the Bible was problematic in its translations, began calling for a Jewish translation of the Old Testament (Lemon et al. 2009). The 1860 publication of *Essays and Reviews* further acknowledged the increasingly unstable place of the Bible within British culture. Benjamin Jowett's essay, 'On the Interpretation of Scripture', clearly articulates the textual and hermeneutic issues that challenge traditional readings of the Bible and even Christian doctrine, but the entire collection of essays asked exactly the sorts of questions Arnold would later address. Taken as a whole, *Essays and Reviews* moves away from aligning the truth claims of Christianity to historical fact, preferring instead the moral power of the text as an indicator of its truth. But this emphasis on moral truth rather than historical fact is highly problematic within Christian theology. Traditionally, Christian doctrine has been built upon two historical claims: the incarnation of God in Jesus and the bodily resurrection of Jesus. Thus, while reading the Bible as a moral allegory may free it from a particular set of textual issues, a moralistic hermeneutic also comes with profound doctrinal consequences. While *Essays and Reviews* inevitably created some doctrinal problems, it also created particular opportunities for thinking about the Bible through literature and as literature. This idea of the Bible as literature would provide the foundation for Arnold's thinking in *Literature and Dogma*. As Arnold ultimately reasons, if the truth of the Bible lies in the moral impact of its stories, then the moral impact of new stories can mark them as equally true and even culturally authoritative.

Given the cultural power of stories that Arnold articulates, it should come as no surprise that novelists were raising questions about the Bible and its proper interpretation long before the scholars in *Essays and Reviews*. Charlotte Brontë's *Jane Eyre* is many things, not least of which is a novel about the Bible's moral authority. While Jane never questions the Bible's sexual ethics in her relationship with Rochester, traditional readings of the Bible's teachings on heaven, hell and salvation are challenged through the stoicism of Helen Burns and Jane's own questions about God's love and wrath. More significantly, in volume three, the authority of the Bible to guide Jane's vocational choices comes into sharp relief through Jane's reflections upon St John. In listening to his preaching, Jane confesses that the 'heart was thrilled, the mind astonished, by the power of the preacher: [yet] neither were softened' (Brontë 2008: 352). As St John proposes marriage and a missionary life, Jane repeatedly acknowledges, 'Religion called – Angels beckoned – God commanded – life rolled together like a scroll – death's gates opening showed eternity beyond', yet her feelings would not allow her to act in accordance with such calls (Brontë 2008: 418). Ultimately, it is the mysterious and supernatural voice of Rochester that proved to be the calling that Jane answers, not the calling of the biblical text as wielded by St John. Brontë frames the question of biblical authority differently from Arnold, in that the historicity and miraculous claims of the Bible are not in question. For Arnold, the question is how the moral authority of the Bible might be maintained even if it proves historically inaccurate. For Brontë, the question is whether or not the Bible should have any moral authority at all to guide the individual. Given that *Jane Eyre* predates

FIGURE 3.7: *Light of the World*, by William Holman Hunt, *c.* 1851–3. Amid a changing religious landscape, this painting suggests the authority of the biblical text as the source of Enlightenment. Photo: The Print Collector/Print Collector/Getty Images.

Literature and Dogma by over thirty years, Brontë's appeal to the moral authority of an individual's feelings is particularly striking and helps us better recognize the deeply conservative nature of Arnold's arguments.

Whereas Brontë addresses the question of biblical authority directly in *Jane Eyre*, Charles Dickens takes a more oblique approach to the Bible. Readers of Dickens often note his general lack of religious themes, characters and even biblical language. In fact, the Christian faith and the stories of the Bible that form the cultural backdrop for Victorian literature and create extensive ecclesial, political and social debate throughout the nineteenth century seem largely absent from Dickens's writings. Yet, Dickens indirectly points to the Bible in his ongoing concern with the authority of the written word and the power of a text-based document to shape individual and community action. His novel *Bleak House* (1852–3) revolves around the never-ending court case of *Jarndyce and Jarndyce*. Due to competing wills and the complications of interpreting these wills, the case drags on for years, such that, at its conclusion the legal fees have entirely consumed the estate and there is nothing left to inherit. Ten years later, Dickens remains invested in the power of the word to confuse, complicate and dictate human action. In *Our Mutual Friend*, much of the inheritance plot centres upon the multiple versions of the old John Harmon's will that, in its first draft makes his son's inheritance dependent upon marrying a particular woman. In later wills, the estate goes to the Crown, and ultimately the kind-hearted Boffins. Through these reiterations of the will and subplots revolving around affidavits, Dickens draws further attention to the legally binding nature of the written word, while highlighting the problem of textual transmission, competing texts, textual reliability and ultimately the reasonableness of following an old text in the first place.

Novels questioning the authority and interpretation of the written word are emblematic of literature's relationship with the Bible by the end of the nineteenth century. While the Bible provided a culturally authoritative text to appropriate for new social visions at the beginning of Victoria's reign, the Bible's contested status increasingly worked against such uses as the century wore on. When questions about textual development and historical reliability brought the Old and New Testaments to the centre of theological and cultural debates, the Bible became the focus of literary and cultural anxieties about the power of the written word and the role of narratives to provide a morally authoritative vision for human life (Figure 3.7).

As such, literary discussions about textual authority frequently mirror Victorian theological debates about the Bible's transmission, its historical reliability, its proper interpretation and its authority as a morally directive text, even when the Bible is not mentioned directly. In the end, works such as *Jane Eyre*, *Bleak House* and *Bartleby the Scrivener*, along with novels like *Robert Elsmere* and *In His Steps*, all resonate with the conclusions of Arnold's *Literature and Dogma*, as well as Dickens's own *The Life of Our Lord*. All this biblically haunted literature from the Victorian era suggests that the literary value and cultural power of the Bible lie in its exhortations to love mercy, act rightly and walk humbly through life.

REFERENCES

Adams, K. V. (2001), *Our Lady of Victorian Feminism: The Madonna in the Work of Anna Jameson, Margaret Fuller, and George Eliot*, Athens: Ohio University Press.

Anderson, N. F. (1996), 'Eliza Lynn Linton: The Rebel of the Family', in *The New Nineteenth Century: Feminist Readings of Underread Victorian Fiction*, ed. B. L. Harman and S. Meyer, 177, New York: Garland.

Arnold, M. (1968), 'Literature and Dogma', in *Dissent and Dogma, The Complete Prose Works of Matthew Arnold*, ed. R. H. Super, Ann Arbor: University of Michigan Press.

Avni, A. A. (1973), 'The Bible and Les Fleurs Du Mal', *PMLA: Publications of the Modern Language Association of America*, 88(2): 299–310.

Bassard, K. C. (2010), *Transforming Scriptures: African American Women Writers and the Bible*. Athens: University of Georgia Press.

Benckhuysen, A. W. (2007), 'Reading between the Lines: Josephine Butler's Socially Conscious Commentary on Hagar', in *Recovering Nineteenth-Century Women Interpreters of the Bible*, ed. C. De Groot and M. A. Taylor, 135–48. Leiden; Boston: Brill.

Bercovitch, S. (1989), *The American Jeremiad*, 2nd edn, Madison: University of Wisconsin Press.

Birney, A. L. (1989), *The Literary Lives of Jesus: An International Bibliography of Poetry, Drama, Fiction, and Criticism*, New York: Garland Publishing.

Brontë, C. (2008), *Jane Eyre*. Oxford: Oxford University Press. (Original work published 1847).

Brown, A. B. (1999), *Rewriting the Word: American Women Writers and the Bible*, Westport: Greenwood Press.

Coleman, D. (2018), 'The Bible', in *Herman Melville in Context*, ed. K. J. Hayes, 211–20, Cambridge: Cambridge University Press.

Colley, L. (1992), *Britons: Forging the Nation, 1707–1837*, New Haven: Yale University Press.

Courtmanche, J. C. (2008), *How Nathaniel Hawthorne's Narratives Are Shaped by Sin: His Use of Biblical Typology in His Four Major Works*, Lewiston: Edwin Mellen Press.

Ensor, A. (1969), *Mark Twain and the Bible*, Lexington: University of Kentucky Press.

Fraser, H. and V. Burrows (2001), 'The Feminist Theology of Florence Nightingale', in *Reinventing Christianity*, ed. L. Woodhead, 199–210, Aldershot: Ashgate.

Gatrall, J. J. A. (2014), *The Real and the Sacred*. Ann Arbor: University of Michigan Press.

Gibson, R. H. and T. Larsen (2015), 'Nineteenth-Century Spiritual Autobiography: Carlyle, Mill, Newman', in *A History of English Autobiography*, ed. A. Smyth, 192–206, Cambridge: Cambridge University Press.

Givens, J. (2018), *The Image of Christ in Russian Literature: Dostoevsky Tolstoy, Bulgakov, Pasternak*, DeKalb: NIU Press.

Herringer, C. E. (2008), *Victorians and the Virgin Mary: Religion and Gender in England, 1830–85*, Manchester: Manchester University Press.

Hindmarsh, D. B. (2005), *The Evangelical Conversion Narrative: Spiritual Autobiography in Early Modern England*, Oxford: Oxford University Press.

Hughes, J. A. (2015), 'Dickens's the Life of Our Lord and the Problem of Jesus', in *'Perplext in Faith': Essays on Victorian Beliefs and Doubts*, ed. J. Melnyk and A. Clapp-Itnyre, 268–303, Cambridge: Cambridge Scholars.

Jenkins, R. Y. (1995), *Reclaiming Myths of Power: Women Writers and the Victorian Spiritual Crisis*, Lewisburg: Bucknell University Press. [In English].

Landow, G. P. (2014), *Ruskin*, London: Routledge.

Landow, G. P. (1980), *Victorian Types, Victorian Shadows: Biblical Typology in Victorian Literature, Art, and Thought*, Boston: Routledge & K. Paul.

LaPorte, C. (2011), *Victorian Poets and the Changing Bible*, Charlottesville: University of Virginia Press.

Larsen, T. (2006), *Crisis of Doubt: Honest Faith in Nineteenth-Century England*, Oxford: Oxford University Press.
Larsen, T. (2012), *A People of One Book: The Bible and the Victorians*, Oxford: Oxford University Press.
Larson, J. (1985), *Dickens and the Broken Scriptures*, Athens: University of Georgia Press.
Lemon, R., E. Mason, J. Roberts, and C. Rowland (2009), *The Blackwell Companion to the Bible in English Literature*. Blackwell Companions to Religion, London: Wiley-Blackwell.
Ludlow, E. (2014), *Christina Rossetti and the Bible*, London: Bloomsbury Academic.
Lundin, R. (2014), 'The Tender Pioneer in The Prairies of the Air: Dickinson and the Difference of God', *Religion and Literature*, 46(1): 149–57.
McKeon, M. (2002), *The Origins of the English Novel, 1600–1740*, 2nd edn, Baltimore: Johns Hopkins University Press.
Pals, D. L. (1982), *The Victorian 'Lives of Jesus'*, San Antonio: Trinity University Press.
Showalter, E. (1981), 'Florence Nightingale's Feminist Complaint: Women, Religion, and Suggestions for Thought', [In English]. *Signs*, 6(3): 395–412.
Showalter, E. (1991), 'Miranda and Cassandra: The Discourse of the Feminist Intellectual', in *Tradition and the Talents of Women*, ed. F. Howe, 313–27, Urbana: University of Illinois Press.
Stanley, B. (1990), *The Bible and the Flag: Protestant Missions and British Imperialism in the Nineteenth and Twentieth Centuries*, Trowbridge: Apollos.
Stanton, E. C. (1898), *The Woman's Bible: Comments on the Old and New Testaments, from Joshua to Revelation*, Vol. 2, New York: European Publishing Company.
Stevens, J. (2010), *The Historical Jesus and the Literary Imagination: 1860–1920*, Liverpool: Liverpool University Press.
Sutherland, J. (1990), *Mrs. Humphry Ward: Eminent Victorian, Pre-Eminent Edwardian*, Oxford: Clarendon Press.
Vanden Bossche, C. (1991), *Carlyle and the Search for Authority*, Columbus: Ohio State University Press.
Watt, I. (2001), *The Rise of the Novel*, 2nd edn, Berkeley: University of California Press. (Original work published 1957).
Wilkes, K. (2018), 'Repairing the Ladder to Heaven: Harriet Beecher Stowe's the Minister's Wooing as a Secular Novel', *Christianity and Literature*, 67(3): 436–53.
Zemka, S. (1995), 'The Holy Books of Empire: Translations of the British and Foreign Bible Society', in *Macropolitics of Nineteenth-Century Literature; Nationalism, Exoticism, Imperialism*, ed. J. Arac and H. Ritvo, 102–37, Durham: Duke University Press.
Ziolkowski, T. (1972), *Fictional Transfigurations of Jesus*, Princeton: Princeton University Press.

CHAPTER 4

Visual Culture

SARAH C. SCHAEFER

In late 1885, Vincent van Gogh completed an unusual painting: a dark still life featuring an open Bible at its centre (Figure 4.1). In a number of ways, the painting is a testament to van Gogh's personal and artistic heritage. It follows the tradition of the seventeenth-century Dutch still life, focusing on a set of relatively humble objects that convey profound messages about life and morality: in this case, the candle burned nearly to its end coupled with the copy of Émile Zola's *La joie de vivre* (*The Joy of Life*) at lower right remind the viewer of the ephemerality of earthly existence. The Bible that van Gogh depicts is generally presumed to have belonged to his father, a pastor in the Dutch Reformed Church, who had passed away just months earlier (Hulsker 1996: 208). Although the scriptural text is largely obscured, the words 'ISAIE' and 'Chap. LIII' emerge from the broad swaths of intersecting brushstrokes. The passage indicated is one that van Gogh cited several times in his letters to Theo – his concluding words on 3 October 1876 were 'Do read Isaiah 53'.[1] The Old Testament prophet has, throughout the history of the Christian Bible, provided some of the most significant connective tissues to the life and ministry of Jesus, and Isaiah 53 begins: 'Who hath believed our report? and to whom is the arm of the Lord revealed?'

This painting is often interpreted through the lens of the artist's biography: the moment in which this painting was produced coincides with van Gogh's increasing rejection of the intense personal faith and evangelism that characterized his life to this point (Edwards 2009: 19–25; Hempton 2008: 114–38). The presence of Zola's novel indicates van Gogh's newfound embracing of modern life that can likewise be traced in the artist's numerous letters from this period. And although the painting consists primarily of the muted, earthy tones of van Gogh's early works, the occasional flourishes of turquoise and orange hint at the exuberant color schemes he would employ after seeing Impressionist paintings in Paris the following year.

It is noteworthy that van Gogh produced the painting partially in response to Theo's description of Édouard Manet's *Dead Toreador* (c. 1864).[2] Among the young, avant-garde artists of van Gogh's generation, Manet was the harbinger of a new language of modern painting, and *Still Life with Bible* grapples with many of the concerns that Manet's *oeuvre* brought to the fore. Many of Manet's paintings, including the few that represent biblical subject matter, consist of well-known subjects from art since the Renaissance but persistently challenge the notion that painting should function as an illusion of reality (Driskel 1992: 188–93). In a similar manner, van Gogh's painting is both clearly indebted to the traditions of the Dutch still life, but the precision of representation and messages of universal morality are questioned. The textual inscriptions indicate the book's content,

FIGURE 4.1: *Still Life with Bible*, by Vincent van Gogh, 1885. Oil on canvas, 65.7 cm × 78.5 cm. Van Gogh Museum, Amsterdam. Photo: Fine Art Images/Heritage Images/Getty Images.

and the loose outlines of the columns on the pages remind the viewer of the weighty history of scriptural authority. That weightiness, however, becomes lost in the thick, impastoed brushstroke, forcing a recognition of the canvas as a flat surface, not an illusion of real space. Despite the seeming solidity of the book, the text is materiality subject to the artist's hand.

Besides the obvious thematic link to the present book, I begin with van Gogh's painting because the work is both a continuation of tradition and a break from it, and is thus, as this chapter details, characteristic of biblical imagery in the long nineteenth century writ large. The Bible occupied a central, albeit complex and shifting, role in the production of visual culture in the nineteenth century, despite the challenges to its authority and authenticity that were increasingly asserted among sceptics. This is the period in which we see the emergence of some of the clearest characteristics of 'modernity': increasing industrialization and urbanization, questioning and outright rejection of traditional institutions of authority like the monarchy and the church, and the rise of liberal, democratic political infrastructures based on capitalistic enterprise. The visual culture of this period tends to follow similar trends: industrialization expanded the quality and variety of images available to audiences of all economic classes, the power of established institutions like the official academies and exhibition societies waned, and artists embraced new subjects and stylistic approaches and openly questioned inherited traditions (not infrequently with the specific aim of provoking shock and outrage among audiences).

Until relatively recently, art historians who studied this period primarily focused on the avant-garde and modernist artists that emerged in Europe (especially France), and generally considered works with religious content only when they could be interpreted as critiques of traditional institutions, dogmatic ideologies or artistic standards. Gustave Courbet's *Burial at Ornans* (1849–50) is an oft-cited example: when first exhibited, the painting was widely reviled for its frank and unsightly representation of death, as many of the mourners appeared bored and uninterested in the coffin or the priest reading from the Bible.[3] In recent years, scholars have expanded their approaches and points of inquiry: artists outside of Europe and America have gained more attention, as has the immense amount of visual culture that did not necessarily operate within the realms of avant-garde or modernist movements. In this context, religious imagery has been the subject of greater focus; as we will see, the Bible, a source that came under unprecedented scrutiny from sceptics and believers alike, proved to be a constant, contested and malleable source from which artists persistently drew.

This chapter examines the impact of the Bible on art and visual culture in the long nineteenth century, considering how biblical imagery operated in the realms of both high art and popular culture. Above all, it demonstrates the ways in which images not only *reflect* the changing perceptions of the Bible in modernity but also how images, in fact, *shape* the ways in which modern subjects perceive and understand the Bible.

THE ACADEMY, HISTORY PAINTING AND THE RISE OF ROMANTICISM

At the turn of the nineteenth century, as the age of Enlightenment brought drastic reconfigurations to the intellectual, political and cultural landscape, the dominant artistic institutions and ideologies remained, in many ways, rooted in tradition. Throughout Europe, aspiring artists sought acceptance into the academies – elite, state-sponsored institutions responsible for artistic education and promotion. Their inherent connections to the established structures of power assured a certain degree of conservatism in terms of subject matter and style. The highest aim to which a painter might aspire was history painting, a genre that included mythological and religious subjects. However, commissions for these often large and expensive works came primarily from state, civic and religious institutions which, broadly speaking, sought to maintain the status quo.

Benjamin West, an American expatriate who served as president of the British Royal Academy at the turn of the nineteenth century, produced a number of works that demonstrate the shifting status of the Bible and its role in art in this period of rupture. Beginning in the late eighteenth century and continuing through the end of his life, West repeatedly devoted attention to the subject of the biblical apocalypse as it is relayed in the book of Revelation, the final book of the Christian Bible. His representations of these subjects are significant in demonstrating both adherence to established artistic norms and shifts in artistic ideology that relate to broader cultural dynamics (Figure 4.2) (Erffa and Staley 1986: 387–98). On the one hand, these works are indebted to some of the major tenets of the Academy of which West was the steward: acceptable source material and close attention to precise, detailed renderings, particularly of the (male) figure. West's paintings also served as models

FIGURE 4.2: *Destruction of the Beast and the False Prophet*, by Benjamin West, 1804. Oil on canvas, 99.06 × 143.51 cm. Minneapolis Institute of Art, The William Hood Dunwoody Fund. Photo: Bettmann Archive/Getty Images.

for visual satirists like James Gillray, who mobilized the apocalyptic subject matter to assess and critique political ruptures (Bindman 1999: 212–19). West initially engaged with this material as part of a project commissioned for King George III, but by the mid-1790s the subject had become indelibly tied to the increasingly tyrannical events of the French Revolution, and the commission was ultimately rescinded (Bermingham 2013: 153–70).

West's apocalyptic paintings also suggest the influence of emerging Romantic tendencies within even the most conservative artistic institutions. The destruction and chaos of these images are at odds with the morally uplifting tone and subject matter that was at the core of academic history painting to this point. It was, indeed, among artists associated with Romanticism that the Bible found new life at the beginning of the nineteenth century (Prickett 1996: 216–20). The Romantic reception of the Bible is perhaps most profoundly manifest in the work of William Blake, who was drawn to the imaginative and mystical characteristics of the Scriptures. Throughout his life, Blake returned again and again to the biblical narratives, focusing especially on prophetic and miraculous subjects. His images, composed primarily of watercolour on paper, are often luminous, ethereal and unorthodox in relation to established iconography. The *Illustrations of the Book of Job*, Blake's most commercially successful print project, demonstrates his imaginative approach to biblical subject matter (Figure 4.3). It also shows the influence of medieval manuscript illumination on Blake's work, which frequently combines word and image on a single page.

FIGURE 4.3: *Job's Evil Dreams*, by William Blake (plate 11 from *Illustrations of the Book of Job*), 1825. Line engraving on medium, slightly textured, cream wove paper, 37.8 × 27.9 cm. Yale Center for British Art, Paul Mellon Collection. Photo: Culture Club/Getty Images.

Although the Christian texts heavily informed Blake's artistic formation and career, he was nonetheless steadfast in his critiques and condemnations of the manner in which the foundations of religious faith had been corrupted over time. In crafting his own cosmology, Blake drew inspiration from the Bible but reconceived it through visionary language and imagery that nonetheless spoke to the imperatives of his present day. It is perhaps in part due to Blake's frank and well-known antagonism towards the Academy that his art remained a somewhat marginalized aspect of his creative output until relatively recently (this despite the fact that Blake insisted on the inseparability of word and image in his work).

However, Romantic trends more broadly, especially an emphasis on color and the expressive application of paint, would wend their way into academic practices over time. In the first decade of the nineteenth century, Joseph Mallord William Turner exhibited several biblically-themed works at the Royal Academy. *The Fifth Plague of Egypt* (erroneously titled as it actually represents the seventh plague) is an example of 'historical landscape', in which the subject matter is of the variety one would find in history painting, but the majority of the composition is given over to landscape elements (Figure 4.4). Turner's works are in many ways compositionally indebted to the staid, classicizing historical landscapes of seventeenth-century artists like Nicolas Poussin; however, the subjects and styles of Turner's paintings evoke the Sublime, a concept popularized in the eighteenth century that refers to the awe-inspiring and even terror-inducing aspects of nature (Ibata 2018). In *The Fifth Plague of Egypt*, Turner uses the expressive brushstrokes and vivid colours associated with Romanticism to depict an intense scene of destruction as a swirling torrent threatens the city in the distance. Turner's application of paint would

FIGURE 4.4: *The Fifth Plague of Egypt*, by Joseph Mallord William Turner, 1800. Oil on canvas, 48 x 72 in. Indianapolis Museum of Art, Gift in memory of Evan F. Lilly. Photo: Fine Art Images/Heritage Images/Getty Images.

become increasingly dramatic over the course of his career, culminating in the apocalyptic works of the 1840s (Jasper 1999: 56–71).

Many artists also looked for sources outside of the established canon, and it is in this period that the works of Dante, Milton and Shakespeare began to be culled for large-scale painting (as well as illustration). Henry Fuseli, a Swiss émigré who gained a prominent position in the Royal Academy despite his penchant for eccentric subjects, created a series of paintings based on the works of Milton that he exhibited in a commercial gallery space in London. Although the endeavour was a commercial failure, the paintings and reproductive prints demonstrate the impact Romanticism was having on the representation of biblical subjects (Figure 4.5). Fuseli never himself identified as a Romantic, and his commitment to neoclassical precision in rendering the human form is evident in these works. However, the tumultuous exuberance of the compositions, as well as the emphasis on inner, transcendent experience, nonetheless aligns these images with Romantic aesthetics.

The Romantic appropriation of the Bible in France emerged at the turn of the nineteenth century with the publication of influential texts like Chateaubriand's *The Genius of Christianity* (Prickett 1996: 164–79). However, representations of biblical subjects are less common among French Romantics, with the notable exception of Eugène Delacroix. In his later career, Delacroix frequently painted subjects from the Gospels, devoting particular attention to several versions of the Crucifixion and Christ asleep during the storm (Polistena 2008). As is often the case in France (and in Catholic countries more generally), Old Testament scenes are far less numerous than those relating to the life of Christ and the lives of the saints. However, among Delacroix's most significant works are the three paintings he produced for the Chapel of the Holy Angels in the Church of Saint-Sulpice in Paris. This complex and dramatic mural programme consists of two subjects from the Old Testament (*Jacob Wrestling the Angel* and *Heliodorus Vanquished from the Temple*) and one from the New (*Saint Michael Vanquishing the Demon*). Although these paintings are in many ways indebted to similar representations by old masters like Raphael and Titian, Delacroix's loose handling of paint and vibrant colours adhere to the Romantic aesthetics he had pursued throughout his career.

In early-nineteenth-century France, Romanticism existed side-by-side with the neoclassical style established by Jacques-Louis David during the revolutionary era and advanced by his most important student, Jean-Auguste-Dominique Ingres. Where David's work often evinces a heroic yet austere sense of drama, Ingres, who was heavily influenced by the early career of Raphael, pursued a more elegant, serene simplicity in his paintings – Ingres, moreover, was pegged as the academic foil to Delacroix's Romanticism. Although Ingres produced a number of significant religious works, they are generally extra-biblical (for instance, his five paintings representing the *Virgin Admiring the Host*). However, Ingres had an immense impact in the education and administration of the Academy, and his style is most evident among painters like Hippolyte Flandrin, Victor Orsel and Ary Scheffer. Though relatively obscure today, these artists were highly praised in their time, and received significant commissions as part of the revitalization of dilapidated churches in and around Paris (Driskel 1992: 99–163). As with Ingres, their works are indebted to Raphael, as well as the hieratic austerity of late-Byzantine and early-Renaissance fresco painting (Figure 4.6). Although their paintings draw from the Bible to a greater extent than we see with Ingres, gospel subjects still tend to predominate.

The works of these French artists also parallel the efforts of two other groups devoted to revitalizing the perceived nobility of late-medieval and early-Renaissance religious

FIGURE 4.5: *The Dream of Eve* by Henry Fuseli, 1804. Stipple etching, etching and aquatint, ink on paper, 58.5 × 47 cm. Victoria and Albert Museum, London. Photo © Victoria and Albert Museum, London.

art. In Germany, the Brotherhood of St Luke (also referred to as the Nazarenes) were influenced by Italian artists like Fra Angelico as well, importantly, as their German forebears like Lucas Cranach and Albrecht Dürer (Grewe 2015). Unlike their French contemporaries, the Nazarenes rejected the neoclassicism associated with European academies; however, the simplified elegance and precise renderings of their compositions dovetail with the Ingresque style, and Victor Orsel especially admired the works of Nazarene painter Friedrich Overbeck (Driskel 1992). The Nazarenes also depart from

FIGURE 4.6: *Entry of Christ in Jerusalem*, by Hippolyte Flandrin, 1843–6. Church of Saint-Germain-des-Prés, Paris. Photo: Christophel Fine Art/Universal Images Group via Getty Images.

their French contemporaries in the extent to which they engage in close analysis of biblical sources and the complex symbolic and typological representations that result. Franz Pforr's *Shulamit and Mary* (Figure 4.7), for instance, displays exemplars of female virtue from both the Old and New Testaments, each situated within her own framed space. Conceived as a 'friendship picture' dedicated to Overbeck, the work also exemplifies each artist's particular stylistic approach. On the left, the landscape and Raphaelesque Shalumit represents the Italian style of the work of Overbeck (whom Pfrorr represented gazing at Shalumit from a distance). On the right, Mary is dressed and situated in an interior space that is recognizably of the late-medieval German period in which Dürer worked, from which Pforr drew much of his artistic inspiration (Grewe 2009: 61–98).

The style of late-medieval and Renaissance painting associated with the students of Ingres and the Nazarenes is also manifest in the work of the Pre-Raphaelite Brotherhood (PRB), a group of artists and writers founded in England in 1848 who opposed the vapid and sentimental characteristics of much Victorian art. Among their aims was a revival of the nobility and authenticity of religious painting. Two of the central PRB artists, John Everett Millais and Dante Gabriel Rossetti (as well as painters in the social orbit of the group like William Dyce and Ford Maddox Brown) depicted images with complex symbolic programmes (Giebelhausen 2006: 67–126). The subjects as well as the luminosity and chalky finish of Rossetti's work are drawn from early Italian Renaissance fresco painters like Giotto and Fra Angelico. The reliance on symbolic elements and the close attention to precise, hyperrealistic surface detail can also be linked to the PRB's

FIGURE 4.7: *Shalumit and Mary* by Franz Pforr, 1811. Oil on canvas, 34.5 × 32 cm. Museum Georg Schäfer, Schweinfurt, Germany. Photo: Alamy.

admiration of Jan van Eyck, whose *Arnolfini Portrait* was acquired by the National Gallery in 1842.

As we have seen thus far, the major trends that dominated artistic production in early-nineteenth-century Europe were thoroughly rooted in a variety of art historical sources, despite their stylistic variations. One of the most significant developments of this period is the notion that artistic creation and experience could itself function as a form of spiritual transcendence. Although this idea was closely linked to the emergence of Romantic aesthetics, it would ultimately extend beyond that movement and shape the popular understanding of artistic value for decades to come, and will heavily impact modernist aesthetics, as will be discussed at the end of the chapter.

BIBLICAL ARCHAEOLOGY AND IMAGES OF THE HOLY LAND

While artists working within both the neoclassical and Romantic modes mobilized the transcendent and visionary aspects of the Bible, many other artists approached biblical representation with an aim towards historical authenticity. This development coincided with the expansion of British, French and American imperial and colonial enterprises into the regions in which the events of the Bible took place. A major component of the Napoleonic campaigns in Egypt involved the documentation and cataloguing of ancient monuments, which would subsequently be disseminated in the immense *Description de l'Egypte*. Later in the century, new archaeological campaigns in the Middle East illuminated the visual cultures of Mesopotamia, offering unprecedented insight into the kingdoms of decadent biblical kings like Nebuchadnezzar and Sennacherib. Ancient fragments unearthed in these campaigns were transported back to Europe and put on view at newly founded public institutions like the British Museum and the Louvre (García 2007: 131–66; Silberman 1982).

Artists like John Martin incorporated these findings into their works, offering fuller and more ostensibly accurate representations of biblical events, particularly the dramatic accounts of encounters between the Israelites and decadent monarchs in the Old Testament. The public eagerly consumed Martin's immense paintings as well as his rich, vibrant mezzotint reproductions, in which the biblical narratives play out within detailed, panoramic architectural landscapes. For British audiences, the destruction Moses called forth with the ten plagues and the prophetic visions of Daniel served as a warning against falling into similar realms of decadence (Coltrin 2019).

Archaeological campaigns and investigations soon reached the locales associated with the events of the New Testament, and these inquiries were mobilized within the contentious debates surrounding the life of Christ. The authenticity of a visual record was often suggested through the notion of 'on-the-spot' documentation. Where artists like John Martin relied on secondary sources, others like David Roberts, William Holman Hunt, Frederic Church, Horace Vernet and Jean-Léon Gérôme made high-profile excursions to the Holy Land, which subsequently underscored the perceived authenticity of their works in the public imagination (Figure 4.8) (Gill 2003: 164–86; Pointon 1989). However, the extent to which artists crafted images that conformed to existing, often problematic, ideologies has been steadily confirmed, especially since the publication of Edward Saïd's influential *Orientalism* in 1978 (Nochlin 1989: 33–59). It was not uncommon, for instance, for artists to represent Jesus and his followers with identifiably European attributes, while his prosecutors embodied the characteristics of Middle Eastern communities. These representations thus reinforced stereotypes and prejudices against the indigenous populations, and could subtly or overtly justify imperial conquests.

The demand for 'authentic' visualizations of biblical sites became even more complex with the emergence of photography in the mid-nineteenth century. First introduced at a joint session of the French Academies of Art and Science in 1839, photography was rapidly embraced in a variety of fields for its ostensibly mechanical, 'objective' capturing

FIGURE 4.8: *The Pool of Bathesda* from *The Holy Land, Syria, Idumea, Arabia, Egypt and Nubia: From drawings made on the spot*, by David Roberts, 1842–9. Lithograph, 32.5 × 49 cm. From the New York Public Library. Photo: Alamy.

of reality. As the technology improved over the next several decades, photography was subsumed into archaeological, diplomatic and touristic campaigns to the Middle East and North Africa. Photographers like Francis Frith, Auguste Salzmann and Maxime du Camp captured biblical sites with a heretofore unprecedented level of authenticity, although their stylistic approaches nonetheless varied widely (Nir 1985). Frith, for instance, generally adhered to the norms of picturesque compositional arrangements, much like one finds in the drawings of David Roberts: architecture is presented at a comfortable distance from the viewer, and locals are incorporated into the scenes to both give a sense of scale and to underscore the 'exotic' nature of the location. Others embraced the particular characteristics offered by photography as opposed to other visual forms. As Abigail Solomon-Godeau has argued, for instance, Salzmann's compositions render the Holy Land in a much flatter, more abstracted manner. This distances his images from strategies associated with artistic traditions like the picturesque, and thus subtly conveys a more 'documentary' approach (Figure 4.9) (Godeau 1991: 150–68).

The investigations, documentations and disseminations of the remains of ancient sites that proceeded throughout the nineteenth century were persistently mobilized as a way of confirming, clarifying and authenticating the biblical narratives, rather than negating

FIGURE 4.9: *Jerusalem, Tomb of the Judges*, by Auguste Salzmann, 1854. Salted paper print from paper negative, 44.8 × 60.1 cm. The Metropolitan Museum of Art, Gilman Collection, Gift of The Howard Gilman Foundation, 2005.

them. Photography and related media like stereoscopy and the magic lantern did more to shape the popular understanding and perception of the lived experience of biblical times than perhaps any other modern development. Despite what we now recognize as the inherently subjective acts of photographic documentation, the realism that this technology offered was crucial to the persistent relevance of the Bible in a period of heated debate and scepticism.

BIBLE ILLUSTRATION

It is likewise crucial to note that at this time, the Bible was being translated, printed and circulated at an exponentially greater rate than ever before (Noss 2007: 24). The industrialization of image-making in the nineteenth century resulted in a similar flourishing of biblical imagery at a popular level through a dramatic increase in printmaking enterprises. From the second quarter of the nineteenth century onwards, artists and publishers frequently undertook major Bible illustration projects (Boase 1966). In many cases, publishers drew from an existing corpus of biblical imagery – the Bible published by the French firm Furne in 1841 includes images by old masters like Raphael and Murillo as well as more contemporaneous works by Pierre-Paul Prud'hon and Friedrich Overbeck. In 1834, British publisher John Murray released *Landscape Illustrations of the Bible*, which included a number of Roberts's 'on-the-spot' images of the Holy Land, as well as works by renowned artists like J. M. W. Turner and Charles Barry.

Histories of printmaking in the nineteenth century have traditionally focused attention on the development and flourishing of lithography, most likely due to its recognition as an 'artistic' form of printmaking, particularly at the hands of French practitioners like Delacroix, Honoré Daumier and Henri de Toulouse-Lautrec. However, the circulation of lithography was dramatically eclipsed by that of wood engraving, which was the primary medium for illustrating books and periodicals in the nineteenth century. Introduced in the late eighteenth century in the works of Thomas Bewick, wood engraving had the capacity to render precise details and, unlike lithographs or etchings, could be printed alongside text using the same press (Mainardi 2017: 73–118).

The growth of audiences for illustrated Bibles was due in no small part to the advent of organizations like the British and Foreign Bible Society (BFBS) and the American Bible Society (ABS), whose missions were to make the Bible widely accessible on domestic and international levels (Fea 2016; Howsam 1991). Many of the illustrated Bible projects of the nineteenth century thus aimed at visual and textual comprehensibility. The *Cassell Family Bible*, first published in 1862, offered a range of visual approaches: some images incorporated the findings of biblical archaeologists, while others emphasize the emotion and drama of the biblical narratives. The Cassell company was particularly committed to maintaining affordability, making large projects like the Bible available through inexpensive subscriptions.

In producing its Bible, Cassell commissioned a number of contemporary artists, the most notable of whom was Gustave Doré. Already a successful illustrator with works like Dante's *Inferno* and *The Legend of the Wandering Jew*, the French artist was invited to produce two illustrations for the *Cassell Family Bible*. Shortly thereafter, Doré began working with the French company Alfred Mame et fils on the production of a lavish, two-volume, richly illustrated Bible. Doré's images focus primarily on dramatic narratives, ranging from sweeping, tumultuous landscapes and battle scenes to intimate character studies (Figure 4.10). Doré worked swiftly and produced his images directly onto woodblocks but maintained a close relationship with his handpicked engravers to effectively translate his visions into printed form. The Doré Bible was eagerly consumed by French audiences, particularly those of the educated, urbane, lay classes – this reception underscores the extent to which the Bible and its imagery were increasingly viewed for their artistic value, often completely independent of any theological significance. It was through Cassell, however, that Doré's images gained international renown. Immediately upon its release in France, Cassell purchased the rights to reproduce Doré's Bible illustrations, and would continue to do so at frequent intervals over the next half-century. Doré's biblical imagery has become among the most widely circulating in the history of Judeo-Christian Scripture, notably informing the production of the spectacular biblical epics of Cecil B. DeMille and D. W. Griffiths. Doré also produced a number of large-scale paintings on biblical subjects, which were exhibited at a gallery in London bearing his name. The Doré Gallery, established in 1868, became a lauded site for modern religious art and remained so well after the artist's death in 1883 (Kaenel 2014: 13–33).

Doré's was one of a number of significant nineteenth-century Bible illustration projects that were produced under the heading of a single artist. The 1860s also saw the publication

FIGURE 4.10: *Moses Breaking the Tables of the Law*, by Gustave Doré and Laurent Hotelin, 1865. Wood engraving. Bibliothèque nationale de France. Photo: Alamy.

of Julius Schnorr von Carlsfeld's *Bibel in Bildern*, which earned international acclaim. Like Doré, Schnorr worked in the medium of wood engraving and drew primarily from the most narratively driven parts of the Bible. However, Schnorr maintained compositional and stylistic consistency across his images, with the action generally centralized in the immediate foreground (Figure 4.11). Schnorr was associated with the Nazarenes, and

FIGURE 4.11: *Moses Breaks the Commandment Tablets*, by Julius Schnorr von Carolsfeld, 1860. Wood engraving. Photo: Alamy.

his Bible images, though often dramatic and detailed, maintain a kind of austerity and elegance through simple hatching and crosshatching (Grewe 2009: 203–50).

It was also in the 1860s that the Brothers Dalziel, the immense wood engraving and publishing firm, initiated their own set of Bible illustration projects, working closely with some of the most esteemed British artists of the period. In 1864, they released *The Parables of Our Lord and Saviour Jesus Christ*, with illustrations after designs by John Everett Millais, one of the founding members of the Pre-Raphaelite Brotherhood. Although the PRB only functioned as a defined unit for about five years, they had a profound effect on the next generation of British painters, many of whom were commissioned by the Dalziels to produce designs for an immense illustrated Bible. The *Dalziel Bible Gallery* would not be published until 1881, and in a less comprehensive form than was originally intended. Ultimately a commercial failure, the *Dalziel Bible Gallery* is nonetheless a powerful encapsulation of the approaches to biblical imagery among the more aesthetically progressive artists of the day, including Frederic Leighton, Ford Maddox Brown and Simeon Solomon (Boase 1966: 363–5). Many of the images are indebted to the inroads being made by British archaeologists, particularly with respect to ancient Assyria (Esposito 2006: 267–96; Bohrer 2003). The Dalziel firm's capacity for translating details of artist's designs into wood engravings is especially evident in these images, and although the project as a whole incorporates the work of numerous artists, the illustrations remain relatively unified visually through a consistency of graphic syntax.

Illustrators like Doré and Schnorr are both notable for devoting extensive attention to the entirety of the Christian Bible, but many nineteenth-century artists focused especial attention on the New Testament, particularly in the wake of Ernest Renan's controversial *Vie de Jésus* (first published in 1863). In this text, Renan emphasized Jesus's humanity and explored the social, political and religious circumstances of first-century Galilee. Renan's rejection of Jesus's divinity and the miracles described in the Gospels was one of a number of studies in this period that questioned the crucial aspects of the Christian faith but purported to do so as a means of restoring its foundational ideology – other major works include David Friedrich Strauss's *Das Leben Jesu* (1836) and Albert Schweitzer's *The Quest of the Historical Jesus* (1906). The first illustrated version of Renan's *Vie de Jésus* appeared in 1870, with sixty images by Godefroy Durand. Removing the trappings and signifiers of traditional Christian iconography, Durand represented Jesus as a man of his time, markedly similar to all those around him. In some instances, however, the frankness with which Durand translates Renan's descriptions becomes quite jarring – in the Crucifixion, for instance, Christ's arms are raised straight up and nailed to the top of a narrow T-shaped cross, emphasizing his emaciated form which is placed at ground level. Drawn directly from Renan's text, this visualization is at odds with centuries of Christian iconography and creates an unfamiliar, disturbing sense of torture and execution (Figure 4.12) (Driskel 1992: 201–3).

Other illustrators produced works that adhere to the more 'authentic' vision of the life of Jesus while maintaining some relationship to familiar iconographic traditions. In his illustrations for the New Testament published in 1875, Alexandre Bida incorporated the architectural and natural elements he would have observed on his earlier trips to the Holy Land. However, Jesus is consistently represented in accordance with traditions that extend back to the Renaissance, wearing light, classicizing drapery with some form of illumination framing his head (Driskel 1992: 200–1). The style of Bida's illustrations (and contemporaneous artists like the German painter Heinrich Hofmann) would heavily influence American religious visual culture of the twentieth century, most notably the work of Warner Sallman (Doss 1996: 67–9).

James Tissot, a French artist who spent much of his career based in London, produced one of the most extensive and acclaimed sets of illustrations of the life of Christ, which oscillated between the observational and documentary to the emotive and mystical. Following a visionary experience in 1885, Tissot made two trips to the Holy Land during which he produced extensive studies and notes of his observations. These works formed the basis of 350 watercolours that were initially published as the two-volume *Vie de Notre-Seigneur Jésus-Christ* in 1896–7 by Alfred Mame et fils – the same firm that had commissioned Doré's Bible illustrations thirty years earlier (Dolkart 2009; Driskel 1992: 214–18). The gritty realism of much of Tissot's imagery is made all the more palpable through his highly unusual compositional arrangements. In an oft-cited instance, Tissot depicts the crowds at Golgotha from the elevated perspective of Christ on the cross; his blood-soaked feet nailed to the cross is just visible at the bottom of the picture (Figure 4.13).

Tissot's watercolours of the life of Christ were on public view in London in 1896–7; the space in which they were displayed was, notably, the Doré Gallery. They would subsequently travel to the United States to be shown in New York, Boston and Chicago,

FIGURE 4.12: *The Crucifixion*, by Godefroy Durand, 1870, from Ernest Renan's *Vie de Jésus*. Wood engraving. Photo: Alamy.

FIGURE 4.13: *What Our Lord Saw from the Cross*, by James Tissot, 1886–94. Opaque watercolour over graphite on gray-green wove paper, 24.8 × 23 cm. Brooklyn Museum, purchased by public subscription. Photo: Alamy.

and ultimately were sold to the Brooklyn Institute of Arts and Sciences (now the Brooklyn Museum) in 1900. Several firms produced English versions of the Mame publication, *The Life of our Saviour Jesus-Christ*, around the turn of the twentieth century, and it became features of the ever-expanding market for biblical imagery in the United States (Morowitz 2009: 193–4).

MASS VISUAL CULTURE IN AMERICA

The Bible was a fixture of nineteenth-century American life, and it became a crucial component of various networks of commercial enterprise in an era of industrialization (McDannell 1995: 67–102). Illustrated Bibles like Doré's, Tissot's, Schnorr's and the *Cassell Family Bible* were in high demand in this context. It is important to note that international copyright law for images was not established until the Berne convention of 1898, and many small-scale publishers took advantage by reproducing well-known images with abandon. Even a firm like Cassell, which maintained (albeit limited) operations in the United States, could do little to check the circulation of images for which they owned the rights (like Doré's). As a result, these works appeared in a seemingly limitless quantity of cheap publications.

Mass production of religious imagery in the United States was indelibly linked to denominational expansion of Protestant ideology, particularly in the wake of the Second Great Awakening. Despite the resistance to religious iconography that was at the foundation of Protestantism, images were thoroughly mobilized for didactic and devotional purposes in this period. The millenarian thread that ran through many Protestant communities generated a sense of urgency, which is palpable in the images that convey the imminent end of days and need for spiritual repentance. Millenialist sectors like the Millerites and the Seventh-Day Adventists circulated charts that visualized interpretations of biblical prophecies and placed the apocalypse just on the horizon (Figure 4.14). The profusion of text and visual ordering of the information in these charts conveys the sense that the interpretations are thoroughly grounded in rational inquiry. At the same time, the illustrations are routed in the fantastical imagery described in the books of Daniel and Revelation and underscore the frightening consequences of the prophecies (Morgan 2007: 43–198).

Images also played a crucial role in promoting biblical literacy and Christian morality among children, a contingency that was thoroughly targeted by the expanding networks of religious organizations in the nineteenth century. Illustrated Bibles, primers, prayer cards and other ephemera were produced in immense quantities. However, the images in these contexts generally functioned in conjunction with the texts that they were intended to illustrate, rather than autonomous entities that could become subject to idolatrous mentalities (Morgan 1999: 201–34).

The American context also saw the flourishing of biblical imagery within the plethora of new visual technologies that emerged in the nineteenth century. The histories of stereoscopic photography, the panorama, magic lantern shows and film are saturated with subjects from the Bible, and they demonstrate the significant overlap between entertainment and religious pedagogy in the American cultural landscape. Stereoscopic imagery became a staple of the American home, provoking intimate experiences of moralizing subjects and transporting the viewer to faraway sites like the Holy Land. In numerous cases, American artists and entrepreneurs mobilized new and spectacular forms of mass visual culture as a means of establishing more and more authentic experiences of the biblical narratives. Visitors to the Chautauqua Institute in upstate New York and the 1904 World's Fair in St. Louis had the opportunity to inhabit recreations of Holy Land sites. The magic lantern became a frequently used tool on the expansive lecture circuits that grew out of the Chautauqua movement; among the catalogs of lantern slides available in this period, biblical subjects and Holy Land travel images form two of the most significant categories (Schaefer 2017: 275–300). The possibilities offered by spectacular forms of entertainment and education like the magic lantern presentations

FIGURE 4.14: *A Chronological Chart of the Visions of Daniel and John*, 1843. Photo: Wkimedia Commons/Alamy.

and the moving panorama prompted their usage among a number of celebrity preachers. One significant example, *The Photo-Drama of Creation* (1914) consisted of a filmed magic lantern presentation accompanied by an audio recording of the voice of 'Pastor Russell', which was seen by millions of viewers (Nelson 1992: 230–5).

The pervasiveness of biblical imagery in nineteenth-century America carried over into and heavily informed the realm of 'fine art' (Schwain 2017). Landscape painters like Thomas Cole and Frederic Church incorporated the spectacular and observational realism of panorama painting; in the case of Church, his firsthand observations of the Holy Land resulted in a series of large-scale paintings that were exhibited at the Goupil Gallery in New York City and were marketed as a kind of virtual tour – much like moving panoramas, but in the context of a more artistic enterprise (Davis 1996: 53–72). African American artist Henry Ossawa Tanner, who received his artistic education under Thomas Eakins before moving to Paris, produced a number of significant biblical paintings that demonstrate the influence of Eakins's Realism while highlighting the mystical, transcendent aspects of the Gospels. The subjects Tanner chose to represent – the annunciation and the resurrection of Lazarus, for instance – underscore the significance of *seeing*, of *witnessing*, in the development of spiritual faith (Schwain 2008: 42–70).

THE BIBLE AND THE NARRATIVES OF MODERNISM

Many of the artists and images that I have discussed thus far fall outside the dominant narratives of nineteenth-century art history. Surveys of this period inevitably place the rise of the avant-garde as the preeminent development. This is certainly understandable, given that the emergence of avant-garde movements coincides with and is in dialogue with the revolutionary uprisings around 1848. As Linda Nochlin, one of the foremost art historians of the late twentieth century, argues, the key avant-garde movement, French Realism, was significant in that it was both politically *and* stylistically radical (Nochlin 1989: 1–18).

The centrality of progressive politics to the narratives of nineteenth-century art is a major factor in the lack of attention given to biblical imagery produced at this time. It is also of note that in the late twentieth century, when many of the dominant narratives were written, scholars focused their attention primarily on France, a nation that still identified as largely Catholic and for which close analysis of the Bible at an individual level was discouraged or even forbidden. Thus, when French avant-garde artists like Gustave Courbet and Édouard Manet approached Christian subject matter, it often related more broadly to religious institutions and practices than to biblical stories, and these works are frequently interpreted as critiques of tradition.

However, the landscape of art historical scholarship has shifted significantly in recent years, illuminating a much more complex picture of nineteenth-century visual culture than is available when looking solely through the lens of the Parisian avant-garde. Moreover, in this expanding field of study, the categorical distinctions between traditional/conservative/academic art and the avant-garde are revealed to be much more ambiguous. In this context, the Bible takes on a much more significant and complex role. Recent investigations of movements like the Nazarenes and the Pre-Raphaelite Brotherhood have argued determinedly for their place within the avant-garde. Although the style of these artists may not seem particularly radical to our eyes, they were reacting against artistic institutions that catered to the tastes of the powerful and wealthy (Barringer et al. 2012).

It certainly was the case that biblical imagery would be more readily found in conservative institutions like the academies than in avant-garde exhibitions. An Old Testament subject

FIGURE 4.15: *Vision of the Sermon (Jacob Wrestling the Angel)* by Paul Gauguin, 1888. Oil on canvas, 72.20 × 91.00 cm. National Galleries of Scotland, purchased 1925. Photo: National Galleries of Scotland/Getty Images.

would have been completely out of place at the Impressionist exhibitions (1874–86), in which modern life was embraced and represented through radical stylistic means. However, by the turn of the twentieth century, we see artists continuing to pursue radical stylistic approaches, but returning to subjects of a mystical, spiritual or transcendent nature. Symbolist artists throughout northern Europe embraced the prophetic, visionary elements of the Bible that the Romantics had explored earlier in the century, but in ways that were consistent with avant-garde principles. Paul Gauguin, for instance, produced radically flat representations of biblical stories like Jacob wrestling the angel (Figure 4.15). These paintings were stylistically derived in part from Japanese prints, which had exerted an immense influence on avant-garde artists like Manet, James Abbott McNeil Whistler, Edgar Degas and Mary Cassatt. In Gauguin's work, the flatness, cropping and odd perspective of Japanese prints are employed to generate a jarring visual experience in which the boundary between the real and the visionary is highly ambiguous.

What is crucial here is that many of the modernist developments of the late nineteenth century are thoroughly embedded in the notion of art as a form of transcendence, a spiritual experience that could take the place of the institutionalized forms of religion that were questioned in the wake of the Enlightenment. For someone like Gauguin that spiritual transcendence could be located especially in the more 'authentic' experiences of provincial communities, whether in the French countryside or the Pacific islands. At the turn of the twentieth century, modernist artists would continue to pursue 'pure' aesthetic experience through abstract means, but again, these experiments are fundamentally tied to the traditions of biblical representation.

THE EARLY TWENTIETH CENTURY

By the end of the nineteenth century, Symbolist approaches to art had taken root in many areas of Europe. This dovetailed with the codification of national identities that pervaded the European landscape on the eve of the First World War. In eastern Europe, where industrialization occurred at a slower pace, art was often mobilized as a means of exploring and reinvigorating particular regional traditions. The visual language used by artists like Nicholas Roerich and Natalia Goncharova is informed by contemporaneous modernist developments, but their works also draw heavily from traditional forms like icon painting and Byzantine frescos and incorporate the stylized forms and religious subject matter of these precedents (Hardiman and Kozicharow 2017). Goncharova, a significant figure in the early-twentieth-century Russian avant-garde, merged tradition and contemporaneity in the series *Mystical Images of War: Fourteen Lithographs*. In these prints, Goncharova explores the subject of modern warfare while frequently relying on the figures and symbols drawn from the book of Revelations (Figure 4.16). Her images use the bold, graphic stylization associated with the inexpensive, popular prints (*lubok*) that circulated widely in Russia (Sharp 2006).

Goncharova was also one of the earliest members of *Der Blaue Reiter* ('The Blue Rider'), a group that formed around Wassily Kandinsky and Franz Marc, and which was central to the development of Expressionism in and around Germany. Like Goncharova, Kandinsky drew from folk imagery and religious subject matter, but he also strongly advocated for the spiritual value of art and its ability to transform society. In particular, Kandinsky saw the potential of radical abstraction as a means of rebirth and rejuvenation and tied these concepts to apocalyptic imagery and language. Paintings like *The Day of the Last Judgment* (Figure 4.17) utilize color and brushstroke to relay these broader themes; however, as scholars have noted, there are formal connections between Kandinsky's abstract motifs and popular religious imageries the artist saw and discussed in his writings (Long 1975).

The story of modern art in the first half of the twentieth century is largely dominated by the pursuit of radical abstraction. However, as we see with Kandinsky, the development of modernism is in many ways fundamentally tied to the Bible and the history of its visual representation. Although Kandinsky's formal choices may be rooted in motifs drawn from the biblical narratives, his works are nonetheless part of a wider shift away from representational art and towards thinking about art in its purest forms and as a means of spiritual transcendence.

Many of the trends that I have traced in this chapter continue to dominate popular culture through the beginning of the twentieth century. Magic lantern presentations give way to the early biblical epics of Cecil B. DeMille and D. W. Griffiths, and the growth of industry in the United States led to exponential growth in the production of biblical print culture. These developments may seem at odds with the avant-garde aesthetics that flourished in the early twentieth century. However, as this chapter has shown, the development of modern art proceeded directly alongside and very much in dialogue with a continued interest in the Bible.

FIGURE 4.16: *Angels and Airplanes*, by Natalia Goncharova, 1914. Lithograph. University of Notre Dame, Hesburgh Library, The Department of Rare Books and Special Collections. Photo: Alamy.

FIGURE 4.17: *The Day of the Last Judgement*, by Vassily Kandinsky, 1912. Painting with water and Chinese ink under glass, 33.6 × 45.3 cm. Paris, Centre Pompidou – Musée national d'art moderne – Centre de création industrielle. Photo: GrandPalaisRmn Photo Agency.

NOTES

1. Letter 092, *Vincent van Gogh – The Letters*, accessed 16 April 2019, http://vangoghletters.org/vg/letters/let092/letter.html.
2. Letter 0537, *Vincent van Gogh – The Letters*, accessed 16 April 2019, http://vangoghletters.org/vg/letters/let537/letter.html. Manet's *Dead Toreador* is in the collection of the National Gallery of Art, Washington, DC (accession number 1942.9.40).
3. Musée d'Orsay, Paris (accession number RF 325).

REFERENCES

Barringer, T., J. Rosenfeld, and A. Smith, eds. (2012), *Pre-Raphaelites: Victorian Art and Design*, New Haven and London: Yale University Press.

Bermingham, A. (2013), 'Apocalypse at the Academy: Death on the Pale Horse and the Revelation of Benjamin West', in *Living with the Royal Academy: Artistic Ideals and Experiences in England, 1768-1848*, ed. S. Monks, 153–70, Burlington: Ashgate.

Bindman, D. (1999), 'The English Apocalypse', in *The Apocalypse and the Shape of Things to Come*, ed. F. Carey, 208–31, London: British Museum Press.

Boase, T. S. R. (1966), 'Biblical Illustration in 19th-Century English Art', *Journal of the Warburg and Courtauld Institutes*, 29: 349–67.

Bohrer, F. N. (2003), *Orientalism and Visual Culture: Imagining Mesopotamia in Nineteenth-Century Europe*, Cambridge and New York: Cambridge University Press.

Coltrin, C. (2019), 'Picturing Political Deliverance: Three Paintings of the Exodus by John Martin, Francis Danby, and David Roberts', *19th-Century Art Worldwide*, 10(1). Accessed 5 April 2019. http://www.19thc-artworldwide.org/index.php/spring11/paintings-of-the-exodus-by-john-martin-francis-danby-david-roberts.

Davis, J. (1996), *The Landscape of Belief: Encountering the Holy Land in Nineteenth-Century American Art and Culture*, Princeton: Princeton University Press.

Dolkart, J. F., ed. (2009), *James Tissot: The Life of Christ: The Complete Set of 350 Watercolors*, London and New York: Merrell Publishers; New York: In association with Brooklyn Museum.

Doss, E. (1996), 'Making a "Virile, Manly Christ": The Cultural Origins and Meaning of Warner Sallman's Religious Imagery', in *Icons of American Protestantism: The Art of Warner Sallman*, ed. D. Morgan, 61–94, New Haven and London: Yale University Press.

Driskel, M. P. (1992), *Representing Belief: Religion, Art, and Society in Nineteenth-Century France*, University Park: Pennsylvania State University Press.

Edwards, C. (2009), *Mystery of the Night Café: Hidden Key to the Spirituality of Vincent van Gogh*, Albany: State University of New York Press.

Esposito, D. (2006), 'Dalziels' Bible Gallery (1881): Assyria and the Biblical Illustration in Nineteenth-Century Britain', in *Orientalism, Assyriology and the Bible*, ed. S. W. Holloway, 267–96, Sheffield: Sheffield Phoenix Press.

Fea, J. (2016), *The Bible Cause: A History of the American Bible Society*, New York: Oxford University Press.

García, M. D.-A. (2007), *World History of Nineteenth-Century Archaeology: Nationalism, Colonialism, and the Past*, Oxford: Oxford University Press.

Giebelhausen, M. (2006), *Painting the Bible: Representation and Belief in Mid-Victorian Britain*, Aldershot and Burlington: Ashgate.

Gill, H. (2003), *The Language of French Orientalist Painting*, Lewiston: Edwin Mellen Press.

Godeau, A. S. (1991), *Photography at the Dock: Essays on Photographic History, Institutions, and Practices*, Minneapolis: University of Minnesota Press.

Grewe, C. (2009), *Painting the Sacred in the Age of Romanticism*, Farnham and Burlington: Ashgate.

Grewe, C. (2015), *The Nazarenes: Romantic Avant-Garde and the Art of the Concept*, University Park: Pennsylvania State University Press.

Hardiman, L. and N. Kozicharow (2017), *Modernism and the Spiritual in Russian Art: New Perspectives*, Cambridge: Open Book Publishers.

Hempton, D. (2008), *Evangelical Disenchantment: Nine Portraits of Faith and Doubt*, Haven: Yale University Press.

Howsam, L. (1991), *Cheap Bibles: Nineteenth-Century Publishing and the British and Foreign Bible Society*, Cambridge and New York: Cambridge University Press.

Hulsker, J. (1996), *The New Complete Van Gogh: Paintings, Drawings, Sketches*, Amsterdam: J. M. Meulenhoff; Amsterdam; Philadelphia in association with John Benjamins.

Ibata, H. (2018), *The Challenge of the Sublime: From Burke's Philosophical Enquiry to British Romantic Art*, Manchester: Manchester University Press.

Jasper, D. (1999), *The Sacred and Secular Canon in Romanticism: Preserving the Sacred Truths*, Basingstoke: Macmillan; New York: St. Martin's Press.

Kaenel, P., ed. (2014), *Gustave Doré (1832–1883): Master of Imagination*, Paris: Musée d'Orsay: Flammarion; Ottawa: National Gallery of Canada.

Long, R.-C. W. (1975), 'Kandinsky's Abstract Style: The Veiling of Apocalyptic Folk Imagery', *Art Journal*, 34(3): 217–28.

Mainardi, P. (2017), *Another World: Nineteenth-Century Illustrated Print Culture*, New Haven and London: Yale University Press.

McDannell, C. (1995), *Material Christianity: Religion and Popular Culture in America*, New Haven: Yale University Press.

Morgan, D. (1999), *Protestants and Pictures: Religion, Visual Culture, and the Age of American Mass Production*, New York: Oxford University Press.

Morgan, D. (2007), *The Lure of Images: A History of Religion and Visual Media in America*, London and New York: Routledge.

Morowitz, L. (2009), 'A Passion for Business: Wanamaker's, Munkácsy, and the Depiction of Christ', *The Art Bulletin*, 91(2): 184–206.

Nelson, R. A. (1992), 'Propaganda for God: Pastor Charles Taze Russell and the Multi-Media Photo-Drama of Creation (1914)', in *Une invention du diable?: Cinema des premiers temps et religion*, ed. R. Cosandey, A. Gaudreault, and T. Gunning, 230–55, Sainte-Foy: Presses de l'Université Laval.

Nir, Y. (1985), *The Bible and the Image: The History of Photography in the Holy Land, 1839–1899*, Philadelphia: University of Pennsylvania Press.

Nochlin, L. (1989), *The Politics of Vision: Essays on Nineteenth-Century Art and Society*, New York: Harper & Row.

Noss, P. A., ed. (2007), *A History of Bible Translation*, Rome: Edizioni de storia e letteratura.

Pointon, M. (1989), 'The Artist as Ethnographer: Holman Hunt and the Holy Land', in *Pre-Raphaelites Reviewed*, ed. M. Pointon, 22–44, Manchester: Manchester University Press.

Polistena, J. (2008), *The Religious Paintings of Eugène Delacroix (1798–1863): The Initiator of the Style of Modern Religious Art*, Lewiston: Edwin Mellen Press.

Prickett, S. (1996), *Origins of Narrative: The Romantic Appropriation of the Bible*, New York: Cambridge University Press.

Schaefer, S. C. (2017), 'Illuminating the Divine: The Magic Lantern and Religious Pedagogy in the USA, ca. 1870–1920', *Material Religion: The Journal of Objects, Art and Belief*, 13(3): 275–300.

Schwain, K. (2008), *Signs of Grace: Religion and American Art in the Gilded Age*, Ithaca: Cornell University Press.

Schwain, K. (2017), 'The Bible and Art', in *The Oxford Handbook of the Bible in America*, ed. P. Gutjahr, 405–23, Oxford and New York: Oxford University Press.

Sharp, J. A. (2006), *Russian Modernism between East and West: Natal'ia Goncharova and the Moscow Avant-Garde*, Cambridge: Cambridge University Press.

Silberman, N. A. (1982), *Digging for God and Country: Exploration, Archaeology, and the Secret Struggle for the Holy Land, 1799, 1917*, New York: Alfred A. Knopf.

von Erffa, H. and A. Staley (1986), *The Paintings of Benjamin West*, New Haven, CT and London: Yale University Press.

CHAPTER 5

Faiths, Confessions and Denominations

LYDIA WILLSKY-CIOLLO

Standing at the turn of the twentieth century and surveying the events of the previous, J. Estlin Carpenter observed that 'we cannot imagine either our history or our religion without the Bible' (1903: 454). Over a series of eight lectures, Carpenter unpacked the progression of historical criticism on various books of the Bible and the text as a whole, as well its intellectual roots. In the eighth lecture, he turned his focus upon the practical fallout of this intellectual trajectory on 'the Church'. Speaking as a British Unitarian and a professor of comparative religion, Carpenter described the church generally and monolithically, so as to illustrate the impact on Christianity as a whole and, ultimately, to make an ecumenical and moralistic plea to all Christian thinkers to 'reshape' theology 'in the light of present knowledge' (1903: 459). He drew upon non-Christian religions and scriptures to highlight the universality of Christian principles as well as the potential reality that many of the stories contained in the Bible were born from earlier non-Christian religions and not from the mouth of God. For Carpenter, the writing was on the wall: Christians, specifically, and people of the book, more broadly, must attend to the historical and material nature of their supposedly timeless and eternal text, as well as the fact that truth was more universal than a narrowly biblicist Christianity had allowed. Not all saw things as Carpenter did, however. Different Christian denominations and traditions claimed supremacy over others by arguing for their 'brand' as eminently biblical. At the same time as competition intensified, the Bible's vaunted status became increasingly unstable. How various religious groups coped with, recovered from, and in certain cases, ignored a world where biblical authority was being recalibrated, is the focus of this chapter.

The reasons or forces behind this ever-shifting world in which the Bible and its proponents found themselves are multifold. Just as it would require volumes to delineate every denomination's understanding of the Bible during this time, it would be futile to pretend to any sort of comprehensiveness in covering the various contextual, intellectual, and practical factors that helped to produce such interdenominational variety. For the purposes of this chapter, I identify five major factors that helped shape different traditions in their use of and beliefs about the Bible during the nineteenth century: the abundance of printed Bibles (including new translations); the splintering of old and the creation of new denominations; competition between established philosophical systems (Scottish Common Sense) and new historical-critical methods; scientific discovery; and the overarching question of biblical authority.

Perhaps there is no invention more significant for the modern world than the printing press. For the Bible, this is certainly the case. While the printing press had been revolutionizing Christianity since the fifteenth century, the nineteenth century witnessed an explosion of bibles, both in terms of their availability and their variety. Presses, both independent and denominational, abounded; more importantly, *cheap* bibles became the norm (Perry 2018: 20). Often, bible societies began as interdenominational initiatives aimed at spreading Protestant Christianity. The notion that the more people with a Bible in hand would equate to more, devoted Christians was taken for granted, particularly when many Protestants operated on the assumption that the Bible's message was perspicuous (Tanner 1987). Complicating, while not confounding this belief, was the profusion of biblical commentaries and guides intended to help the reader, particularly those who were uneducated, to understand the 'plain' text (Perry 2018: 50–8). This concern for clarity transformed in the latter part of the century into efforts for new, improved translations of the Bible. At the beginning of the nineteenth century, for most Protestants, the King James Version was still standard (for Catholics, it was the Douay-Rheims). The end of the century would witness the production of the new revised version, a translation whose contentious history is testament to the conflict between those who hoped that a better Bible would inoculate the text from its critics and those who feared that more bibles claiming to be 'the Bible' would dilute its power and potency (Thuesen 1999). There were also bibles advertised for particular demographic groups or occasions, such as the family Bible or the 'travel' Bible (Ferrell 2008: 192–220). The Bible was everywhere in the nineteenth century and ripe for the claiming by denominations competing for supremacy and converts.

Protestantism is inherently schismatic (it's in the name, after all) and the doctrine of *sola scriptura* has played a major role in perpetuating this tendency. Despite Martin Luther's intentions to check rogue biblical interpretations by the community of faithful Christians, the notion of Scripture alone took on its own life, propelled by political, intellectual and social forces that made possible the idea that individual interpretations of the Bible could blossom into new confessions. In *The Lively Experiment*, Sidney Mead explored the phenomenon of 'denominationalism' in the American context, rooting it first and foremost in the notion that each denomination believes itself to be the true, biblical faith. In the nineteenth century, the religious marketplace overflowed with such claims – fueled in the United States by disestablishment and the prevailing Enlightenment assumption that people had the capability to discern truth for themselves (1963: 103–33). This is true not only of Protestant denominations; Catholics have never relinquished the idea that it is they, not the Protestants, who are the true keepers of the Bible. As do Jews, whose biblicism and link to the story of the Hebrews served as a bridge to Christians, particularly Protestants, during the nineteenth century, just as their system of rabbinical exegesis and adherence to the oral Torah complicated notions of *sola scriptura*. However, the nineteenth century also witnessed divisions among Jews (some of which would manifest into denominational or geographical schism) that highlighted the influence of Protestantism, specifically in the elevation of the written over the oral Torah among certain groups (Sarna 2017: 506–7). Alongside these changes in established religious traditions, new denominations, such as the Church of Jesus Christ of Latter-day Saints, arose *because*, not in spite of this veritable smorgasbord of religious options. Joseph Smith was prompted to seek counsel from the Bible, because he could not determine which Christian sect was, in fact, the correct, and therefore biblical, faith (Bushman 2005). As the century progressed, the Bible was increasingly found at the centre of intradenominational debates, particularly when European intellectual currents found purchase on the continent and across the Atlantic. Most denominations born from schism and splintering would continue as it became clearer that dominant philosophical assumptions regarding truth were facing challenges.

Intellectual histories of the nineteenth century note the ascendancy of the system of Scottish Common Sense Realism, particularly in the United States. This system, which posited that knowledge emerges primarily from sense data (*a posteriori*), rather than previously held intellectual assumptions (*a priori*), helped to form the buffer employed by Protestants, primarily, between the Bible and new fields of historical and scientific inquiry (Bozeman 1977). The notion that the Bible could be considered a storehouse of 'facts', intuitively grasped and easily understood, helped establish the 'plain Bible thesis', which, in turn, would strengthen the idea that the Bible, when read properly (led by the Spirit, usually) was inerrant and infallible, not simply perspicuous in meaning (Noll 1986: 11–31; Marsden 1983). Multiple factors conspired to challenge this thesis during the nineteenth century, including Romanticism, which emphasized the possibility of seeking divine truth through the intuitive and imaginative capacities of the human mind and heart. Suddenly, it mattered less what form the sacred text took than how it made a person feel, what greater connection it developed between God and the individual (Kittelstrom 2015: 135–42; Coleridge 1829: xii–lxi). However, perhaps no two intellectual challenges were more threatening than historical criticism and the advance of certain scientific theories and discoveries.

Historical criticism (or 'higher' criticism, as contrasted with 'lower' criticism, or the examination of variations between versions of the Bible with the aim of finding the 'original autograph'), particularly that issuing from Germany proposed that the Bible was, like any book, historically located and must be examined as such (Satta 2007: 57). This premise alone was revolutionary, given that the Bible's universality and timelessness were taken for granted by many. The conclusions that arose from such an examination further challenged these assumptions by detecting, among other things, multiple authors for texts typically attributed to a single scribe, redactions showing that texts were often compiled from several sources and references to historical events occurring at the time of writing, even if that time was different than the events reported in the text. As scholars have shown, many Protestants embraced higher criticism, arguing that it did not impact the message of the Bible, only its form; however, others felt the need to challenge these views, creating entire systems that accounted for the alleged discrepancies uncovered by the higher critics (Satta 2007: 67–73).

Harder to ignore, particularly by those who wished for the Bible to speak authoritatively in areas of history, science and theology, were advances in geology in the early nineteenth century and the theories of Darwin in the mid- to late nineteenth century. Some argued that scientific discoveries, such as the earth's age could be accounted for in the biblical text if, for example, the 'day' designated in the Genesis account of the creation were taken to mean an epoch or some greater unit of time. Others sought to maintain the literal meaning of a day by proposing alternative theories of time or simply by denying the discoveries of science – something that contribute to the modern phenomenon of fundamentalism in the early twentieth century (Chapman 2015). How human beings evolved, through Darwinian gradualism or by immediate creation, would also require explanation, which, for some, led to further parsing of biblical from scientific truth or to a merging of the two (Satta 2007: 47–50). Taken together, these potential challenges to the 'facts' of the Bible, coupled with interpretive clashes that undermined the Bible's so-called plainness (such as during slavery debates during the Civil War), meant that, at the least, the philosophical grounding for the Bible and biblical truth was shifting.

Though it is hard to know whether it produced or emerged from the changes occurring in and around the Bible during the nineteenth century, at their centre were questions regarding the Bible's authority. This did not simply break down between those who believed that the Good Book served as viable religious authority and those who did not. Rather than a categorical split, people and denominations existed along a spectrum from the arguably very few who had dispensed with the Bible, to those who felt that only *parts* of the Bible were authoritative while others were not, to those who saw the Bible as an authority but who welcomed other such sources, including other sacred texts and to those who believed that the Bible was the one and only source of divine authority on earth. Further nuancing this spectrum were innumerable and complicating questions, including: Was the Bible an authority only if it was proved to be inerrant? Or only if it could speak definitively to all human questions of any relevance, including science? Or only if it could speak to everyone precisely in the same way? Or if it could stand alone, without scaffolding, addition or new edition? And finally, *which* Bible? Arguably, at the start of the nineteenth century, the Bible stood – or at least appeared to stand – on relatively stable ground. By its end, not Bible but *bibles* was the reality, in a material sense meaning more physical bibles, but also in a confessional and personal sense. It was no longer given that what one person meant by 'the Bible' was shared by others, both in and outside of specific religious traditions.

To illustrate the shift from the Bible as a relatively stable source of truth and authority to a sacred text whose purpose and meaning were increasingly multiform and dynamic, the rest of this chapter examines four denominations for which the Bible played a central role, but which diverged from each other in their understanding, application and use of the Bible: the African Methodist Episcopal Church, the Unitarian Church, the Presbyterian Church and the Roman Catholic Church. Here the focus skews American, though a number of these denominations, most notably Roman Catholicism, contended with questions regarding the Bible's status in multiple theatres.

THE AFRICAN METHODIST EPISCOPAL CHURCH

The 'Slave Bible' was published in London in 1807 by the Society for the Conversion of Negro Slaves. As initially conceived, this was a gesture of benevolence. Why should slaves be deprived of Christian education? In fact, the conversion of slaves to Christianity became a popular retroactive justification for the slave trade since it 'saved' them from their heathen religions and cultures in the present and from damnation in eternity (Johnson 2015). Of course, the text itself revealed the cognitive dissonance of white Christians: since the message of Christianity was, arguably, one of liberation and the Bible was replete with passages attesting to this fact, the need to keep slaves docile needed to be balanced against the need to save their souls. Fears over not only the message of the Bible but of literacy in general prompted slave owners to push back against missionaries eager to proselytize among their slaves. To accomplish this, publishers responded to the pleas of both missionaries and slave masters and purposefully omitted segments of the sacred text, such as the Exodus story, and retained all mentions of obedience to one's masters, such as Paul's letter to the Ephesians (6:5). This book, publishers hoped, would be palatable to slave masters and missionaries alike (Callahan 2006: 9–10).

In spite of these efforts to circumscribe the impact of the Bible, the King James Bible found black slaves. The text spoke to them in a way that missionaries and white preachers did not – a fact that along with the oral rather than written mode in which the Bible was transmitted – has prompted the common label for the Bible in African American Christian circles as 'The Talking Book' (Callahan 2006: 2, 11). For their part, the publishers of the slave Bible were right: what the text said to African Americans undermined the institution of slavery and the system of racialized oppression intended to degrade, dehumanize and disenfranchise those of African descent. Not only did the text reveal that they were not, in fact, sub-human (or 'cursed'), it told them that it was *they* who were chosen; redemption was not just possible, but inevitable if one understood the direction of the providential history recorded in the text (Smith 2017: 201; Callahan 2006: 26–9). This notion underscored the belief that African Americans were keepers of true Christianity over against what Frederick Douglass famously termed 'slaveholding Christianity'. Entire denominations were forged upon this understanding, the African Methodist Episcopal Church key among them.

Known as the first fully independent black denomination, the A.M.E. Church was steeped in Protestant biblicism understood through the lens of black suffering and struggle. The Church grew out of the Free African Society established in the late eighteenth century by Richard Allen and other free blacks. Ordained as a Methodist exhorter and ultimately a bishop in 1799, Allen presided over Bethel Chapel in Philadelphia from its dedication as a Methodist Church in 1794. Methodism would explode in membership during the nineteenth century; the evangelical model which focused on the conversion experience and often occurred *en masse* at revival meetings, seemingly democratized Christianity. Suddenly, it was an experience of God, rather than seminary training that qualified someone to preach the Gospel and to interpret the meaning of the Bible for an audience expecting talented preaching, not instruction (Frey and Wood 1998: 118–48). This type of Christianity made inroads among slaves in the American South where high church denominations, such as the Episcopalian Church, had failed. Scholars of African American Christianity have famously noted that slaves mixed African culture and rites with the redemptive message of evangelical Christianity to create their own religious traditions, which were uniquely suited to their plight, level of literacy and cultural milieu (Raboteau 1978). Denominations like Methodism also provided pathways to religious leadership unavailable in others – a fact of which men like Richard Allen would take full advantage.

Allen had been born a slave, ultimately purchasing his freedom in the 1780s, and bristled at the persistent and heavy-handed white dominance of his free black congregation. In 1807 and then again in 1815, Allen petitioned to free the church from white control and to establish a free black denomination; in 1816, he succeeded. In his retelling of events from his earliest inclinations to preach the creation of the A.M.E. Church, biblical passages provide the language, model and authority for his narrative – a process which black preachers refer to as 'taking a text' (Callahan 2006: xi). In *Life Experiences and Gospel Labors*, Allen invokes the Bible in his early preaching days, citing Christ's admonishment to 'Come unto me, all ye that are weary and heavy laden, and I will give you rest' (Allen 1985: 139). Such passages not only acted as justification for his activities as a black preacher (he was simply emulating Christ, after all), but invoked the struggle of slaves under slavery as definitively biblical. Who could be more 'weary and heavy laden' than slaves? This was their text to be spoken, spread and taken.

Perhaps none 'took' the text quite like Jarena Lee, whose path to preaching highlights the ways that biblical expertise opened doors for black women, not simply free or enslaved black men, to claim religious leadership. Facility with the Bible (and a pronounced, natural charisma), in the case of Lee, trumped race and sex. In her own autobiography, Lee invokes the traditional Methodist conversion narrative, which, prompted by a 'reading of the Psalms', led to a pronounced period of despair, followed by the conviction of her salvation (Lee 2000). Her experiences, as recorded, were common fare – not just for Methodists but for Protestant conversion stories in general – particularly in citing the Bible as the catalyst for the conversion process. However, it was Lee's use of the Bible to make her case to preach that highlights how the Bible could operate for the degraded during the nineteenth century and how, in a denomination where the population was comprised of free and enslaved blacks, a woman could invoke the authority of the text to establish her own authority.

In a meeting with Richard Allen, Lee petitioned the Bishop to preach. Allen was reluctant, noting that 'our Discipline knew nothing at all about [women preaching] – that it did not call for women preachers'. Though this initially caused her a certain relief, the urge to preach did not leave her; for recourse, she turned to the Bible, writing:

> 'If the man may preach, because the Saviour died for him, why not the woman, seeing he died for her also? . . . Did not Mary *first* preach the risen Saviour and is not the doctrine of the resurrection the very climax of Christianity – hangs not all our hope on this, as argued by St. Paul? Then did not Mary, a woman, preach the gospel? For she preached the resurrection of the crucified Son of God'. (Lee 2000: 169)

Contradicting the Pauline injunction against female preaching, Lee cited the example of Mary, which emphasizes her facility with the text and the emergence of an early feminist hermeneutic. As a black woman – a set of identity markers that meant that she was doubly subjugated in the American context – the Bible operated as a proof text for both racial and gender liberation, even while claiming that God chose preachers 'by inspiration only' (Wills 1982: 138). In this way, Lee bridged the two modes of the talking book: as a text that spoke to blacks and as a text from which blacks spoke. As the physical remnant of revelation, the text spoke to her, unfolding its narrative of redemption, just as God spoke to her, commanding and commending her to preach, just as she 'talked' from the text, threading her own narrative with biblical allusion and justification.

The A.M.E. Church's pairing of the distribution of the Bible to the preaching of the Gospel and the missionary expansion of Christianity to the African continent and to blacks in the south was complicated by context. Almost since its start, the A.M.E. Church foresaw evangelism in Africa; preaching the Gospel was a natural extension of the church's theological and racial heritage (Raboteau 2001: 33). Going south was another story. In a debate with Frederick Douglass over the question of whether to distribute Bibles among slaves in the south, A.M.E. preacher Henry Highland Garnet was confident that the text could speak to slaves without the commentary or scaffolding provided by preachers or institutions. This was a feature of the A.M.E. Church, which 'stood within the circle of theological populism' (Holifield 2003: 306). Douglass was dubious, fearing that the 'justice of the Bible was not self-evident' and that the text, if placed in the hands of slave holders (who undoubtedly would have a say in whether Bibles even made it to their slaves), would continue to serve as a tool of oppression rather than liberation. Douglass had his own experience to cite by way of example: he first heard the Bible read aloud by his white mistress, which incited his own desires to learn the text, just as laws were passed that prevented unsupervised readings of the Bible (Callahan 2006: 9–10, 24).

Just as many would ask throughout the nineteenth century, American blacks, in general, and members of the A.M.E. Church, had to wonder: Can the text *truly* speak for itself?

For the most part, the answer among A.M.E. members at least, was a resounding yes. Daniel Alexander Payne, a bishop in the Church as well as an accomplished theologian, spoke resoundingly on the self-sufficiency of the Bible. He told his congregants to 'Rest not' until they had 'learned to read the Bible', which was itself the 'only safe guide' (Noll 2002: 404). The reference to the safety of the text reflected the collective experience of African Americans, who could trust very few sources of authority in the protection of their best interests. Only the Bible remained stalwart. Yet, even while touting its stability and sufficiency – ideas that were often paired with the idea of its 'plainness' – A.M.E. preachers and theologians interpreted its words through the lens of their own experiences. Bishop Henry MacNeal Turner had long declared the need for blacks to find revolutionary motivation in the Bible, particularly in figures like Moses. It would not take him long to declare Jesus and, with him, God, to be black; his reading of the Bible had told him as much (Callahan 2006: 169, 231).

UNITARIANISM

American Unitarians represent a fascinating test case for examining the evolution of biblical authority among Protestants. In the earliest histories of the denomination, written at the turn of the twentieth century, Unitarianism is portrayed as reactionary: revolting first from Calvinism, then from Transcendentalism (Cooke 1902; Wilbur 1925). This view is seemingly reinforced by the fact that the Unitarian denomination did not formally coalesce as an institution until the National Convention (later Conference) of Unitarian Churches until the mid-nineteenth century and even then a universal 'statement of faith' was not adopted until 1893 (Cooke 1902: 224–46). Others, particularly those more critical of Unitarianism, view Unitarianism as a way station to Transcendentalism, as more post-Christian than Christian at its very inception (Brownson 1889). There is truth in all of these interpretations. Yet, all can be nuanced by a better understanding of how, in those first decades, Unitarians understood the place of the Bible. To see the Unitarians as inherently biblicist from the outset is to understand them as fundamentally engaged with the greater questions plaguing Protestantism of their day, namely: How do we know what is true? How can an inanimate object, a book, continue to speak for God – particularly as its historicity, singularity and authenticity came under critique?

Unitarianism began as a movement among liberal Congregationalists to incorporate the prevailing European intellectual currents of the age – primarily those emanating from the UK and, later, Germany – into their reading of the Bible. Emphasizing the concept of 'self-culture', Unitarians challenged traditionally Calvinist readings of human ability, which required grace prior to understanding. All human beings, as creations of God, were equipped with the appropriate faculties to understand the truth of the Bible, they simply needed to train them through study and repeated readings of the text. It was why in his 1819 sermon at the ordination of Jared Sparks in Baltimore, better known under the title 'Unitarian Christianity', William Ellery Channing stated that 'the Bible is a book written for men, in the language of men' and 'its meaning is to be sought in the same manner as that of other books'. Reading it also required looking 'beyond the letter to the spirit', which involved seeking 'in the nature of the subject and the aim of the writer his true meaning; and, in general, to make sure of what is known for explaining what is difficult, and for discovering truths' (Channing 1884: 278–9). The notion that a

Bible reader is dependent upon their natural interpretive (reasoning) abilities, as well as their experience and knowledge, made the reading of the Bible possible for all people, but truly open to those who exercised their mental faculties and constantly inquired after truth. Unitarians did not eschew the guidance of the Holy Spirit; they, as Frederic Henry Hedge would explain, argued that it acted through and with human faculties, a divine and miraculous feature of people's innate, intuitive capacities (Willsky-Ciollo 2015: 161–93). That this sermon is touted as Unitarianism's coming-out party casts the movement as fundamentally Bible-focused in its original intent. Further, the majority of exchanges between the Unitarians as the 'liberal' Christians and orthodox or conservative counterparts presumed a common facility with the Bible, making debates about points of Unitarian theology – their denial of the doctrine of human depravity, for example – about proper interpretation of Scripture.

Though he is unfortunately remembered as a stick in the mud, whose evisceration of German Idealism and transcendental thought in *Discourse on the Latest Form of Infidelity* (1839) seemed to prove Ralph Waldo Emerson correct that the current state of Unitarianism was 'corpse-cold', Andrews Norton held together the tenuous link between Unitarian intuitionism, rationalism and biblicism for decades (Emerson 1971: 10: 381). As the Dexter Lecturer, later Professor, of Biblical Literature at Harvard, he viewed his task as establishing the standard of Unitarian biblical interpretation, which linked his beloved liberal movement indelibly to Christianity as the church of the future. All signs, intellectual trends and markers seemed to point to this inevitability. In his exchange with Moses Stuart, his orthodox counterpart at Andover Newton Theological Seminary, Norton laid out the various reasons that the Unitarian position was *the* biblical position, employing much of the language regarding human reasoning ability and God's benevolence found in Channing's sermon to make his case. Norton confronted specific points of Calvinist doctrine, such as the dual nature of Christ, on the grounds that the doctrine was abiblical: since any language related to Christ's mutual humanity and divinity do not appear in the Bible, it required a tremendous leap of logic, which asked a lot of human reason and painted God as fickle. 'Do you think that we should be left to collect the proof of a fundamental article of our faith, and the evidence of incomparably the most astonishing fact that ever occurred upon our earth, from some expressions scattered here and there, the greater part of them being dropt [sic] incidentally', asked Norton in his response to Stuart's letter about Channing. Biblical language, and language in general, Norton agreed, lent itself to figurative reading and multiple interpretations, but no person who considered a word or sentence in its context as well as through the lens of experience and sense, could come to be certain of the theological conclusions held by the orthodox (Norton 1819: 28–9, 40–2, 47).

It was Norton's magnum opus, *The Evidences of Genuineness of the Gospels*, written and published over the course of two decades that represented both the heyday of Unitarian biblicism and his status as one of the greatest American Bible scholars of his generation (matched only by his orthodox Congregationalist counterpart Moses Stuart, perhaps). At its core was the central Unitarian belief that the Gospels were essential and their inoculation, against the insidious claims of De Wette and the 'extravagances' of Strauss, was vital (Norton 1852: 301). In truth, he was not especially bothered by historical criticism when its proponents focused on the Hebrew Bible, perceiving this as a boon to true Unitarian Christianity, which privileged the New Testament (Willsky-Ciollo 2015: 93–129). Over two volumes, Norton set about the task of 'asserting [the Gospels'] genuineness', by which he meant that they remained 'essentially the same as they were originally written; and that they [had] been ascribed to their true authors' (Norton 1837: 10) By this, he was not coming out as a believer in verbal inspiration – Norton was no literalist. Indeed, he frequently referenced the poetic nature of biblical language, which attests to his belief that divergent interpretations were an intended feature of the sacred text – though not on things that were 'essential' to faith, such as the existence of God (Norton 1852: 73–4). Rather, he hoped to show that, even though words may have changed or different versions favored some over others, that the essential meaning and purpose of the Gospels had not wavered from their original composition.

There were two essential obstacles inherent in the Unitarian approach to the Bible. At base, they failed to realize their privilege when making assumptions about the self-evidence of their intellectual and theological claims. Channing, Norton and many other Unitarians were white men of status and means, with the time and resources to devote to study, and with their finger on the pulse of the latest philosophical trends. They, the elites, took for granted their ability to pursue perpetual education (even for upper-class white women, formal schooling stopped at the age of fourteen or fifteen), their access to books and scholarship (as well as their ability to read them), and the leisure they had to spend countless hours devoted to the singular task of self-culture (whereas those of other races, genders and classes may not have been so fortunate). Unitarianism was biblicist, certainly, but had inadvertently built the Bible into an ivory tower, while proposing to open its contents to the minds of all willing to read it.

The second obstacle was that by arguing that human beings were capable of reading and understanding the Bible on their own, Unitarians opened the door to alternative sources of religious authority. Arguably, this was the narrative of Protestantism in general: by providing greater access to the text it increased the idea (and the incidence) that readers could be the arbiters of truth. In Unitarian hands, however, the elevation of human reasoning abilities made possible the Bible's supplantation as the, or even *a*, source of authority. Transcendentalist Unitarians, the so-called radical branch of the movement, made waves during the 1830s with several claims affecting the vaunted status of the Bible. First was Ralph Waldo Emerson's assertion in his 1838 address to the graduating class of Harvard's Divinity School that human beings were the 'wondermakers', thus diminishing the singularity of Christ as a human miracle worker and the Bible as a text that recorded his miracles (Emerson 1957: 112). This was followed by a series of pamphlet debates and exchanges regarding the miraculous nature of the Bible, waged primarily between Andrews Norton and his former student and original member of the transcendental club, George Ripley. If, Norton argued, the Bible were stripped of its miraculous nature then not only would Unitarianism founder, but so would all of Christianity. Ripley, joined later by Theodore Parker, believed that Christianity pre-existed the Bible, hence the Bible's conditional status as a sacred text. The Bible only served humanity insofar as it brought truth and knowledge to people and failing in that, the Bible should cease to serve as a viable source of authority, even as Christianity or 'Absolute Religion' endured (Ripley 1839; Parker 1908).

For those Unitarians who wished to maintain the Bible's status, the implications of their liberal biblicism were hard to swallow, particularly later in the century when it seemed that the more radical branch had won. In the 1893 statement of faith (which was still too much 'creed' for some) there was no mention of the Bible, simply the 'religion of Jesus' as being uniquely authoritative. The Bible became one among many viable sources, something that has often led to aspersions cast on the denomination as being 'post-Christian'. Though this may have been the view of some both inside and outside of Unitarianism, there were quite a few who, like Channing, Norton and other liberal Congregationalists-turned-Unitarians, viewed their denomination as the culmination of Christianity. Though the Bible was still used above any other text during the late nineteenth and even into the early twentieth century – a survey of sermons during this time indicate as much – the seeming dilution or diminishment of the Bible's 'specialness' would come as a hard blow.

PRESBYTERIANISM

For nineteenth-century Presbyterians, the Bible stood at the centre of their attempts to globally expand and to assert that Presbyterianism was *the* Christian denomination, even as internal challenges to the Bible's authority threatened to undermine these very efforts. From a European Presbyterian standpoint, the nineteenth century was the 'Evangelical Century', defined by missions and the need to spread, particularly since they were being outpaced by other denominations. The distribution of bibles and denominationally sanctioned 'Scripture readers' overseas grounded missionary efforts. Such efforts were seemingly stymied when evangelical Presbyterians, those inspired by the revival culture of American Presbyterianism, locked horns with those who worried about the excesses of such exercises (Shaw 2019: 126–8, 130). Both sides (which map, to a degree, onto the Old School and New School Presbyterians in the United States) believed they were employing the Bible as it was meant to be employed: one buffeted by the Spirit-driven and ecstatic interpretations of the text and the other adherent to confessional regularity and the need to check rogue interpretations with sound theology (always based on the Bible, they believed). For the most part, these internecine battles did not stop the spread of Presbyterianism throughout the nineteenth century, which saw gains in membership in various Asian countries such as India and Thailand, and on the African continent, for example, spurred in great part by the distribution and translation of bibles, thus enabling indigenous Presbyterian churches to emerge. Even in places where schism was pronounced and permanent, such as in the United States, numerical gains were made among Presbyterians, ultimately boasting one of the largest concentrations of Presbyterianism worldwide (Lucas 2019: 51). However, these gains would become partisan, as the authority of the Bible became increasingly vulnerable.

The 1891 heresy trial of Charles Augustus Briggs is often viewed as the harbinger of things to come for mainline Protestantism in the next century. His refusal to recognize the doctrine of inerrancy and his outright denial that this was the orthodox, and therefore traditional, position of the church (broadly understood) foreshadowed the twentieth century's Fundamentalist–Modernist controversy (Satta 2007: ix, 75–96). It was also a watershed moment for the Presbyterian Church, which, like many mainline denominations, had been tested as the nineteenth century progressed on its understanding of the Bible. What makes the Briggs trial so seminal is that all parties involved, from the accused, to the Prosecuting Committee, to the General Assembly, believed they were right and that it was they who served as custodians of the Presbyterian Church. Though the problem child was chastised, Briggs's conviction for heresy and defrocking failed ultimately in its greater goal of dampening his viewpoint (and those of potential sympathizers) and preventing further schism of a denomination that had already fractured during the Civil War. Both fractures were rooted in debates over the Bible; one regarded the correct interpretation of the sacred text and the other regarded the nature of the text itself.

At the dawn of the nineteenth century in the United States, Presbyterianism stood among four primary or 'mainline' traditions – the others being Congregationalism, Methodism and the Baptist Church – whose fortunes would shift over the next decades, but whose ascendancy would remain relatively stable. Presbyterianism had been imported to the United States during the eighteenth century, primarily by Scottish immigrants, where it existed as the state church, and stood as the largest Reformed tradition in the dawning republic. Presbyterians began the nineteenth century united: they spearheaded efforts to create the American Bible Society, by joining with Congregationalists in their mutual aim of bringing the Bible to as many people as possible and by investing fully in the rhetoric that a proper understanding of the Bible was necessarily American (Perry 2018: 36; Lucas 2019: 59). As early as the 1820s, however, Old and New School factions were warring over questions of theology, ultimately splitting and creating their own General Assemblies in the 1830s. The two sides still retained a certain fellowship, until divergence over the question of slavery and the Bible's stance upon it would break the New, and predominantly northern, branch from the Old, predominantly southern, branch of the denomination. Mark Noll has argued decisively that the Civil War brought to a head the assumption that the Bible spoke plainly to all since both pro- and anti-slavery proponents marshalled biblical texts to make their cases (2002: 248–386). Similar schisms occurred in most of the major Protestant denominations, many of which would never heal, though this did not stop attempts at reunions. Following the Civil War, Northern Old and New School Presbyterians seemed to come together tentatively as the Presbyterian Church of the United States of America (PCUSA), resulting in the largest Presbyterian denomination in the country. Yet, while the fracture over theology and slavery would not prove permanent for all, the inerrancy and literal truth of the Bible would.

Scottish Common Sense Realism had paved the way for the idea that the Bible could be treated as a collection of facts to be deduced. As the century wore on and the challenge of higher criticism loomed, Presbyterian and Princeton theologian Charles Hodge argued that even the most symbolic language in the Bible could be taken literally (Marsden 1983: 90–1). Such doubling down on the Bible's plainness would increase the growing fissure between those in the denomination who felt increasingly concerned that tethering the Bible to inerrancy could ultimately undermine it altogether and those who feared the opposite, that without adhering to the doctrine of inerrancy and infallibility, the Bible's authority would be undermined and with it Christianity's claims to exclusive truth. So, when Charles Briggs began to argue that the Bible's 'inconsistencies' not only existed, but helped to prove its authenticity, the conservative factions foresaw disaster. Heresy trials ensued and Briggs was punished. Though with the Presbyterian denomination, now factionalized, no one seemed to come out the winner (Satta 2007: 75–6, 79).

THE ROMAN CATHOLIC CHURCH

The Roman Catholic Church has never doubted, nor relinquished the notion, that it is the true biblical faith. Beginning with the Council of Trent, convened, depending upon one's interpretation, as a natural outgrowth of Church protocol or as a defensive manoeuvre against the Protestant Reformation, the Church has sought to balance access to the Bible with adherence to theological orthodoxy or 'tradition' (Neuner 2015: 537–8). The Church has defied the notion that *sola scriptura* is possible, or even necessary, but has taken particular issue with the claim that individual interpretation based on reason could trump centuries of careful interpretation and application by Church fathers, scholars and officials. The notion that the text should be distinct from the institution that had housed it was a dangerous fallacy that could undermine Christianity and Catholics could point to the years of schism among Protestants as testament to this. The Catholic Church's stance on the Bible fuelled Protestants historically, but also particularly during the nineteenth century, in their assertions that the Catholic Church privileges institution over text, rather than viewing both as two inseparable halves of the same whole.

In Quebec, for example, Protestants believed and publicized the view that Catholics were prohibited from reading the Bible – an accusation that proved false, but which fit Protestants' missionary platform. Ever consistent with the Catholic Church's platform of Bible tethered to tradition, Quebecoise bishops objected to 'false' bibles, or those without the Apocrypha and 'formally sanctioned annotations', as well as 'laissez-faire' Bible reading, or reading undertaken by those unfamiliar with Scripture and proper interpretive technique (Jones 2001: 33–4). The same was true for American Catholics who were prohibited from reading the King James Version of the Bible because it was not a translation of the Latin Vulgate. Gerald Fogarty notes that Protestant Americans did not distinguish between prohibitions against private 'interpretation' of the Bible and private reading of the Bible – for Catholics, only the former was prohibited (Fogarty 1982: 166). From a Protestant standpoint, the prohibition of one was effectively the prohibition of the other, since the right of the individual reader to determine, unaided, the message of the Bible had become sacred doctrine itself. This perspective, of course, took for granted the fact that their own reading was rarely unaided – Protestants were equally shaped by the theological conclusions of their particular denomination, and the abundance of 'guides' for reading the Bible indicated that Protestant theologians were equally concerned with 'right' reading of the so-called plain text (Perry 2018: 44–6). Nonetheless, preservation and promotion of the Bible was consistently cast as a Protestant birthright over against the alleged anti-biblicism of the Catholic Church. Thus, for Catholics, the nineteenth century was characterized by what Tracy Fessenden calls 'Bible wars' (2007). On one side, they had to contend with the impact of higher criticism and scientific discovery, just as their Protestant compatriots did. On the other, they also had to combat an intransigent anti-Catholicism perpetuated by Protestant culture, particularly in North America, which very often involved debates over the Bible or, more accurately, *which* Bible would reign supreme.

Historians of Catholicism often describe the nineteenth century as a time when conservatism won, particularly during its last few decades. In fact, the declaration of papal infallibility at the First Vatican Council (1869–70), could be viewed as a defensive manoeuvre taken after the previous decades witnessed a profusion of critique against both the Church and the Bible that was exacerbated by higher criticism and advances in geological science. The doctrine was seemingly promoted in direct defiance of more liberal factions within the Church. What the first Vatican Council's stance did that the Council of Trent did not, according to Peter Neuner, was to formally elevate the 'decrees of the magisterium to stand alongside the Scriptures rather than the previous view that placed Scripture as the norm in relation to the decrees of the magisterium'. The Church had always held tradition and the Bible together, but with the increasingly precarious position of the Bible as the arbiter of all truth, such a stance seemingly inoculated the Catholic Church against the debilitating debates occurring in many Protestant denominations (Neuner 2015: 541–2). Internal critics of the doctrine of infallibility often cited the early church fathers, none of whom took such a posture – in other words, the doctrine represented a breach of tradition, rather than its continuation. For internal proponents, this view of the Pope's infallibility was nothing new and had been argued for centuries prior even if it had not been formalized. Regardless, its promulgation was timely for what it says about the context in which the Catholic Church found itself. It was also a precursor of the next century's debates between Catholic liberals and conservatives – debates that mapped onto, though did not replicate exactly, those between Protestant modernists and fundamentalists (Neuner 2015: 543–6).

Internal debates over the authority of the Bible were matched in pitch and fervor by the ongoing drama of anti-Catholic sentiment felt most keenly in the United States, where anti-Catholicism had been a rhetorical mainstay of the rebelling colonists during the recent Revolutionary War. Anti-Catholicism, in other words, was built into the very fabric of American life, even at the same time that religious freedom was supposedly codified in the First Amendment. Could Catholics – whose love of hierarchy, consolidated power and institutional control, so the stereotype went – be good Americans? This question took on a new kind of urgency when Catholic immigration to the United States spiked during the nineteenth century; where there had been only about a half a million Catholics in 1800, by 1900 there were around 12 million, most hailing from western Europe. The solution, besides a targeted propaganda campaign undertaken by people like Josiah Strong, was the public school system. Schools, as the training ground for the next generation of citizens, could feasibly strip children of undesirable traits and fill them with proper American values. Yet, as Fessenden notes, public schools had a distinctly Protestant character, as evidenced by the use of the King James Version. For Catholics, this was not the approved translation, and was therefore full of error. Even more worryingly, it was being passed off as non-sectarian and perfectly American (Fessenden 2007: 69). Conflict over the use of the King James Version eventually broke out into violent riots in 1844.

In spite of the street fights that ensued in the 1840s, the Catholic response to the Protestant ethos of the surrounding culture was complex. They objected to the imposition of the King James Version, as a definitively Protestant translation, by arguing for its removal from public schools and for the creation of their own parochial schools where young Catholics could be educated without fear of Protestant indoctrination. Yet, they were also not immune to the Protestant biblicism that surrounded them, a fact that can be seen in the explosion in printing of Catholic bibles. During the nineteenth century, there were reportedly eighty-six different editions of the entire Bible and forty-five editions of the New Testament in the United States alone (Ohlhausen 2006: 1). Though the Douay-Rheims (the Catholic English translation of the Vulgate) had stood as the definitive version for centuries, and continued to be spoken of with reverence, the notion that new translations were needed to clarify the text as well as to ensure its accuracy gained purchase among a growing number of Catholics. American Catholic theologians, those who would be primarily responsible for the production of these new editions of the Bible, were desirous of entering the field of Bible scholarship, particularly that of lower criticism – the race to achieve the definitive original text would not be one-horse race if they had their way. At the same time, they recognized the importance of vernacular bibles both from an perceptual and a practical point of view. But they were fighting a losing propaganda war after the 1840s riots were laid squarely at their feet ('why were Catholics so averse to teaching the Bible in school?' became the clarion call of anti-Catholicism). The production and distribution of Catholic bibles were meant in part to insulate them from such critiques. Additionally, having a ready supply of cheap, easily distributable vernacular bibles derived from the Vulgate would also facilitate a specifically Catholic text in an overtly biblicist American context, thereby preventing Catholic flight from the ancient church to newer, Protestant pastures.

The pursuit of a vernacular Bible was met with resistance from an increasingly conservative Catholic Church, not simply for the historic reason of pairing Bible with tradition, but also because some viewed the need for a vernacular Bible as clear evidence of Protestant (and American) influence (Fogarty 1982: 173–4). Though American Catholics viewed a vernacular Bible as a necessary and preventative measure, those at the top feared what this could mean from the standpoint of traditional and institutional authority. Without a singular edition, would the Catholic Church go the way of Protestant denominations? Would there be multiple 'Catholic' churches – an oxymoron by any other name? Arguably, this was already occurring – perhaps an inevitability for a truly global church. And yet the Church's stance following the First Vatican Council, whether preventative or reactive, reflected a desire to remind Catholics that there was only one Catholic Church, even though there may be myriad bibles.

A BIBLE IN EVERY HOME–AND FOR EVERY DENOMINATION

At the close of the nineteenth century, one could argue that the Bible was everywhere and nowhere. As a material artefact, it seemed to be replicating at an extraordinary rate; accessibility to the Bible was at a high; lower critics continued to search for the original text, promising that this Urtext was within their reach; and more people seemed to possess, read and interpret the Bible than ever before. These facts were complicated by the fact that denominations sparred with each other and within themselves as to what the Bible was, *which* Bible to use, how far the scope of the Bible's authority extended and how the Bible should be read. All claimed to know the Bible, in other words, but few knew the Good Book the same way. This was not a strictly nineteenth-century problem for Christians, of course. The nineteenth century, for all of its innovation, industry, global expansion, and (depending upon one's definition of the word) progress, simply exacerbated lines of fracture once maskable.

Unitarian minister J. Estlin Carpenter, whose book *The Bible in the Nineteenth Century* began this essay, wrote with an air of acceptance at the Bible's demotion. 'Neither then in the shape of a sacred book or a sacred tradition, on the one hand, nor in the emphatic delineation of the phases of the soul's inner life, upon the other, can the authority of the Church be said to guarantee itself', wrote Carpenter, uncoupling the authority of the church from the authority of the Bible (Carpenter 1903: 507). From the only source of truth, to one among many, he could speak about the Bible at the turn of the twentieth century in ways that would have been unthinkable for a Christian preacher at the turn of the nineteenth century. Its authority was not assumed, its singularity was challenged, and its universality was undermined. For Carpenter, these were features of the world in which he lived – a world informed by the discoveries of the previous century. For others, however, the treatment of the Bible as one among many was unthinkable and the twentieth century was rife with people combatting the more deleterious trends of the nineteenth century. Presbyterians were but one example of Protestants compelled to recalibrate their theological and historical commitments to the Bible. In the next century, these fractures would spill out into the so-called Fundamentalist–Modernist controversy, at least in the United States, where the Bible would again take centre stage. Suddenly belief in the inerrancy of the Bible became, for some, the barometer of Christian identity. In the nineteenth century, though the word Fundamentalist was not yet known, the ideas that would ground this broad, ultimately cross-denominational movement, found purchase in early debates regarding the nature of the Bible and its ability to speak as both a historical and divine text.

Not all had been or would become swept up in such debates. Historically black denominations such as the African Methodist Episcopal Church, even while maintaining the sufficiency of the Bible, had rarely been reliant on singular readings or understandings of any text, a feature of the circuitous methods by which the text found its way to black ears. The text 'spoke' to many, which meant it spoke variously – it had always been many texts in one. And though the Roman Catholic Church was certainly not immune to the forces that seemed to destabilize the position of the Bible – one reason behind the declaration of papal infallibility – its emphasis on tradition and Vulgate-derived translations, coupled with the centralized power of Rome, protected it from broad scale schism. Thus, where the Bible stood within a given denomination at the close of the nineteenth century depended a great deal upon what the denomination had been at the century's start. Questions of authority, an exploding print industry, intellectual trends and scientific discoveries, and denominational profusion spurred adaptation among these people of the book, while the denominational character and the makeup of congregations determined which direction such adaptations would take.

REFERENCES

Allen, R. (1985), 'Life Experience and Gospel Labors', in *Afro-American Religious History: A Documentary Witness*, ed. M. C. Sernett, 139–54, Durham: Duke University Press.
Bozeman, T. D. (1977), *Protestants in an Age of Science: The Baconian Ideal and Antebellum American Religious Thought*, Chapel Hill: University of North Carolina Press.
Brownson, O. (1889), *The Convert; or Leaves from My Experience*, New edn, New York: D & J Sadlier & Co.
Bushman, R. L. (2005), *Joseph Smith: Rough Stone Rolling*, New York: Alfred A. Knopf.
Callahan, A. D. (2006), *The Talking Book: African Americans and the Bible*, New Haven: Yale University Press.
Carpenter, J. E. (1903), *The Bible in the Nineteenth Century: Eight Lectures*, New York and Bombay: Longmans, Green, and Co.
Channing, W. E. (1884), *The Complete Works of William Ellery Channing: Including the Perfect Life and Containing a Copious General Index and a Table of Scripture References*, London and New York: Routledge & Sons.
Chapman, M. (2015), 'Liberal Readings of the Bible and their Conservative Responses', in *The New Cambridge History of the Bible. Volume 4, From 1750 to the Present*, ed. J. Riches, 208–19, Cambridge: Cambridge University Press.
Coleridge, S. T. (1829), *Aids to Reflection*, London: William Pickering.
Cooke, G. W. (1902), *Unitarianism in America: A History of its Origin and Development*, Boston: American Unitarian Association.
Emerson, R. W. (1957), *Selections from Ralph Waldo Emerson*, ed. S. E. Whicher, Boston: Houghton Mifflin.
Emerson, R. W. (1971), *The Journals and Miscellaneous Notebooks of Ralph Waldo Emerson*, ed. W. H. Gilman et al., 16 vols. Cambridge, MA: Harvard University Press.
Ferrell, L. A. (2008), *The Bible and the People*, New Haven: Yale University Press.

Fessenden, T. (2007), *Culture and Redemption: Religion, the Secular, and American Literature*, Princeton: Princeton University Press.

Fogerty, G. (1982), 'The Quest for a Catholic Vernacular Bible in America', in *The Bible in America: Essays in Cultural History*, ed. N. O. Natch and M. A. Noll, 163–80, Oxford: Oxford University Press.

Frey, S. R. and B. Wood (1998), *Come Shouting to Zion: African American Protestantism in the American South and British Caribbean to 1830*, Chapel Hill: University of North Carolina Press.

Holifield, E. B. (2003), *Theology in America*, New Haven: Yale University Press.

Johnson, S. (2015), *African American Religions, 1500–2000: Colonialism, Democracy, and Freedom*, New York: Cambridge University Press.

Jones, P. (2001), 'Protestants, Catholics and the Bible in Late-Nineteenth-Century Quebec', *Fides et Historia*, 33(2): 31–8.

Kittelstrom, A. (2015), *The Religion of Democracy: Seven Liberals and the American Moral Tradition*, New York: Penguin Press.

Lee, J. (2000), 'A Female Preacher among the African Methodists', in *African American Religious History: A Documentary Witness*, ed. M. C. Sernett, 164–84, Durham: Duke University Press.

Lucas, S. M. (2019), 'Eighteenth- and Nineteenth-Century Presbyterianism in North America', in *The Oxford Handbook of Presbyterianism*, ed. G. S. Smith and P. C. Kemeny, 51–72, New York: Oxford University Press.

Marsden, G. M. (1983), 'Everyone One's Own Interpreter? The Bible, Science, and Authority in Mid-Nineteenth-Century America', in *The Bible in America: Essays in Cultural History*, ed. N. O. Hatch and M. A. Noll, 79–100, New York: Oxford University Press.

Mead, S. (1963), *The Lively Experiment: The Shaping of Christianity in America*, New York: Harper & Row.

Neuner, P. (2015), 'The Reception of the Bible in Roman Catholic Tradition', in *The New Cambridge History of the Bible. Volume 4: From 1750 to the Present*, ed. J. Riches, 537–62, Cambridge: Cambridge University Press.

Noll, M. A. (1986), *Between Faith and Criticism: Evangelicals, Scholarship and the Bible in America*, San Francisco: Harper & Row.

Noll, M. (2002), *America's God: From Jonathan Edwards to Abraham Lincoln*, New York: Oxford University Press.

Norton, A. (1819), *Statement of Reasons for not Believing the Doctrines of Trinitarians Respecting the Nature of God, and the Person of Christ Occasioned by Professor Stuart's Letters to Mr. Channing*, Boston: Wells and Lilly.

Norton, A. (1837), *The Evidences of the Genuineness of the Gospels*, Boston: American Stationers' Company.

Norton, A. (1852), *Tracts Concerning Christianity*, Cambridge: John Bartlett.

Ohlhausen, S. K. (2006), *The American Catholic Bible in the Nineteenth Century: A Catalog of English Language Editions*, Jefferson: McFarland & Company.

Parker, T. (1908), *The Transient and the Permanent in Christianity, Delivered at the Ordination of Rev. Charles C. Shackford in the Hawes Place Church, Boston May 19, 1841*, Boston: American Unitarian Association.

Perry, S. (2018), *Bible Culture and Authority in the Early United States*, Princeton: Princeton University Press.

Raboteau, A. (1978), *Slave Religion: The 'Invisible Institution' in the Antebellum South*, New York: Oxford University Press.

Raboteau, A. (2001), *Canaan Land: A Religious History of African Americans*, New York: Oxford University Press.

Ripley, G. (1839), *'The Latest Form of Infidelity' Examined: A Letter to Mr. Andrews Norton, Occasioned by his 'Discourse Before the Association of the Alumni of the Cambridge Theological School,' on the 19th of July, 1839*, Boston: James Munroe and Company.

Sarna, J. D. (2017), 'The Bible and Judaism in America', in *The Oxford Handbook of the Bible in America*, ed. P. C. Gutjahr, 505–16, New York: Oxford University Press.

Satta, R. (2007), *The Sacred Text: Biblical Authority in Nineteenth-Century America*, Eugene: Pickwick Publications.

Shaw, I. J. (2019), 'Presbyterians in Britain and Europe', in *The Oxford Handbook of Presbyterianism*, ed. G. S. Smith and P. C. Kemeny, 117–40, New York: Oxford University Press.

Smith, A. (2017), 'The Bible in African American Culture', in *The Oxford Handbook of the Bible in America*, ed. P. Gutjahr, 195–215, Oxford: Oxford University Press.

Tanner, K. E. (1987), 'Theology and the Plain Sense', in *Scriptural Authority and Narrative Interpretation*, ed. G. Green, 59–78, Philadelphia: Fortress Press.

Thuesen, P. J. (1999), *In Discordance with the Scriptures: American Protestant Battles Over Translating the Bible*, New York: Oxford University Press.

Wilbur, E. M. (1925), *Our Unitarian Heritage: An Introduction to the History of the Unitarian Movement*, Boston: Beacon Press, Inc.

Wills, D. W. (1982), 'Womanhood and Domesticity in the A.M.E. Tradition', in *Black Apostles at Home and Abroad*, ed. D. W. Wills and R. Newman, 133–46, Boston: G.K. Hall.

Willsky-Ciollo, L. (2015), *American Unitarianism and the Protestant Dilemma: The Conundrum of Biblical Authority*, Lanham: Lexington Books.

CHAPTER 6

Science

MATTHEW J. KAUFMAN

In the nineteenth century the earth and all the teeming life it harbored acquired a history rooted in deep time. While the suggestion that the planet might have existed across a span of millennia of almost unimaginable vastness was not entirely new, it was not until this century that the idea that life on earth might possess an antiquity far greater than previously imagined really began to take root. A watershed moment in that progression occurred in 1812 when French naturalist Georges Cuvier made a compelling case for past mass extinctions. His groundbreaking proposition contested the longstanding belief that life was not only stable but completely unchanging. The realization that life could change, and that species could vanish, implied that life itself possessed a history. This shift in perspective laid a foundation for new theories and approaches to emerge – most notably Charles Darwin's ideas about natural selection – which would go on to radically transform the Victorian understanding of the natural world and the place of human beings in it. And that had very serious implications for the Bible.

Debate over whether to treat the Bible as a reliable historical record spurred religious reaction and readjustment throughout much of the nineteenth century. New perspectives on the Bible emerged, inspired by new understandings of nature. Questions posed about nature were driven by mindsets shaped by Scripture, and questions asked of Scripture were shaped by developing ideas about nature. Of overriding importance was how to understand what the Bible taught about humanity and how to situate humanity in nature. Different understandings of the Bible developed in response to science's historicizing of life on earth and of the Bible. Whether or not one believed that the Bible taught facts about the natural world, reading it had to take into account changes in the scientific understanding of nature. At the same time, exploring the Bible for its moral teaching inevitably engaged with the natural sciences.

Some were committed to a literal reading of the biblical text. In their view, the onus to resolve any incompatibilities with scientific discoveries lay with the naturalists – and emphatically not with the Bible. Others firmly believed that natural history forced a reevaluation of scriptural claims. The onus to resolve any incompatibilities lay with interpreters of the Bible – and not with natural history. Still others preferred to separate natural history and Scripture into discreet realms of inquiry, thus removing any need to address apparent inconsistencies. And because the Bible remained ubiquitous in Victorian life, its presence permeating virtually every aspect of social and political culture, one could hardly fail to earnestly take one (or more) of these positions on the issue (Barbour 2000; Larsen 2011; Rupke 2013).

While activities that we call 'scientific' or 'religious' have a long history, the boundaries separating science from religion were first mapped in the nineteenth century. The meaning of the term 'science' as we understand it today crystallized by becoming differentiated from the term 'religion' (Harrison 2015; Brooke 1991; Brooke and Cantor 2000; Lindberg and Numbers 1986). At the dawn of that century, for example, the nascent science of geology grappled with whether and how Scripture might be related to a newly historicized view of the earth. In the third decade of the nineteenth century, the stratigraphic record seemed to support the assumption that the earth's history could be divided into pre- and post-biblical flood periods. And religious observers showed no great discomfort with an extended timescale for the earth.

Efforts were made, particularly in Britain and the United States, to harmonize the biblical stories of the six-day Creation of the earth and of the Flood using the geological evidence of an ancient earth that suggested a series of major catastrophes had occurred in the remote past. This stemmed from a tradition of natural theology deeply rooted in the Anglophone world that framed the 'Book of Nature' as a kind of commentary on the 'Book of Scripture', a popular two-book metaphor that imagined nature to be a revelation complementing that of Scripture. God could become known through the study of either book. Indeed, it was a view of some considerable antiquity, reflected even in the earliest writings of the New Testament. St Paul, in his letter to the Romans, wrote 'For the invisible things of him from the creation of the world are clearly seen, being understood by the things that are made, even his eternal power and Godhead' (Rom. 1.20, KJV) – suggesting that the natural world could reveal truths about God. It was only a small step to add that the insights thus gained could complement and enrich one's own reading of the Bible (Rudwick 2014: 159; Paley 1802).

Harmonization efforts were rarer in the German states, which had pioneered biblical criticism. Reading the Bible with an eye towards recovering its original literary elements or its historical contexts had already conditioned the German-speaking world not to expect the Bible to serve as reliable witness to natural history. Beyond mainland Europe, however, there was no tradition of biblical critical inquiry until 1860 (Moore 1986; Rudwick 1986; Yarchin 2008: 50–1). That year saw the publication in England of *Essays and Reviews*, a collection of essays by liberal Anglican clergy that presented to the Anglophone world for the first time the historical-critical apparatus of biblical interpretation that had already taken root in the German-speaking world. The validation of biblical criticism by these clergymen created a firestorm of controversy that eclipsed that surrounding Charles Darwin's *On the Origin of Species by Means of Natural Selection*, published only the previous year. Three of the essayists in *Essays and Reviews* were prosecuted for heresy, a degree of formal censure that was not pursued against those who accepted or promoted Darwin's theory (Temple 1860; Darwin 1996; Shea and Whitla 2000).

Biblical criticism was perceived as a greater threat to faith than theories of natural history. Until mid-century, in fact, two theories that harmonized the idea of an ancient earth with the Genesis narrative were particularly popular among scientific practitioners in the Anglophone world. These were the so-called 'day-age' and 'gap' theories. 'Day-age' theory proposes that each of the six days of creation signifies a geological age. 'Gap' theory posits a geological time interval that was not recorded in the Bible between the creation of the heavens and the earth and the Edenic six-day creation. Indebted to the culturally entrenched mythology of poet John Milton, it assumes that the formless void and darkness of the second verse of Genesis depicts the ruin of nature in which all of earth's mass extinctions occurred, followed by the restoration of creation beginning with the creation of light on the first day. The lack of human fossil evidence seemed to support the view that the biblical narrative began its story only with the recent entrance of human beings in earth's history.

For Anglican clergymen-naturalists at Oxford and Cambridge, the intellectual heart of the Church of England, the Book of Nature affirmed the authority of the Bible, and the Book of Scripture confirmed the authority of geology because of its alignment with the biblical narrative (Rudwick 2014: 121). In 1821, for example, William Buckland, an Oxford geologist and palaeontologist (and future Dean of Westminster), explored a cave just uncovered by workmen in Kirkdale, Yorkshire, and he found fossilized bones revealing it to have once been a hyena den.

The discovery that hyenas had once roamed Great Britain was momentous enough, but this discovery showed far more than that. It also contained evidence of what they ate, thus hinting at what the world around the cave must have looked like as well. Buckland eventually realized that he had before him the fossilized evidence of an entire ecosystem in which the hyenas had lived. It was suddenly possible to picture whole vanished ecosystems in earth's history. At this stage (he later abandoned this position), Buckland believed that the fauna had all been wiped out by a relatively recent geological deluge – Noah's flood (Rudwick 2014: 124–5).

Geology and palaeontology imparted a sense of the concrete reality of Genesis and even seemed to confirm Milton's imagined ruined nature (Figure 6.1). It was not necessary to explore the deep past to sense God's providence at work. That was quite easily done through personal observation. Evangelical Christians inspired by the Methodist Keswick holiness movement, for example, were inspired by the beauty and

FIGURE 6.1: *Duria Antiquior* by Henry De la Beche (1830). This was the first portrayal of a fossil environment in its entirety painted with watercolour. Photo: Wikimedia Commons.

power of nature to reflect on God as Creator and Redeemer (Smith 2010: 317). They noted with awe nature's beauty and barrenness, its beauty and its fallen state. Christian truth, they averred, was evident in nature. Contemplating nature could enhance one's appreciation for God's providence, or alternatively, awaken awareness of one's sinful nature.

One rural Anglican pastor and naturalist reflected after forty years of ministry that the more than 70,000 companionless miles he walked never felt lonely. Nature constantly prodded him to 'infinite speculations and inquirings' about the power, wisdom and goodness of the Creator. The winter landscape appeared to him as bejewelled with 'frost-gems' set by 'nature's jeweller', inspiring him to 'regard the enginery [sic] from which they resulted'. Nature could also be harsh, but this helped instill in one a kind of stoic virtue. Reflecting on two young boys who survived a perilous December night lost on the moor, he was awed by their courage and resilience. For rural parsons such as this, walking in nature offered a particular revelatory experience unavailable to those in urban settings. Their interactions with the natural world afforded spiritually transforming possibilities (Atkinson 1891: vii, 370, 383; Sheils 2010: 376).

A Romantic theology of nature infused a wide cross-section of Victorian life. For many, it survived into the post-1860 era of historical criticism. Its spiritual pull was not dependent on a literalist interpretation of Scripture. Rather, it rested on a continued belief in the immortality of the soul and in the capacity of believers to experience God's grace. There was significant opposition to biblical literalism because it was felt to distract from the Christian spiritual message of sin and redemption by focusing attention instead on the correspondence of Scripture to the physical structure of the world.

Evangelicals were more concerned with how natural history was presented to the reading public than they were with the scientific activity itself. They were discomfited by secular popular science publications that presented natural history without reference to Christian teachings. Evangelicals believed that natural history told a story of salvation. The Religious Tract Society (RTS), the largest of the evangelical publishers, was created to fulfil that goal. The RTS focused on instilling in its readers moral lessons revealed through nature. Its audience learned that not only did the natural world reveal God's wisdom and goodness, but discerning minds might also divine its hints at the Gospel's message of sin and salvation (Fyfe 2004: 116).

One treatise, for example, describes the infection of a species of New Zealand caterpillar by a fungus that kills it and transforms it into a vessel to house itself. Echoes of the classical perspective that nature is an allegory for religious teachings may be seen in the author's view that this physical degradation in nature teaches a powerful lesson about moral degradation. To him it served as an example of 'the warnings of the gospel addressed to unbelievers'. It 'forcibly implies the possibility of those who are to the last under an uncured and unpardoned taint of sin, rising to shame and contempt' (Sidney 1846: 27–8). Nature was invested with theological meaning, and the transformation wrought by the fungus manifested a divine warning about the sin of unbelief.

There was no single interpretive lens through which Victorian evangelicals sought natural knowledge, but a common thread that runs throughout the staggering variety of views of nature is that natural knowledge was not expected to produce belief – that was the job of Scripture – but it was expected to provoke a religious response akin to what Elihu hoped to inspire in Job when he admonished him to 'stop and consider God's wonders' (Job 37.14). This was as true of rural pastors as it was of the Anglican clergymen-naturalists at Oxford and Cambridge (Topham 1998: 238). In 1836, for example, Buckland argued that the massive cumulative evidence of finely wrought perfections in the physical form of extinct species preserved in the fossil record made it 'impossible to resist the conclusions as to Unity of Design in a common Author' (Buckland 1836: 403; Rudwick 2014: 162). God may have made changes in the natural order over the millennia, but for Buckland, these revelatory relics attested to God's ongoing providential design.

The 1830s saw geologists and palaeontologists like Buckland present a progressivist synthesis of earth history even as they now abandoned attempts to link geological theory to the biblical Flood (Rupke 1983: 17). Buckland, who, as we have seen, believed in the 1820s that his finds corresponded to a pre-Flood world, had, by the end of the 1830s, abandoned that line of reasoning and accepted Louis Agassiz's argument that an ice age better explained how the earth had changed over time (Rudwick 2014: 179). His theology of nature, however, remained unaffected.

Buckland's theological views reflected a general consensus among the elite gentlemen of science. This view is memorialized in the extraordinarily popular and influential Bridgewater Treatises – so-called because the eighth Earl of Bridgewater had bequeathed a considerable sum of money to commission a work entitled 'On the Power, Wisdom, and Goodness of God, as manifested in the Creation' (Figure 6.2).

Published piecemeal from 1833 to 1836, eight treatises were written on sciences such as astronomy, geology and comparative anatomy. They introduced massive amounts of evidence that aimed to make the case inductively for God's power, wisdom and goodness. Although critics viewed the series as a religious apology (one outspoken critic referred to them disparagingly as the 'Bilgewater Treatises'), they were in fact serious scientific treatises by eminent scientific practitioners (Robson 1990: 74). The authors did not seek to prove God's existence or attributes through natural theology, as the classic model of natural theology sets out to do, but they did presume that Christian belief could be bolstered through the evidence of nature.

Although the treatises contain few scriptural allusions, the Bible's authority is implicit. William Whewell, who coined the term 'scientist' in 1833, authored a treatise on astronomy. He wrote that he regretted that natural theology is

> utterly insufficient for the great ends of Religion; namely, for the purpose of reforming men's lives, of purifying and elevating their characters, of preparing them for a more exalted state of being . . . . [T]his can, I well know, be achieved only by that Revealed Religion of which we are ministers, but on which the plan of the present work did not allow me to dwell. (Whewell 1833: vi–vii)

In significant respects, natural theology in the wake of the Bridgewater Treatises helped to pave the way for a Christian audience to be receptive to evolutionary theory because it reassured the public that a developmental view of nature was consistent with Christian belief (Topham 2010: 112). Faith, however, must derive from the foundation of Scripture, not from nature's evidences.

Natural theology took various forms. Some believed that God created a common blueprint for the forms that created creatures would take. Still others grounded their theology of nature in an aesthetic sensibility, struck by the beauty of fossil forms that appeared to anticipate the same architectonic principles that architects use. More common was the view that nature revealed God's designed laws. Still, many were concerned lest this belief in a law-abiding cosmos lead to atheism. Perhaps nothing better demonstrates the double-edged sword of this perspective than the appearance of the Victorian publishing sensation, *Vestiges of the Natural History of Creation* (1844). It presented

FIGURE 6.2: Memorial to Francis Henry Egerton, 8th Earl of Bridgewater in the Church of St Peter & St Paul, Little Gaddesden, Hertfordshire, England. Photo: Wikimedia Commons.

a sweeping speculative narrative that brought together ideas of progression and change culled from cosmology, geology and biology in a grand synthesis designed to demonstrate how all of nature developed out of natural law. And it gripped the Victorian imagination. Reader reactions to it reveal the broad spectrum of responses in the general public to the findings of natural science. Some found it to affirm God's divinely designed laws, while others condemned it for promoting what they believed to be a thinly veiled materialism (Chambers 1844; Secord 2000; Numbers 2002). Certainly something of this ambiguity lingered in Darwin's later *Origin of Species*, which leaves open to interpretation whether the laws of nature are purely natural in origin or are divinely created.

That *Vestiges* drew upon the nebular hypothesis of Pierre-Simon Laplace, a theory which proposed that the cosmos formed out of a primordial gaseous cloud, would have struck many as confirmation of the author's atheism, for Laplace had famously said of God that he had no use for that hypothesis. The English were exquisitely sensitive about French atheism. But for some Christian readers, *Vestiges* suggested the possibility that the extended progressive development of the cosmos was a feature of divine law. From this point of view, it was not unpalatable to Christian sensibilities that the organic world might have arisen from a similar extended process of gradual development guided by divine intention. In this way, *Vestiges* paved the way for the public acceptance of Darwin's theory of evolution, finally introduced at the end of the next decade. Natural theology proved to be a very versatile and resilient way to construct nature in relation to religious faith (Numbers and Susalla 2002: 242–3; Brooke and Cantor 2000: 160–1).

Nevertheless, there can be little doubt that *Origin of Species* disrupted natural theology. Darwin's theory of evolution by means of natural selection described how incremental changes over the course of deep time could account for the marvellous intricacies and perfections of nature without necessitating recourse to divine design (Figure 6.3) (Brooke 2002: 171).

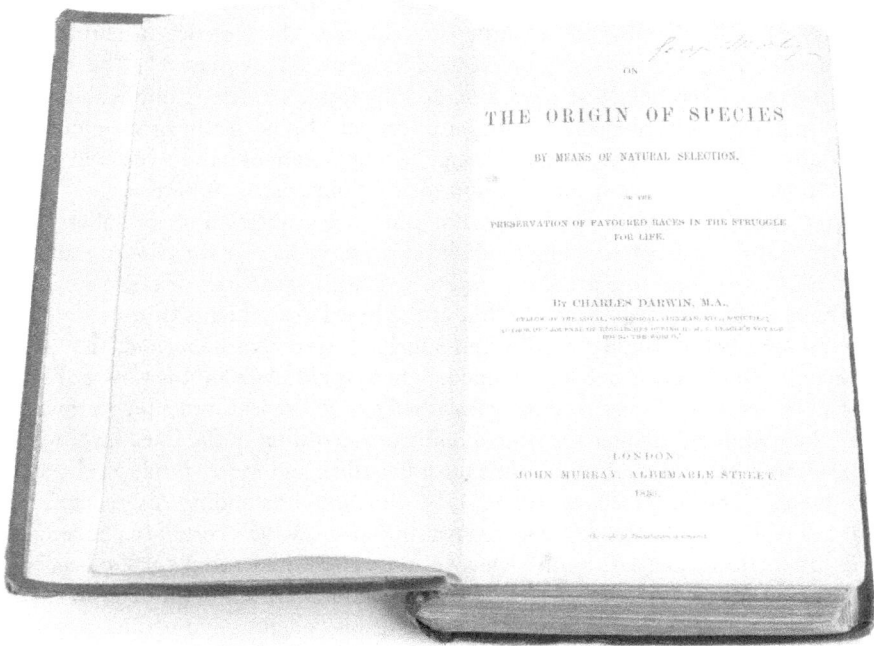

FIGURE 6.3: *On the Origin of Species by Means of Natural Selection* by Charles Darwin. Photo: Wikimedia Commons.

This was no idle speculation. It grew out of a rigorous and methodical analysis of the mass of information that he had recorded and collected during his voyage to South America in the 1830s. He had come to believe by the autumn of 1838 that the popular belief in the special creation of myriads of variations of species was less plausible than the possibility that variations developed as a consequence of adaptation to specific ecological niches. Animals, he realized, were not instantaneously created perfectly suited for a given ecological niche; they had adapted and changed over vast amounts of time in response to the demands of the ecological niche.[1] Species variation had best to be explained by descent from a common ancestor. But he waited another twenty years before presenting his musings to the reading public, finally pushed by the inconvenient happenstance that another naturalist, Alfred Russel Wallace, had hit upon precisely the same idea and might have published it before him.

As Darwin developed his theory in the late 1830s, he also began to express his growing doubts about religion. Darwin's religious doubts, however, were not those of an atheist. He rejected that label, preferring instead, in his later years, that of agnostic. But after his return from the *Beagle* voyage, he did renounce the Christian orthodoxy that he had embraced during his Cambridge years. Darwin's religious journey is generally understood to have proceeded from being an aspiring country clergyman to a deist and finally to an agnostic. That Darwin lost faith in Christianity is beyond dispute, but that did not mean that he no longer found the Bible to be a source of moral inspiration or that he rejected the existence of God.

But by the late 1830s, Darwin had already confided his scepticism about the Bible's divine origins to his fiancée Emma Wedgwood, who was greatly alarmed that her future husband's salvation might be in jeopardy. Darwin was methodologically committed to withholding belief in the absence of sufficient evidence. The violence of nature that he had witnessed during his travels, coupled with his growing awareness of the staggering number of extinctions that must have already taken place, made it impossible for him to reconcile himself with natural theology's portrayal of a perfectly harmonious nature under a kind and benevolent God. If anything, the tragic death of his ten-year-old daughter Annie in 1851 must have confirmed for him the random cruelty of nature.

Origin of Species, however, took direct aim only at the doctrine of special creation. It rejected the notion of an intervening God, but it preserved a role for God in the form of a non-biblical Deism and it expressed reverent awe at the grandeur of creation. 'When I view all beings not as special creations, but as the lineal descendants of some few beings which lived long before the first bed of the Silurian system was deposited, they seem to me to become ennobled', Darwin concluded. 'There is grandeur in this view of life, with its several powers, having been originally breathed by the Creator into a few forms or into one, and that, while this planet has gone circling on according to the fixed law of gravity, from so simple a beginning endless forms most beautiful and most wonderful have been, and are being, evolved' (Darwin 1996: 359–60). Notwithstanding his recognition of the realities of the brutal struggle for survival in nature, which certainly challenged his belief in a beneficent deity, Darwin's view of nature still had room for God as creator and designer. Darwin's well-known agnosticism came later, although even in his most agnostic phases his beliefs still fluctuated, making his religious sympathies notoriously hard to pinpoint (Brooke 2010: 391–405).

Darwin may have rejected Paleyian natural theology, but the possibility of reading in *Origin of Species* a modified version of natural theology that took into account a developmental view of life and grappled with the problem of evil made his views palatable for many religious thinkers. Nevertheless, Darwin's growing conviction that human beings were not specially created as Adam and Eve, and that humans had, with apes, descended from a common simian ancestry, forced a fundamental religious revaluation of humanity's place in the natural order (Darwin 1871). Some, of course, rejected the notion out of hand as antithetical to religious teaching (Figure 6.4).

For Darwin himself, the notion of humanity's evolution would become an important factor in his eventual agnosticism in part because he reasoned that if the mind is not a perfect creation but is the product of evolution, then the phenomenon of religious conviction might itself have arisen as a by-product of natural processes. Darwin's personal conclusions, however, were not the final word in how his theory was more generally received and interpreted.

The storied revulsion of religion at the noxious notion of the descent of man from simian ancestry bears little relation to reality. But caricatures abound. One legend, for example, has it that the bishop of Oxford, Samuel Wilberforce, was publicly humiliated by Darwin's bulldog, the zealously anti-clerical Thomas Henry Huxley, who had in 1860 proclaimed that '[e]xtinguished theologians lie about the cradle of every science as the strangled snakes beside that of Hercules; and history records that whenever science and orthodoxy have been fairly opposed, the latter has been forced to retire from the lists, bleeding and crushed, if not annihilated; scotched, if not slain' (Huxley 1896: 52). At the 1860 meeting of the British Association for the Advancement of Science, the story goes, Wilberforce cheekily asked Huxley if he would rather be descended from an ape on his grandfather's or his grandmother's side. Huxley reputedly struck back by saying that although he would not personally feel ashamed to be of simian ancestry, he would be ashamed to find that he was connected to a bishop who obscures the truth. An uproar ensued. A lady fainted. This largely invented story has played a dramatic role in furthering the narrative of the progressive triumph of secular science over benighted religion, but the reality is that the engagement of science with religion proved to be of a far more nuanced and textured character than this (Lightman 2001).

For those religious thinkers who were prepared to accept the idea of human descent from more humble origins, a new theology of nature began to emerge that viewed God not as an artisan but as an artist (Brooke and Cantor 2000: 163). The universe was imagined not so much as an intricate mechanism created by God but as a canvas of emerging creative possibilities. And the religious imagination would refocus its energies on discerning the unfolding of a moral teleology rather than on finding in nature physical evidence of biblical miracles or divine intervention. Darwin himself does seem to have believed that evolution had a moral goal, although his eventual agnostic confession would ensure that he did not contribute to these theological developments (Lightman 2007; Lightman 2016; Richards 2009). In general, religious students of nature did not perceive Darwin as having challenged the moral authority of the Bible.

Protestant reactions to Darwin varied greatly. Christian thinkers used various strategies to reduce the cognitive dissonance produced by Darwin's theory of natural selection. Most Protestants and Jews were able to accommodate some evolutionary progressivism (with varying degrees of attachment to the mechanism of natural selection) if it did not threaten the elevated spiritual and moral status of humanity (Moore 1979; Roberts 1999; Swetlitz 1999). The matter was more complicated with the Catholic Church, however. Although the Holy See never formally condemned evolutionary theory (perhaps deliberately so), the pope was wary of endorsing a scientific theory that could lead Catholic communicants astray with respect to the doctrinal status of the special creation of human beings, the

FIGURE 6.4: *A Venerable Orang-outang*, a caricature of Charles Darwin from *The Hornet* (1871). Photo: Wikimedia Commons.

human soul and original sin. There may not have been an explicit Catholic decree against evolutionary theory, and some may have even thought to reconcile theological doctrine with evolutionary theory by, for example, invoking the traditional philosophical distinction between primary and secondary causes (with the forces of nature being relegated to the latter category), but the dominant view was that evolutionary theory was too difficult to harmonize with church doctrine concerning the place of humanity in the cosmos (Artigas et al. 2006).

Catholic concerns with the theological implications of evolution were not initially a feature of Protestant criticism of evolutionary theory. Protestant critics instead attacked the science on the basis of philosophical and methodological issues. A main concern was their perception that Darwin had strayed from the Baconian methodology of inductionism which calls for avoiding speculation. Baconian methodology, they believed, was the only certain path to knowledge regarding the natural world. Darwin's evolutionary hypothesis was, to them, mere speculation, not legitimate science. Only after scientific naturalism took a firmer hold over scientific minds in the last quarter of the nineteenth century did theological concerns about the implications of Darwinism begin to assume an increased urgency (Roberts 1988).

Although some Christians maintained that special creation was central to their faith and they therefore opposed evolutionary theory, there was little organized anti-evolutionism before the 1920s, when the fiery rhetoric of a powerful politician named William Jennings Bryan helped to galvanize it in America. A national spotlight was trained on the issue during the infamous Scopes Monkey Trial of 1925, at which Bryan was called as a witness (Numbers 1997; Conkin 2001; Larson 1998). For most religious thinkers until then, the doctrine of the inerrancy of Scripture was not necessarily seen as challenged by Darwin. Nevertheless, for many, Darwin's theory was an affront to the spiritual dignity of humankind. A number of scientific and religious thinkers responded by differentiating the human condition from the general course of nature, whether by maintaining a belief in the special creation of humanity or (as was increasingly popular in the last quarter of the century) in the divine gift of a special moral consciousness.

As these developments in England were being debated, a new science of energy arose in Scotland around the time of the 1843 'Disruption' that split the Scottish church into established and free branches. A group of Scottish physicists and engineers developed new concepts such as 'actual' and 'potential' energy and the science of thermodynamics. They presented their scientific theories in a manner designed to counter what they perceived as the excessive biblical literalism of the Free Kirk as well as the perceived atheistic threat of scientific naturalism coming from England. William Thomson, Lord Kelvin, after whom the Kelvin temperature scale is named, believed that energy constituted a divine gift that should be harnessed to benefit humanity. At the same time, however, experiments on mechanical energy led him to conclude that energy dissipation is inevitable. The implication was that creation itself has a finite lifespan. And, if it had a definite end, then it had a definite beginning, a moment of creation. It was a view that seemed compatible with the doctrine of a fallen world, for the dissipation of energy seemed to imply a 'fall' in nature that only God could reverse (Smith 1998: 6, 102).

Nature, they believed, was irreversibly unidirectional except for the intervention of God's grace. For them, the dissipation of energy provided a link between the natural and moral order (Smith 1998: 240). Since energy is the evidence of God's providence, aligning our will with God's will entails making proper use of that energy. Indeed, it was a moral duty. At the same time, they affirmed the Calvinist doctrine that God's grace is necessary for salvation, for dissipation is a reminder of the ephemerality of existence and the spiritually fallen status of humanity.

This focus on the moral dimension in religion was already well attested in Europe. It grew in popularity in England in the wake of the introduction of historical criticism there. For many, reading the Bible strictly for its moral teachings provided a roadmap to separate religion from science (Brooke 1991: 209). Religion would no longer concern itself with the natural world's physical structure. Instead, it would reframe the natural world as having been designed in such a way as to facilitate moral progress, thus aligning nature with God's will.

Although natural theology played an important role in framing a harmonized relationship between science and religion in the Christian context, it played virtually no role in shaping Jewish attitudes towards scientific naturalism. There was no Jewish tradition of a Book of Nature to complement the Book of Scripture (Efron 2007, 2012). The twin revelations of oral and written Torah remained far and away the more important resource for sensing God's presence in the world than evidence adduced from the world of natural theology (Cantor 2005: 309). The lack of any sustained Jewish theological engagement with nature is also due to the traditional emphasis on Jewish praxis (the observance of *mitzvot*) rather than on creedal affirmation.

Rabbis in mainland Europe, Britain and America began to engage with the question of the transmutation of species in earnest only in the last quarter of the nineteenth century. A unique aspect to their engagement with evolutionary theory was their overriding concern with how its reception affected the prospects for the normalization and equalization of Jewish life among Christians. This is not to suggest there was an absence of theological discussion, but the far-reaching changes taking place in Jewish communal life were a more pressing concern. After all, the possibility of equal Jewish participation in national political life and in academic and scientific circles was only beginning to emerge. Many Jews saw a connection between the dismantling of social barriers and the rise of scientific naturalism. Science, it seemed, was at the vanguard of major social change, advancing the cause of a tolerant, meritocratic society. Rabbinic responses to Darwinism in the latter half of the nineteenth century were thus often connected to practical concerns like Jewish–Christian relations, attracting religiously disaffected Jews, and disarming anti-religious adversaries (Cantor 2011: 56; Cohen 1984; Efron 2014; Swetlitz 1999).

Both Orthodox and Reform rabbis accepted a theistic version of evolution. The Jewish mystical tradition known as *kabbalah* was seen to support such a position because of its progressive view of the cosmos (Cherry 2001). On the other hand, most rabbis rejected non-teleological natural selection into the twentieth century. That was seen as posing a threat to the elevated status of humanity and the sanctity of the human soul. One prominent Reform rabbi referred to Darwinism as 'Homo-Brutalism' (Figure 6.5) (Wise 1876).

Jews, like Christians, resisted the materialist implications of biology. One common accommodation that served many Jews and Christians equally well was the idea that human beings may have evolved physically but that their spiritual and moral essence was providentially created. For many Christians and Jews, what was objectionable about the idea of human evolution was not so much Genesis as it was ethics. Nature could not be trusted to vouchsafe for moral perfection.

Reading the Bible as a repository of moral wisdom is nothing new, but the post-1860 historicized perspective of the Bible and the natural world led to a new emphasis on moral knowledge as the proper and only meaningful way to read the Bible. This led

FIGURE 6.5: Caricature of Charles Darwin from the *London Sketch-Book* (1874). Photo: Wikimedia Commons.

to new controversies. Did the Bible teach that humankind had fallen from a state of moral perfection or that it was rising towards it? Evolution seemed to imply a rise from a state of savagery rather than a fall from grace. Some Christians reconciled the traditional doctrine of the Fall with evolution by maintaining that Adam and Eve were not created in a state of moral perfection but were created perfectly innocent. For them, the story of Adam and Eve's departure from the Garden of Eden is not one of degeneration, nor is human history a saga of inevitable progress. Moral development proceeds from free will and correctly aligning one's conscience with God's will. Evolutionary theory seemed compatible with such a world view.

One powerful reading strategy applied to Genesis that aligned religious sensibilities with biblical criticism and evolutionary theory was that preferred by Samuel R. Driver, author of the immensely influential *The Book of Genesis* (1904). Of him it was said that he taught the faithful criticism and the critics faith. He argued that the story of Adam and Eve was symbolically true. It communicated spiritual truths in a compelling narrative format that speaks to human experience (Driver 1904; Livingston 2007: 183).

Conservative Protestants, however, recoiled at what they perceived to be a denial of the sinful human condition and the need for grace. For theologians like P. T. Forsyth, for example, humanity exists in a state of sinful rebellion against God, and so is not naturally inclined to moral improvement. Forsyth's understanding of the process of moral progress began with a negative assessment of human nature, fundamentally challenging natural theology's optimistic assessment of a correspondence between natural history and divine providence. He warned his coreligionists against making such peace with evolution that they ended up reducing Christ to an evolutionary stage that might be outgrown. 'The danger is greater as the theory grows more religious', he warned in 1909. He nevertheless maintained that evolution was not incompatible with Christianity. Without the moral anchor of Christ, though, evolutionary change was merely meaningless motion. 'Evolution is within Christianity, but Christianity is not within evolution', he wrote. 'Man has in Christ the reality of his destiny, and not a prophecy of it' (Forsyth 1909: 10–12). The emphasis placed by conservative Protestants on human moral transformation through volition and piety helped to carve out a space for religion independent from scientific assessment.

The doctrine of the Fall was a specifically Christian concern, and so these theological discussions had little impact on how Jews interpreted the Bible. Nevertheless, Jews followed the trend, dominant in Christian society, of reading the Bible as concerned strictly with morality and not with the structure of the natural world, a reading that was conditioned as a response to science. The terms were different, however. In its 1885 Declaration of Principles, Reform Judaism expressed concern not with salvation from sin, but with promoting moral progress through fulfilment of what it believed to be its mission that followed from being chosen by God. What particularly distinguished this group of Jews from more traditional groups was their explicit specification that only those Mosaic laws concerned with moral issues would continue to have relevance for them.

Driven by their desire to reformulate Judaism in keeping with what they perceived to be the modern scientific mindset and to promote Jewish acceptance in non-Jewish society, Reform Jews read Torah's moral teachings in a manner untethered to their traditional mooring within a ritual and legal (*halachic*) framework. Whereas traditionalists, who believed that living in accord with the divine will required living by *halachic* norms, would insist that ethical living demanded inclusion of those *halachic* norms, Reform Jews now declared that they would no longer accept the authority of biblical and rabbinic laws pertaining to ritual observances such as diet and purity.

General considerations of human evolution and its relation to moral and spiritual concerns purport to speak to something universal about the human condition. In practice, however, musings about the universal human condition were usually coded to white people of European and Christian extraction. Scientific and religious opinions concerning the human condition varied depending on which part of humanity was under consideration. People debated whether human racial differences began before or after Adam and Eve.

Preadamists believed that Adam and Eve were the ancestors of whites and that other human races were earlier special creations with a different lineage altogether. In what might be construed as a creative, if deeply racist, reconciliation with the idea of human evolution, some polygenist religious apologists for the biblical narrative reasoned that Adam and Eve may not have been the first human beings – they were just the first to have a soul (Figure 6.6).

Some monogenist religious observers, however, felt that preadamism was corrosive to faith. But their belief that all humanity descended from Adam and Eve did not immunize them from racist views. Some argued that racial differences derived from the so-called 'curse of Ham' (Haynes 2002; Livingstone 2008: 80–108, 137–68). Noah had cursed his son Ham, after the latter discovered him drunk and naked, telling him he would be the lowest of slaves.

In Britain, abolitionists tended to be drawn from the ranks of the monogenists, while pro-slavery advocates tended to be polygenists. But in America, some slaveholders in the South on the eve of the Civil War used Genesis to support the ideology of slavery. Arguing that Blacks were descendants of Ham, they found in Genesis divine justification for the enslavement of Africans. In the South, one's position regarding human origins had little predictive value concerning one's position regarding slavery, in large part because the southern white mindset was not conditioned to evaluate slavery through Scripture. It was the other way around. It was conditioned to interpret Scripture through the institution of slavery (Sivasundaram 2010: 122).

The question of human origins had profound political and moral reverberations. For some conservative Christians, the only way to securely anchor oneself to the Bible's moral teaching required retaining a tight correspondence between natural history and the biblical narrative. For the 'creationists', evolutionary theory was morally repugnant. But organized opposition was slow in coming. Even *The Fundamentals* (1910–15), a collection of essays that sparked the creation of the fundamentalist movement, viewed biblical higher criticism as a far greater threat to orthodox faith. Its editor had said that although having an ape for an ancestor was a repugnant idea, he was prepared to accept it if it were proven to be true (Numbers 2006: 32, 53).

George McCready Price, a Canadian-born Seventh-Day Adventist with virtually no scientific training, sowed the seeds of what would later become known as 'creation science' in the mid-twentieth century. A popularizer of the erstwhile discarded theory of 'Flood geology', which posits that the Flood had buried the fossils, Price understood that without the foundation of deep time to support it, the argument for evolution fell apart. By attacking the foundations of geological time, he simultaneously undermined organic evolution, which depends on the passage of vast amounts of time (Numbers 2006: 92–119). Fundamentalists like Price believed that the findings of natural science could not contradict what they understood to be the literal meaning of the text. Faithful fidelity necessitated reinforcing a strong correlation between the physical structure of the

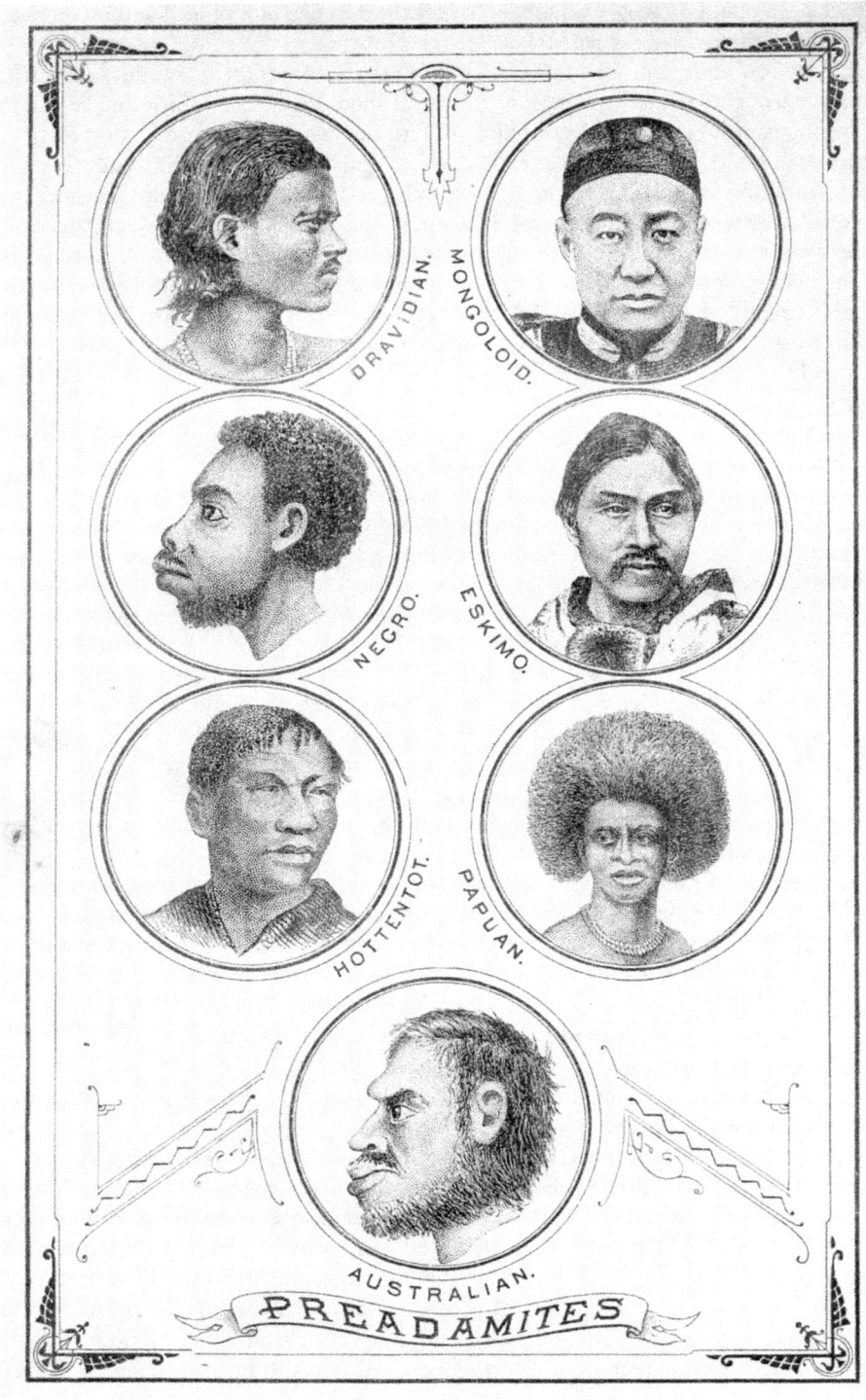

FIGURE 6.6: *Preadamites* by Alexander Winchell. Photo: Alamy. Image ID P9PRY6.

world and the biblical narrative. Ironically, the purported literal meaning of the text was determined by evaluating its effectiveness at undermining the evolutionary argument. Thus, just as liberal Christianity's outlook was shaped by developments in natural science, so too was fundamentalist thought conditioned by it.

Momentous developments in the field of natural history during the Victorian era posed new questions about the meaning of the human condition. Faith communities had to grapple with the earth and all life in it having a story rooted in deep time, which spurred new ways of reading the Bible. Some liberal Protestants understood Genesis to be concerned only with moral and existential concerns, while other conservatives were concerned with how sin and salvation correspond to natural history. Among Jews, some aligned natural history with the kabbalistic framework of progress. Others sought to distance humanity from the forces of evolution, while for still others, the scientific world view sparked a debate concerning the relationship of ethics to *halachah*. Different faith communities developed reading relationships with Scripture that were conditioned by developments in science, and this would transform their self-understanding.

NOTE

1. Darwin was not the first person to propose a developmental view of life. Jean-Baptiste Pierre Antoine de Monet, chevalier de Lamarck, had already advanced a theory that animals could change in response to their environments. But Lamarck's theory that animals could acquire new traits during their lifetimes and then pass on those characteristics to their offspring lacked adequate evidence, and moreover, his theory smacked of French materialism and atheism, which felt threatening to British naturalists.

REFERENCES

Artigas, M., T. F. Glick, and R. A. Martínez (2006), *Negotiating Darwin: The Vatican Confronts Evolution, 1877–1902*, Baltimore: Johns Hopkins University Press.

Atkinson, J. C. (1891), *Forty Years in a Moorland Parish: Reminiscences and Researches in Danby in Cleveland*, Macmillan and Co.

Barbour, I. G. (2000), *When Science Meets Religion*, 1st edn, Harper.

Brooke, J. H. (2002), 'Natural Theology', in *Science and Religion: A Historical Introduction*, ed. G. B. Ferngren, 163–75, Johns Hopkins University Press.

Brooke, J. H. (2010), 'Darwin and Religion: Correcting the Caricatures', *Science & Education*, 19(4–5): 391–405.

Brooke, J. H. (1991), *Science and Religion: Some Historical Perspectives*, Cambridge University Press.

Brooke, J. H. and G. Cantor (2000), *Reconstructing Nature: The Engagement of Science and Religion*, Oxford University Press.

Buckland, W. (1836), *Geology and Mineralogy Considered with Reference to Natural Theology*, Vol. 1, The Bridgewater Treatises 6, William Pickering.

Cantor, G. (2005), *Quakers, Jews, and Science: Religious Responses to Modernity and the Sciences in Britain, 1650–1900*, Oxford University Press.

Cantor, G. (2011), 'Modern Judaism', in *Science and Religion Around the World*, ed. J. H. Brooke and R. L. Numbers, 44–66, Oxford University Press.

Chambers, R. (1844), *Vestiges of the Natural History of Creation*, John Churchill.

Cherry, M. S. (2001), *Creation, Evolution and Jewish Thought*, Ph.D. thesis, Brandeis University.
Cohen, N. W. (1984), 'The Challenges of Darwinism and Biblical Criticism to American Judaism', *Modern Judaism*, 4: 121–57.
Conkin, P. K. (2001), *When All the Gods Trembled: Darwinism, Scopes, and American Intellectuals*, Rowman & Littlefield Publishers.
Darwin, C. (1859), *On the Origin of Species by Means of Natural Selection, or the Preservation of Favoured Races in the Struggle for Life*, John Murray.
Darwin, C. (1871), *The Descent of Man, and Selection in Relation to Sex*, Vols. 1–2, J. Murray.
Darwin, C. (1996), *The Origin of Species. 1859*, ed. G. Beer, World's Classics, Oxford University Press.
Driver, S. R. (1904), *The Book of Genesis*, 2nd ed., Methuen & Co.
Efron, J. M. (2007), *Judaism and Science: A Historical Introduction* 2011. Greenwood Guides to Science and Religion, Westport: Greenwood Press.
Efron, N. J. (2012), 'Jews and the Study of Nature', in *The Routledge Companion to Religion and Science*, ed. J. W. Haag, 79–90. Routledge.
Efron, J. M. (2014), *A Chosen Calling: Jews in Science in the Twentieth Century*, Baltimore: Johns Hopkins University Press.
Forsyth, P. T. (1909), *The Person and Place of Jesus Christ*, London: Congregation Union of England and Wales.
Fyfe, A. (2004), *Science and Salvation: Evangelical Popular Science Publishing in Victorian Britain*, Chicago: University of Chicago Press.
Harrison, P. (2015), *The Territories of Science and Religion*, Chicago: University of Chicago Press.
Haynes, S. (2002), *Noah's Curse: The Biblical Justification of American Slavery*, Oxford: Oxford University Press.
Huxley, T. H. (1896), *Darwiniana Essays*, New York: D. Appleton and Co.
Larsen, T. (2011), *A People of One Book: The Bible and the Victorians*, Oxford: Oxford University Press.
Larson, E. J. (1998), *Summer for the Gods: The Scopes Trial and America's Continuing Debate Over Science and Religion*, Cambridge, MA: Harvard University Press.
Lightman, B. (2001), 'Victorian Sciences and Religions: Discordant Harmonies', *Osiris*, 16: 343–66.
Lightman, B. (2007), *Victorian Popularizers of Science: Designing Nature for New Audiences*, Chicago: University of Chicago Press.
Lightman, B., ed. (2016), *Global Spencerism: The Communication and Appropriation of a British Evolutionist*, Leiden: Brill.
Lindberg, D. C. and R. L. Numbers, eds. (1986), *God and Nature: Historical Essays on the Encounter Between Christianity and Science*, University of California Press.
Livingston, J. C. (2007), *Religious Thought in the Victorian Age: Challenges and Reconceptions*, New York: T&T Clark.
Livingstone, D. N. (2008), *Adam's Ancestors: Race, Religion, and the Politics of Human Origins*. Medicine, Science, and Religion in Historical Context, Baltimore: Johns Hopkins University Press.
Moore, J. R. (1979), *The Post-Darwinian Controversies: A Study of the Protestant Struggle to Come to Terms with Darwin in Great Britain and America, 1870–1900*, Cambridge University Press.

Moore, J. R. (1986), 'Geologists and Interpreters of Genesis in the Nineteenth Century', in *God and Nature: Historical Essays on the Encounter Between Christianity and Science*, ed. D. C. Lindberg and R. L. Numbers, 322–50, University of California Press.

Numbers, R. L. (1997), *Darwinism Comes to America*, Cambridge, MA: Harvard University Press.

Numbers, R. L. (2006), *The Creationists: From Scientific Creationism to Intelligent Design*, Expanded edn, Cambridge, MA: Harvard University Press.

Numbers, R. L. and P. J. Susalla (2002), 'Cosmogonies', in *Science and Religion: A Historical Introduction*, ed. G. B. Ferngren, 220–34, Johns Hopkins University Press.

Paley, W. (1802), *Natural Theology: Or, Evidences of the Existence and Attributes of the Deity, Collected from the Appearances of Nature*, R. Faulder.

Richards, R. J. (2009), 'Natural Selection and Its Moral Purpose', in *The Cambridge Companion to the 'Origin of Species'*, ed. M. Ruse and R. J. Richards, 47–66, Cambridge University Press.

Roberts, J. H. (1988), *Darwinism and the Divine in America: Protestant Intellectuals and Organic Evolution, 1859–1900*, Madison: University of Wisconsin Press.

Roberts, J. H. (1999), 'Darwinism, American Protestant Thinkers, and the Puzzle of Motivation', in *Disseminating Darwinism: The Role of Place, Race, Religion, and Gender*, ed. J. Stenhouse and R. L. Numbers, 145–72, Cambridge University Press.

Robson, J. M. (1990), 'The Fiat and Finger of God: The Bridgewater Treatises', in *Victorian Faith in Crisis: Essays on Continuity and Change in Nineteenth-Century Religious Belief*, ed. R. J. Helmstadter and B. V. Lightman, 71–125, Stanford University Press.

Rudwick, M. J. S. (1986), 'The Shape and Meaning of Earth History', in *God and Nature: Historical Essays on the Encounter Between Christianity and Science*, ed. D. C. Lindberg and R. L. Numbers, 296–321, University of California Press.

Rudwick, M. J. S. (2014), *Earth's Deep History: How It Was Discovered and Why It Matters*, Chicago: University of Chicago Press.

Rupke, N. A. (1983), *The Great Chain of History: William Buckland and the English School of Geology (1814–1849)*, Oxford: Oxford University Press, 1983.

Rupke, N. A. (2013), 'The Bible and Science', in *The New Cambridge History of the Bible*, ed. J. C. Paget et al., 707–24, Cambridge University Press.

Secord, J. A. (2000), *Victorian Sensation: The Extraordinary Publication, Reception, and Secret Authorship of Vestiges of the Natural History of Creation*, Chicago: University of Chicago Press.

Shea, V. and W. Whitla, eds. (2000), *Essays and Reviews: The 1860 Text and Its Reading*. Victorian Literature and Culture Series, University Press of Virginia.

Sheils, W. (2010), 'Nature and Modernity: J. C. Atkinson and Rural Ministry in England c. 1850–1900', in *God's Bounty? The Churches and the Natural World*, ed. P. Clarke and T. Claydon, 366–95, Studies in Church History, Vol. 46. Ecclesiastical History Society, Boydell & Brewer.

Sidney, E. (1846), *Blights of the Wheat and Their Remedies*, London: The Religious Tract Society.

Sivasundaram, S. (2010), 'Race, Empire, and Biology before Darwinism', in *Biology and Ideology from Descartes to Dawkins*, ed. D. Alexander and R. L. Numbers, 114–38, The University of Chicago Press.

Smith, C. (1998), *The Science of Energy: A Cultural History of Energy Physics in Victorian Britain*, Chicago: University of Chicago Press.

Smith, M. (2010), 'The Mountain and the Flower: The Power and Potential of Nature in the World of Victorian Evangelicalism', in *God's Bounty? The Churches and the Natural World*, ed. P. Clarke and T. Claydon, 307–18, Studies in Church History, Vol. 46. Ecclesiastical History Society, Boydell & Brewer.

Swetlitz, M. (1999), 'American Jewish Responses to Darwin and Evolutionary Theory, 1860–1890', in *Disseminating Darwinism: The Role of Place, Race, Religion, and Gender*, ed. J. Stenhouse and R. L. Numbers, 209–46, Cambridge University Press.

Temple, R. (1860), *Essays and Reviews*, London: J.W. Parker.

Topham, J. R. (1998), 'Beyond the "Common Context": The Production and Reading of the Bridgewater Treatises', *Isis*, 89(2): 233–62.

Topham, J. R. (2010), 'Biology in the Service of Natural Theology: Paley, Darwin, and the Bridgewater Treatises', in *Biology and Ideology from Descartes to Dawkins*, ed. D. R. Alexander and R. L. Numbers, 88–113, Chicago: The University of Chicago Press.

Whewell, W. (1833), *Astronomy and General Physics Considered with Reference to Natural Theology*, London: William Pickering.

Wise, I. M. (1876), *The Cosmic God: A Fundamental Philosophy in Popular Lectures*, Cincinnati: Office American Israelite and Deborah.

Yarchin, W. (2008), 'Biblical Interpretation in the Light of the Interpretation of Nature: 1650–1900', in *Nature and Scripture in the Abrahamic Religions: 1700-Present*, ed. J. M. van der Meer and S. Mandelbrote, Vol. 1, 41–82, Brill's Series in Church History 37, Brill.

CHAPTER 7

Women, Gender and Sexuality

AMANDA PAXTON

Then their eyes met, and they shook hands like cronies in a tavern, and Jude saw the absurdity of quarrelling on such a hypothetical subject, and she the silliness of crying about what was written in an old book like the Bible. (Hardy 1999: 122)

Jude the Obscure

At the moment that Sue Bridehead, a central character in Thomas Hardy's novel *Jude the Obscure* (1895), sees the 'silliness' of crying over the Bible, she has yet to learn the extent to which Victorian religious orthodoxy and its social manifestations would continue to bring her tears. A world of sexual constrictions rationalized by scriptural authority and expressed in legal injunctions surrounding marriage and adultery would press mightily on her and her lover Jude, propelling their story's tragic arc. Indeed, the tale of Sue Bridehead and Jude Fawley calls to mind the words that Virginia Woolf would utter almost thirty-five years after the novel's first publication, this time describing the now-baffling resistance women in the past encountered upon trying to enter the public sphere: 'Opinions that one now pastes in a book labelled cock-a-doodle-dum and keeps for reading to select audiences on summer nights once drew tears, I can assure you' (Woolf 2008: 72). And, to be sure, even if Sue's religious scepticism allows her to reduce the Bible to an 'old book', that determination would not diminish the real impact that the Bible exerted on the lives of nineteenth-century women and men like her and Jude.

In England and North America, the Protestant *sola scriptura* approach to the Bible – positing the authority of Scripture alone, rather than that of any interpretive bodies or texts – constituted a central tenet of public discourse, reflected socially and institutionally (Larsen 2011: 2; Vance 2012: 33; LaPorte 2011: 17). The Bible played a central role in undergirding and justifying social norms, including those surrounding gender, sexuality and the role of women in society. In many ways, biblical texts served as *prima facie* explanations for socially sanctioned constructions of gender, discrepancies in divorce law and voting rights, and understandings of sex and marital duties.

Simultaneously, however, the changing relationships to the Bible developing in the nineteenth century rendered the text a contested site of meaning-making. What came to be called the 'higher criticism', a method of reading the Bible not as divine revelations but rather as a compilation of texts written by individuals at various historical moments and with various political investments, would famously be invoked by Benjamin Jowett in his contribution to the revolutionary 1860 publication *Essays and Reviews*, in which he invites the reader to '"interpret Scripture from itself" as in other respects, like any other book written in an age and country of which little or no other literature survives' – that is, as a historical document (1860: 382). The repositioning of the Bible as a text inspired by historical conditions rather than by God constituted one of many seismic shifts in the way nineteenth-century readers received biblical teachings. Scientific discoveries popularized by figures such as the geologist Charles Lyell and the biologist Charles Darwin complicated the reception of biblical narratives of creation. Furthermore, the growing popularity of Protestant Evangelicalism, with its emphasis on interpreting Scripture independently, encouraged the lay reader to come to her own readings of sacred texts rather than relying on outside authority figures like priests. Moreover, developments in linguistics led to a revision of the standard King James Version English Bible, a further challenge to any remaining conceptions of the Bible as an immutable text.

Concurrent with the tumult surrounding the changing role of the Bible came equally tumultuous changes in social norms surrounding gender and sexuality. Theories of gender, the rights of women and sexual expression and identity became increasingly disputed terrain over the course of the century. As Bruce Dorsey notes, 'both religion and sexuality are crucial to webs of meaning associated with feeling, emotion, bodies, communication, and the constitution of the self' (2015: 347). It should come as no surprise, then, that shifts in biblical reception and shifts in cultural understandings of sex and gender would transpire in tandem, each informing and responding to the other. This chapter will distil a number of the tensions, arguments and paradoxes in a century of shifting readings of Scripture, sex and bodies.

SEPARATE SPHERES AND TWO-SEX BODIES

The notion of 'separate spheres', a model of gender predicated on a binary distinction between men and women, found its height in the nineteenth century, in Europe and North America. Within this model, the conceit that men and women exhibit inherently distinct tendencies, rooted in biology and manifested in behaviors and aptitudes, becomes extended to determine what types of spaces men and women are most suited to occupy: men are seen as most suited to the public sphere of commerce, politics and law; women to the private sphere of the home. The doctrine is perhaps most famously articulated in the words of the English critic and social commentator John Ruskin: 'The man's power is active, progressive, defensive. He is eminently the doer, the discoverer, the defender . . . . But the woman's power is for rule, not for battle, – and her intellect is not for invention or creation, but for sweet ordering, arrangement, and decision' (1882: 90).

Belief in separate spheres predates the nineteenth century, traceable at least to antiquity. Nevertheless, its classical iterations and its nineteenth-century manifestations share a foundation in what a 'sophisticated androcentric metaphysics' presents in the 'Hellenistic Judaism of Philo of Alexandria, rooted in both the Bible and Plato' (Barton 2009: 189). The biblical germ of the dualistic gender model appears in the first Genesis creation story: 'So God created man in his own image, in the image of God created he him; male and female created he them' (Gen. 1.27, KJV). Nineteenth-century models of separate spheres, however, found greater traction in the second creation story, in which God fashions the first woman, Eve, from the rib of the first man, Adam. Importantly, this narrative stipulates that woman was created as a 'help meet' to man (Gen. 2.18). This secondary status informed a host of extrapolations concerning the nature of women in society. In 1859, William Landels, a London-based Baptist minister and eventual head of the Baptist Union, would exemplify this view in his claim that this biblical passage 'defines the mission of woman as such'. For Landels and others, Eve is representative of womankind: 'As *she* was designed to be an helpmeet for *Adam*, so is *woman* designed to be an helpmeet for *man*' (1859: 8). The ensuing description of humanity's fall from Eden in Gen. 3.3-6 did nothing to bolster Eve's reputation, and the account became fodder for later biblical pronouncements on women's fallibility and the consequential restrictions that are to be imposed on them. In 1 Timothy, Paul decrees, 'Let the woman learn in silence with all subjection. But I suffer not a woman to teach, nor to usurp authority over the man, but to be in silence. For Adam was first formed, then Eve. And Adam was not deceived, but the woman being deceived was in the transgression' (1 Tim. 2.11-15). To a nineteenth-century reader of a certain inclination, this declaration affords ample support for the assumption that women's purview is in the home rather than in the public sphere. Similarly, Paul's letter to the Ephesians has historically served as biblical guidance on hierarchy in marriage and continues to appear in 'The Form of Solemnization of Matrimony' in the Anglican Book of Common Prayer: 'Wives, submit yourselves unto your own husbands, as unto the Lord. For the husband is the head of the wife, even as Christ is the head of the church: and he is the saviour of the body. Therefore as the church is subject unto Christ, so let the wives be to their own husbands in every thing' (Eph. 5.22-24).

Importantly, while nineteenth-century thinkers affirmed these biblical texts in their models of gender, they were also quick to note that women's subordinate status was not to be interpreted as degrading. Instead, nineteenth-century iterations of the doctrines of separate spheres and scripturally determined gender hierarchy, coming in the wake of Enlightenment notions of equality and justice, insist on a language of conciliatory chivalric paradoxes. Landels notes that 'Man's inferior we do not call her; man's subordinate she certainly is' (1859: 60). In literature, the mid-century model of female subordination was most famously glorified in *The Angel in the House*, a figure exemplifying idealized feminine domesticity, taken from Coventry Patmore's multi-volume poem of the same name. Patmore's faultless heroine is described as deriving satisfaction from dutiful submission to her husband: 'Her will's indomitably bent / On mere submissiveness to him' (1863: 88). In Europe and the United States, the vision of 'Republican motherhood' ennobled the idea of women's place being in the home, since she was entrusted in the nationalist cause of shaping the state's children. Similarly, the New Testament figure of Mary, the virgin mother of Jesus, was commonly invoked as exemplary of female piety, obedience and motherhood. One commentator remarked, 'We cannot have too many Marys, handmaidens of the Lord, who yield themselves up to God, to be moulded by His Word (Luke 1:38)' (Schroeder 2014: 141).

At the same time that nineteenth-century pundits were deferring to biblical texts to legitimize popular conceptions of gender, the notion of binary gender roles was underwritten by a newer form of orthodoxy: scientific empiricism. Post-Enlightenment scientific models of gender increasingly reflected what Thomas Laqueur calls the 'two-sex' model of gender in which women and men constitute ontologically distinct categories of humanity, a shift from 'one-sex' models preceding the eighteenth century, in which sex differences were thought to represent divergent poles on a singular continuum between male and female (1992: 11). Within the one-sex model, female organs were thought to be inverted male organs. By contrast, the figuration of gender attendant to the new, two-sex model was rigidly binary, entailing two distinct categories of 'male' and 'female'.

The new claim operated nicely in the service of the ideology of separate spheres, adding a biological conceit to notions of women as inherently submissive, maternal and domestic. Under the one-sex model, it was believed that both the male and female partner were required to orgasm during heterosexual intercourse in order to conceive. This belief was sustained into the early nineteenth century until German biologist Thomas L. W. Bischoff found that ovulation does not exclusively occur during intercourse. Bischoff's research was on canine physiology, but the results were extrapolated to human populations, changing the understanding of women's role in reproduction – specifically, the role of female sexual pleasure. That conception was possible without female orgasm, which made way for an emerging understanding of women not only as submissive and domestic but also as free of sexual desire. If anything, women were understood to desire motherhood, leading them to submit to their husbands' sexual advances. In 1876, the American feminist and spiritualist Eliza Duffey would contend that women's sexuality is unique from men's in that it necessitates a mutual 'kindness' and 'self-denial' rather than carnal desire (1889: 208).

The dual pillars of Scripture and biological determinism mounted a platform for what is by now a roundly popularized image of nineteenth-century attitudes towards sex and gender, centred on constraint and middle-class moralism. Given that women constituted the majority of attendees at church services, the alignment of biblical texts with the designation of women's duties might be said to have had a particularly potent significance on nineteenth-century European culture (Larsen 2011: 7). Indeed, ideas of womanhood as necessitating marriage and motherhood were commonly framed with scriptural references meant to confer legitimacy. In Sarah Stickney Ellis's immensely popular 1843 handbook *The Wives of England*, the author posits an essential female inclination for marriage stemming from humanity's exile from Eden:

> It is possible to imagine that the mother of mankind, even when looking her last upon that Eden whose flowers her care had tended, would turn to the companion of her banishment with a deeper and more fervent appeal to his sympathy and affection than she could ever have felt the need of, in those bowers of beauty where a leaf was never seen to fade. Thus out of her very weakness, and from amongst the many snares which have beset the path of woman since that day of awful doom, has arisen a more intense desire, and a more urgent need, for the support of a stronger nature, with which her own can mingle, until it almost loses the bitter consciousness of having forfeited all claim to be still an inhabitant of Paradise. (1843: 141–2)

A marital handbook from almost forty years later would counsel, 'the Bible builds the happiness of married life upon these two great pillars: 1. The Husband's permanent love to his Wife. 2. The Wife's willing and cheerful obedience to her Husband' (Kirton 1882: 202). Moreover, girls were advised to seek out socially prescribed traits of womanhood in scriptural figures: 'Every young lady', notes the 1861 edition of *The Illustrated Girl's Own Treasury*, 'ought to be familiar with the lives of Scripture female characters: they contain wonderful examples of the highest and the gentlest feminine qualities – filial duty, sisterly affection, patriotic self-devotion, domestic virtues, humility, patience, resolution, piety, friendship, and truth' (2). In many ways, the use of Scripture in enforcing the doctrine of separate spheres and binary gender structures supplemented the biological determinism of mainstream science by directing women as to how they were to experience their inner lives and their relationships with the external world.

LEGISLATING DIFFERENCE

Scholars have noted that the doctrine of separate spheres and the two-sex model both papered over discrepancies between the post-Enlightenment belief in liberalism and equality and the lived reality of women's continued social disenfranchisement. Discussing France, Robert A. Nye remarks that the seeds of separate spheres of ideology in the revolutionary period 'was a matter, no doubt, of politics and power. [...] The challenge for the men who were responsible for legitimating a male monopoly of civil authority was to inscribe this essentially biological distinction into the laws and institutions of the new order' (1998: 55). One form this inscription took in France was the 1816 dismantling of divorce laws – seen to ascribe too much power to women, despite still favouring men – which would only be reinstated in 1884. The English context was complicated by the fact that English common law maintained the practice of coverture, dating from the Middle Ages, under which a woman's legal identity (along with her property) was subsumed into her husband's at the moment of marriage. Under this system, the British writer and activist Annie Besant wrote, 'looking at a woman's position both as wife and mother, it is impossible not to recognise the fact that marriage is a direct disadvantage to her' (1882: 33).

Just as marriage was unfavorable to women, so too were divorce laws, which privileged men by, for instance, allowing divorce on the grounds of a wife's infidelity but not on the grounds of a husband's, unless that infidelity was additionally transgressive involving, for example, incest or bestiality (Shanley 1993: 80). Equally, child custody laws stipulated that fathers had sole custody rights after divorce. Although Scripture was not cited in the legislation itself, it was invoked in its defence. In 1884, when MP James Bryce proposed a bill to equalize child custody regulations, Cambridge MP William Fowler – a liberal, though not a radical – declared that he disapproved of the bill because it established equal custody between married parents. Fowler protested, 'The Bill started with the idea that the husband and wife were equal, a theory which was against Scripture and reason' (Shanley 1993: 147). In America, the recourse to Scripture was more overt. As Cassandra Yacovazzi notes, 'While earlier public discourse made more ornamental references to Scripture, by the late eighteenth and early nineteenth centuries, public officials began citing Biblical passages as primary justifications for public policy, from temperance, to common schools, to slavery' (2013: 28). As late as 1895, voices like that of Peter Z. Easton, an American Evangelical preacher, would claim that a reader would 'search in vain for one single word of commendation for emancipated woman' (Schroeder 2014: 142).

Although incremental suffrage gains were made over the nineteenth century and into the twentieth, in most countries full voting rights would not be granted to women until the twentieth century. In the United States this moment came in 1920, in England it came in 1928. French women would wait until 1945. Unsurprisingly, restrictions on suffrage were rationalized with Scripture. In 1878, the Anglo-Catholic poet Christina Rossetti would write that her ambivalence towards women's rights advocacy 'seems to myself a fundamental one underlying the whole structure of female claims. Does it not appear as if the Bible was based upon an understood unalterable distinction between men and women, their position, duties, privileges?' (1997–2004: 2:158). The doctrine of separate spheres and distinct essential gender traits continued to serve for some as an adequate explanation for unequal treatment under the law.

In fact, commentators were apt to claim that biblical texts afforded women greater rights than other traditions. The celebrated 1855 debate between freethinker Joseph Barker and the Reverend Brewin Grant witnessed Grant defend against Barker's assertions that the Bible denigrated women by referring to the Indian practice of *sati*, the self-immolation of a widow on her husband's funeral pyre. The practice was outlawed by colonial English powers in 1828, a turn that Grant attributes to 'our Christian rule' (1855: 147). Indeed, by the 1830s the British and Foreign Bible Society and the colonial East India Company had become 'tacit allies' in the campaign to consolidate India under English and Christian cultural norms, leading to a number of sweeping legislative and judicial changes in that country (Zemka 1995: 128). Arguably, the operation was driven by imperial hegemony rather than religious ideals. For his part, Barker was not convinced by Grant's claims, responding, 'All he quoted about the condition of woman in heathen countries brought to my mind parallel facts mentioned in the Bible, showing that among the earlier Jews, who had God's special revelation, woman was in a worse condition than is even described in those quotations which he read' (Zemka 1995: 150).

WAYS OF READING WOMEN

Despite the number of social and legal restrictions imposed on women and justified through reference to Scripture, many proponents of women's rights also deferred to biblical authority to substantiate their arguments. Shira Wolosky formulates a key distinction between readings of the Bible that informed two broadly conceived hermeneutic positions:

> On the one hand, a 'subordinationist' reading regarded the Bible as a book of hierarchical authority, extending from the text to the church, and urging patient acceptance of one's lot as ordained by God within a fixed order. . . . In contrast stood what may be generally called a liberal interpretation, which defined the Bible's central teaching as the principles of freedom, liberation, individual conscience, and the sacred integrity of every soul created equally by God. (2002: 192)

What Wolosky calls a subordinationist approach can be seen in Rossetti's alignment of separate gender identities with correlative, discrete rights and privileges, or in Fowler's refusal of equal rights for wives and husbands on biblical grounds. A liberal interpretation, by contrast, sees such interpretations as products of specific hermeneutic practices subject to challenge. As Esther Fuchs notes, the liberal approach 'is anchored in the belief that the system itself – in this case, the Bible at its core – is not the problem, but is, rather, a separable and distinct "overlay" that can be removed through proper reading techniques' (2008: 63). An example of this approach appears in Lucretia Mott's 1849 lecture 'Discourse on Woman', in which she takes a rationalist argument against traditional belief in female subordination based on Genesis: 'The cause of the subjection of woman to man, was early ascribed to disobedience to the command of God. This would seem to show that she was then regarded as not occupying her true and rightful position in society' (1850: 4). Notably, Mott does not challenge the status of the Bible itself, but rather its readers' interpretations of the book of Genesis as mandating women's secondary status.

Another model of reparative scriptural interpretation comes in the form of reiterating essentialist principles already present in the dominant culture but inscribing them with implications of female nobility or even superiority. In her 1853 volume *Woman's Record*, the New England author and editor Sarah Josepha Hale opines that 'The Bible is the only guarantee of woman's rights, and the only expositor of her duties. Under its teachings, men learn to honor her' (1853: viii). The rights Hale saw as scripturally afforded to women include, for example, the right to higher education, since 'God designed woman as the preserver of infancy, the teacher of childhood, the inspirer or helper of man's moral nature in its efforts to reach after spiritual things' (1853: viii). Women deserve education because of their inherent relationships with others – in this case, their children and husbands. Like Ruskin, Hale would default to the essentialist patterns that figured women as inherently free of sexual desire and, therefore, more spiritually capable, than men. Declaring women 'the true source of moral power in human nature' (1853: xxxv). Hale challenges Paul's interpretation of Genesis to mean that woman is subordinate: 'Truly she was made "for man," but not in the sense this text has been interpreted. She was not made to gratify his sensual desires, but to refine his human affections, and elevate his moral feelings' (1853: xxxvii). In this vein, Hale figures Jesus's mother Mary as noble in her unselfish submission to God's calling: 'Great indeed, must have been her faith, when it wholly overcame all fear of man, all selfish considerations' (1853: 128). Hale's brand of liberal interpretation adopts a position similar to that of Patmore in his chivalric elevation and idealization of the angel in the house archetype.

Like Mott and Hale, Rossetti takes Genesis as an occasion to reflect on the nature of Eve's transgression. Going further than the former two writers, her interpretation proposes a challenge to standard notions of male and female natures. Despite Rossetti's opposition to women's suffrage, her reading of the narrative of the Fall problematizes standard interpretations that foreground Eve as an icon of female fallibility. In Rossetti's telling, Eve's 'very virtues may have opened the door to temptation. By birthright gracious and accessible, she lends an ear to all petitions from all petitioners' (1883: 17). Eve was subject to a compelling argument, and her fall came about from that characteristic of hers, whereas Adam was subject merely to his domestic affections: 'Eve preferred various prospects to God's will: Adam seems to have preferred one person to God' (1883: 18). Timothy Larsen sees in this moment 'a striking inversion of Victorian gender stereotypes' by which 'Rossetti reads this as the woman being lead [sic] by her "mind" and the man by his "heart"' (2009: 27). Readings like Rossetti's, Mott's and Hale's demonstrate the variety of liberal interpretations of Scripture, whether working within essentialist frameworks or troubling them.

Alongside liberal readings of biblical texts came increasingly radical relationships to Scripture, particularly in terms of hermeneutic authority. Although traditional Pauline doctrine dictated that women not partake in preaching, nineteenth-century movements like the Second Great Awakening and the revival of Evangelicalism invited individuals to read and interpret Scripture on their own, without recourse to mediating pastoral figures. This movement included women, and Protestant communities afforded women space to preach and to be received as legitimate interpreters of the Bible. Rather than deferring to church leaders, women were able to assert independence by virtue of their direct reading of and relationship to Scripture. The case of Indian activist Pandita Ramabai Sarasvati proves particularly telling, as it involves a number of hierarchical and institutional claims. Born into an upper-caste family in 1858, Ramabai converted to Christianity in 1883 while in England. As a woman, a colonial subject and a convert, Ramabai stood at a disadvantage in disputes with missionaries in her home country. Rather than concede to their authority, however, Ramabai asserted authority directly from Scripture writing, 'Obedience to the word of God is quite different from perfect obedience to priests only. I have just, with great effort, freed myself from the yoke of the Indian priestly tribe, so I am not at present willing to place myself under another similar yoke' (Tharu and Lalita 1991: 245).

Early in the century the American Quaker and suffragist Sarah Moore Grimké similarly availed herself of direct scriptural authority by taking issue with the King James translation and the implicit biases she saw embedded in it by its translators: 'King James's translators were not inspired. I therefore claim the original as my standard, believing that to have been inspired, and I also claim to judge for myself what is the meaning of the inspired writers' (1838: 4). Grimké goes on to provide textual analysis at odds with, for instance, traditional readings of the story of the Fall from Eden, faulting the translators for having mistranslated Gen. 3.16, God's decree to Eve that 'thy desire shall be to thy husband, and he shall rule over thee'. 'The Hebrew', Grimké explains, 'uses the same word to express shall and will. Our translators having been accustomed to exercise lordship over their wives, and seeing only through the medium of a perverted judgment, very naturally, though I think not very learnedly or very kindly, translated it shall instead of will, and thus converted a prediction to Eve into a command to Adam' (1838: 7).

A striking example of marginalized women asserting authority through Scripture comes in the cases of women who were unable to read, such as the former slave Sojourner Truth and the black freewoman Rebecca Cox Jackson. When asked if she preached from the Bible, Truth, famous as a travelling preacher and abolitionist, replied in the negative, since she was unable to read the book itself. Her text, she said, was simply called 'When I found Jesus!' The radicalism of this position was reflected in Truth's 'Ain't I A Woman' speech, delivered at the Ohio Women's Rights Convention in 1851, in which she contended, 'If the first woman God ever made was strong enough to turn a world upside down all alone, these women together ought to be able to turn it back, and get it right side up again!' (Wade-Gayles 1995: 154). Rather than echo essentialist patterns of femininity or attempt a mitigation of Eve's transgression, Truth positions Eve as a figure of potency by virtue of the destruction she wrought. She then imports that same potency into her own time in the collectivist potential of the women's movement.

Just as striking is the account given by Jackson, a black freewoman and contemporary of Truth's who also became an itinerant preacher, describing her experience learning to read. Frustrated by her brother's unfulfilled promises to teach her to read, Jackson writes, 'I laid down my dress, picked up my Bible, ran upstairs, opened it, and kneeled down with it pressed to my breast, prayed earnestly to Almighty God if it was consisting to His holy will, to learn me to read His holy word. And when I looked on the word, I began to read' (Humez 1981: 108). The first two people she reports informing of her newfound literacy are her husband and her brother, a notable declaration before two male relations of her newly acquired 'gift of power' (Humez 1981: 140).

The rise of higher criticism led to what might be seen as the most radical interactions with biblical texts, insofar as these readings challenged not subordinationist interpretations of Scripture but the status of Scripture itself. Viewing the Bible as 'a set of documents written, transcribed, and redacted under varying historical circumstances by divergent authors and groups' (Wolosky 2002: 193), higher criticism provokes questions concerning authorial intention and historical context. For instance, John Stuart Mill would address Paul's mandates surrounding female subordination in terms of political expediency rather than transcendental truth:

> We are told that St. Paul said, 'Wives, obey your husbands,' but he also said, 'Slaves, obey your masters.' His business was the propagation of Christianity, and it wouldn't help him in that to incite anyone to rebel against existing laws. His acceptance of all social institutions as he found them doesn't express a disapproval of attempts to

improve them at the proper time, any more than his declaration 'The powers that be are ordained by God' implies support for military despotism as the only Christian form of political government. (1869: 85)

The most famous concerted proto-feminist reading of the Bible through the lens of higher criticism was Elizabeth Cady Stanton's *The Woman's Bible*, published between 1895 and 1898. In response to the new revised version of the Bible issued by the Church of England at the end of the century, Stanton, an American suffragist, supervised the arrangement of a volume of biblical criticism written by a committee of women. Stanton argues in the volume's introduction that such a commentary is warranted given the extent to which Scripture was used to justify any number of legal and social restrictions imposed on women: 'Whatever your views may be as to the importance of the proposed work, your political and social degradation are but an outgrowth of your status in the Bible' (1898: 10). Unlike liberal readers of the Bible, Stanton takes no pains to validate the status of the Bible as divinely inspired. Instead, she equates it to any other text, asking, 'Why is it more audacious to review Moses than Blackstone, the Jewish code of laws, than the English system of jurisprudence?' (1898: 10). Stanton's own contributions to the collection often take a higher critical approach, faulting Genesis, for instance, for flaws in scientific reliability raised by contemporary scholars. If Genesis cannot be trusted on the topic of talking serpents, how should it be received on the subject of human nature and gender roles? Other contributors offer critiques of the tenets drawn from biblical figures. For instance, an anonymous contributor to the second volume protests against the traditional Victorian view of the Virgin Mary as a model of ideal female purity, instead arguing that the doctrine of the virgin birth demeans the natural state of motherhood.

Stanton remains a vexed figure in her legacy regarding abolitionism. An abolitionist in her youth, Stanton would later invoke racist stereotypes in her lobbies for women's rights (DuBois and Smith 2007: 3–5). In some cases, her refutation of biblical depictions of women rests on anti-Semitic arguments about the inferior treatment of women under Judaism.

The radicalism of the committee's work led the National American Woman's Suffrage Association to denounce it publicly for fear that it would discredit their campaign. The tensions at the end of the century at the nexus of science, law, gender and Scripture are perhaps metaphorically reflected in the fact that Sue Bridehead would appear in *Jude the Obscure* the same year that the first volume of *The Woman's Bible* was published.

SONS OF MAN

If nineteenth-century women experienced a varied relationship with Scripture, the same can be said for nineteenth-century men. Robert Priest notes that, amid the conflict surrounding the status of Scripture in light of scientific and hermeneutic developments, 'we are accustomed to contrasting the increasing "feminization" of religion with a male-dominated scientific and anticlerical establishment' (2014: 261). Nonetheless, men remained readers of the Bible and turned to it both for validation of and resistance to popular narratives of masculinity.

In Europe, England and America, nineteenth-century masculinity was predominantly conceptualized around what Robert A. Nye calls the 'bourgeois preoccupation with moral discipline, inner values, and with the control of reproduction and sex' (1998: 32). These values of masculine self-control and fortitude contributed to the middle-class doctrine of separate spheres, which allowed men to circulate and operate in the public realm because of their presumed resilience. The feminine sphere of the home remained a haven for husbands and fathers returning from the callous machinations of the market, and the home also represented a justification for the 'labours of the breadwinner, and perhaps even the moral depths to which he must stoop, to maintain his dependents' (Tosh 2007: 34). Although this arrangement afforded numerous freedoms to men that women were denied, it carried with it a spiritualized division of labor that imposed constraints on both parties. In Barbara Taylor's formulation, 'Having confined all those virtues inappropriate within the stock market or boardroom to the hearts of their womenfolk, middle-class men were then left free to indulge in all those unfortunate vices necessary for bourgeois enterprise' (1983: 26). Within such structures, masculinity came to be associated with the acquisitiveness and indifference of the workplace, while femininity represented a spiritualized oasis apart from such tendencies. In addition to the conventional masculinizing of scientific and critical inquiry, then, men were further removed from spirituality by their association with the cruelty of the marketplace.

In England, the mid-century movement of so-called 'muscular Christianity', associated with figures like the Broad Churchmen Frederick Denison Maurice and Charles Kingsley, arose in tandem with the Christian Socialist movement as a means of fostering modes of masculinity that avoided cutthroat self-interest but that also exceeded standard feminized models of spiritual self-abnegation. This movement, exemplified in Thomas Hughes's novel *Tom Brown's School Days* (1857), valorized sportsmanship, courage and even violence in the service of just causes. Part of the project undertaken by figures like Hughes was to resuscitate Christianity from its association with virtues identified with nineteenth-century ideas of femininity, including humility, gentleness and self-sacrifice. To this end, works such as the Reverend S. S. Pugh's *Christian Manliness* would posit interpretations of Scripture that foreground male biblical figures as embodying bourgeois notions of masculinity. Like Grimké, Pugh invokes questions of translation to support his claim, arguing, for instance, that 'the word "meek," by which Moses is designated, is hardly an adequate rendering of the Hebrew, which should rather be "much enduring"' (1866: 117). Importantly, Pugh also frames Jesus as not only a model of self-sacrifice – all too often coded feminine – but also of masculinized strength: 'But we rise above the contemplation of even angelic excellence in him who is yet the example and type of Christian manhood, "the man Christ Jesus." Too often we leave out of sight the element of strength in his character, and associate with our idea of him only the gentler aspects of humanity' (1866: 129).

In 1879 Hughes published *The Manliness of Christ*, which applies the language of masculinity specifically to Jesus. Hughes begins the book with concern over what he sees as the 'underlying belief in the rising generation that Christianity is really responsible for his supposed weakness in its disciples'. He responds that 'the conscience of every man recognizes courage as the foundation of manliness, and manliness as the perfection of human character, and if Christianity runs counter to conscience in this matter . . . Christianity will go to the wall' (1880: 5). The book goes on to argue for Jesus as a model of manliness, deferring to scriptural narratives such as the description of the Crucifixion for evidence: 'Follow Him through that long night: . . . to the final brutalities in the praetorium while the cross is preparing, and the blood which is dripping from the crown of thorns on his brow mingles with that which flows from the wounds of his scourgings – and find, if you can, one momentary sign of terror or of weakness' (1880: 131).

Despite the elaborate imagery of bloody wounds and scourgings, it must be noted that Hughes's depiction of Jesus's manliness rejects certain facets of traditional bourgeois masculinity. A central feature of Hughes's description of Jesus's manliness lies in yielding to authority rather than self-will. Hughes remarks that 'courage can only rise into true manliness when the will is surrendered', and 'that strong Son of God to whom this cry has gone up in our day . . . has left us the secret of his strength in the words, "I am come to do the will of my Father and your Father"' (1880: 33–4). Hughes's conclusion is spent reflecting on the perversions of popular notions of financial 'success', many of which are inherently predicated on exploitation (1880: 137–60). As a model of manhood, Jesus provided a malleable figure by which to imagine new forms of masculinity, even if their contours remain bound by bourgeois patterns.

SEXING SCRIPTURE

Just as liberal and radical nineteenth-century readers came to question standard models of gender that were justified through scriptural reference, so too did they turn a critical eye on conventional modes of bourgeois sexuality. Whereas Victorian opponents of masturbation, prostitution and extramarital sex all sought support in Scripture, George Drysdale's *Elements of Social Science, or Physical, Sexual, and Natural Region* (1854) presented an alternative voice. A medical doctor, Drysdale pointed to the ubiquity of genital and reproductive medical conditions that went untreated because of what he believed to be a culture of shame surrounding sexuality, a shame he traced to biblical influence. After delivering a list of episodes from the Hebrew Bible in which sexual functions are denigrated or made the occasion of violence (including the death of Onan as punishment for masturbation), he notes the misery of the moral code perpetuated by biblical legacy, particularly as it pertains to women (1861: 160–1). Arguing that the institution of marriage is unnatural and destructive, leading to vices like prostitution, Drysdale remarks that the authority of marriage is averred through reference to Scripture and that 'this *divine right* of marriage . . . has rendered most people blind to the evils of the institution' (1861: 373).

Medical discourse of the nineteenth century exhibited great interest in investigating and classifying sexuality, with particular concern for establishing boundaries between so-called normal and abnormal variants. As famously posited by Michel Foucault, the nineteenth century witnessed the rise of terminology demarcating and often pathologizing categories of sexual desires and practices. In 1869, Karl-Maria Kertbeny coined the term '*homosexualität*', a German term that would eventually be translated as 'homosexuality'. A year later, the German psychiatrist Karl Westphal would identify the phenomenon of 'contrary sexual feeling', the moment identified by Foucault as the birth of the category of homosexuality as its own class of identity or sensibility (1978: 43). Psychiatrists and sexologists of the 1880s and 1890s also relied on the notion of 'sexual inversion' as a mode of understanding same-sex desire. At the same time that these categorizations were being created, aestheticism and decadence, artistic and cultural movements celebrating beauty, 'art-for-art's sake', indulgence, and even perversity, arose in response to industrialism and bourgeois moralism. In many cases, medicalized notions of rigid gender and sexual identity categories were challenged or exploded by the work of artists and writers associated with these movements.

Many of the leading aesthetes and decadents, who would by twenty-first-century measures be considered homosexual, demonstrated fascination with biblical iconography, making use of it in ways that proffered new subversive, playful or paradoxical models of sexuality. The biblical figures King David and Jonathan, for instance, whose love is described as 'passing the love of women' (2 Sam. 1.26), provided a shorthand for male same-sex tenderness that Oscar Wilde invoked as an example of the 'Love that dare not speak its name' in his courtroom address during his trial for gross indecency (Roden 2002). The visual artist Simeon Solomon, associated with the Pre-Raphaelite movement, similarly drew on biblical texts in depictions of male intimacy. In the 1860s, Solomon produced a series of sketches based on the Hebrew Bible book, the Song of Songs. The book takes the form of a love poem featuring exchanges between two voices: a bridegroom (often identified with King Solomon) and a bride (often identified as a commoner, sometimes referred to as the Shulamite). Historically, the text has posed interpretive challenges due to its overt eroticism and seemingly secular content; readings dating as far back as Origen have parsed it as an allegory for God's love of the church or the individual soul.

In Solomon's sketches, the heterosexual couple in the text is joined by a third male figure, identified in one title as 'Sad Love', and in another as the 'friend of the bridegroom'. The earlier sketch, dating from 1865, depicts the three figures standing together, with the bridegroom in the centre. Here, the bridegroom is turned towards the bride, their bodies locked in caress, but the right hand of the bridegroom rests on the genitals of the nude male figure of 'Sad Love', pictured with wings and a halo. With its trio of nude and half-nude figures, the image invites a number of readings that challenge compulsory heterosexuality and suggest bisexual or same-sex desires. A later sketch, titled *The Bride, the Bridegroom, and the Friend of the Bridegroom* (1868), also features a trio of figures. In contrast to the earlier image, here the bridegroom turns away from the bride and towards the second male figure, who bows chivalrously to kiss the bridegroom's hand. Although the figures in this sketch are fully clothed, the sketch suggests a freer expression of its underlying male–male desire.

By virtue of their symbolic ambiguity, the sketches present an eroticism that exceeds the attempts at formal categorization visible in the concurrent medical discourse: simple categories of heterosexual or same-sex desire, masculinity and femininity, are troubled. Solomon, himself of Jewish heritage, further clouds conventional methods of classification by interweaving a New Testament reference into his 1868 sketch: John the Baptist refers to himself as the friend of the bridegroom, 'which standeth and heareth him, rejoiceth greatly because of the bridegroom's voice: this my joy therefore is fulfilled' (Jn 3.29). Solomon himself would be publicly disgraced in 1873 after his arrest for attempted sodomy, lending cruel irony to his use of institutional imagery in the service of imagining sexual freedom (Morgan 1996; Paxton 2018: 51–4).

Sexologists also exhibited interest in identifying and classifying modes of 'deviant' sexual behaviour, broadly construed as any non-procreative sex acts or desires. For instance, in 1890 the German psychiatrist Richard von Krafft-Ebing introduced the terms 'sadism' and 'masochism' to denote desires rooted in imposing or receiving pain. Moreover, Krafft-Ebing and others attached gender associations to these impulses, coding sadism as inherently active and male, masochism as passive and female. Again, as such behavioral classes were being imposed by science, they were simultaneously elaborated and undone by poetry.

Algernon Charles Swinburne's 1866 poem 'Dolores' offers an example of the subversive opportunities afforded by biblical iconography. The poem's titular character is a pagan goddess whose tradition has been superseded by Christianity. The bisexual (or, one might propose, pan-sexual) goddess Dolores, 'Our Lady of Pain', might be called a dominatrix, whose lips the speaker describes as 'Curled snakes that are fed from my breast' before he implores her to 'Bite hard' (2000: 122–3). In a reversal of the typical valorization of the

Virgin Mary, the speaker laments the introduction of the virgin as a bland replacement, 'Most fruitful and virginal, holy, / A mother of gods' who has 'hidden and marred and made sad / The fair limbs of the Loves, the fair faces / Of gods that were goodly and glad' (2000: 133). In this formulation, the purity and maternal abundance of Mary, traditionally prized as models of womanhood, become destructive, the 'splendid and sterile Dolores' (2000: 123) representing a more enticing sinister, seductive enjoyment.

In using the Virgin Mary and her pagan alter ego as a representation of potency and even sadism, Swinburne enlists the cultural tensions surrounding the figure of Mary. Mary was commonly seen as a redemptive force for women, meant to compensate for Eve's transgression. At the same time, the Catholic tradition of Mariolatry spurred backlash from Protestants who found the cult of the virgin mother idolatrous. As both a sign of humanity and of womanhood, Mary was meant to represent feminized virtues such as humility and submission; as an immaculate conception, however, she also retained a status that rendered her powerful in her own right. An 1874 poem by the Evangelical writer Eliza Keary invokes this tension in an address to the virgin titled 'A Saint'. In this text, the virgin is addressed as 'Wounded mother of Him', and then beseeched to 'Wound me, slay me, / Sorrow-ridden / Mother of God' (1874: 120–2). Though not associated with the aesthetic or decadent movements, in her remarkable figuration of Mary, Keary fuses the agonistic traits of Swinburne's dual dominatrix and virginal mother, lending subversion and complexity to the biblical figure.

In invoking violent and even potentially sadistic treatment from the virgin mother, the speaker of Keary's poem troubles traditional gender norms, given the association of sadism with masculinity. The speaker is not identified, but one might reasonably assume the speaker is female, given the predominance of female characters and speakers throughout the rest of Keary's volume. The text therefore also makes possible readings of female same-sex desire, a particularly vexed subject in nineteenth-century discourse. Given the two-sex model's assumption that female sexual desire is either absent or decidedly more subdued than male desire, the notion of what would now be termed lesbianism held no currency, particularly in the mid-century high-water point of the bourgeois cult of respectability (Marcus 2007: 6). Despite the lack of specific nomenclature for female same-sex desire, texts like Keary's demonstrate the way that biblical figures, replete with textured layers of cultural associations, become instruments of voicing such desire. Similarly, Sharon Marcus notes that the figure of Jesus would serve as a vehicle for passion within female relationships, with women's homosocial bonds mediated through professed desire for or attachment to Christ (Marcus 2007: 63–5). Such was the case in certain poems by the Catholic converts Edith Cooper and Katharine Bradley, lovers who wrote and published under the pseudonym Michael Field (Roden 2002: 199).

Perhaps the most celebrated subversion of biblical iconography comes at the end of the century in the form of Wilde's play *Salomé* and the accompanying illustrations by Aubrey Beardsley. Salome appears in the gospels of Mark and Matthew, in which she is only referred to as Herodias's daughter, and is said to have demanded the head of John the Baptist in exchange for dancing before King Herod. As an icon of feminine sexuality and subterfuge, Salome became an especially charged character in the nineteenth century as 'the woman question' – concerning women's role in society – took on increased urgency. The 1876 debut in Paris of Gustave Moreau's sensational series of paintings of Salome – depicting Herod's court as a den of Orientalist exoticism and dangerous sexuality – remains a central moment in the century's fascination with the figure.

From this same basis, Wilde crafted a Symbolist text equally dense with Orientalism and depictions of weaponized female sexuality (Townsend 2008: 154–97). At the same time, the complexity of gender and desire in the play is breathtaking, particularly as Salome, an object of near-universal desire, becomes entranced by the one man who does not desire her, Iokannan (John the Baptist). As is perhaps best exemplified in Beardsley's illustrations for the play's 1894 English edition, Salome and Iokannan represent correspondingly disruptive representations of female and male. In one illustration, titled *John and Salome*, the viewer may be excused for initially taking the figure with long, tousled hair and a coy, retiring posture as the princess, and the figure leaning forward, chin jutting beneath what appears to be a horned helmet as the male prophet; in fact, the identity of the figures is the reverse. Similarly, the famous illustration *The Climax* sees Salome holding the prophet's severed head, the locks of which are now decidedly serpentine, rendering the image evocative of Perseus and the head of Medusa. Originally written in French and banned from London theatres because of legal prohibitions against depicting biblical characters onstage, the play premiered in Paris in 1896, after Wilde's trial, conviction and imprisonment for gross indecency. Like Solomon, Wilde would find in art a freedom of play and flexibility that he would be denied in actuality.

With the end of the century came increasingly complex public responses to Scripture. The concurrent rise of scientism and higher criticism increased scepticism and even outright atheism. Simultaneously, interest developed in alternative belief systems like spiritualism, which held its own means of providing women with positions of authority, as in mediumship, and even enabled alternate means of sexual expression. Marlene Tromp observes, 'Spiritualism's assault on the permanence and rigidity of spirit/matter and self/other disrupted other social binaries that were intimately linked to its structure, like those between the mind/body, spiritual/sexual, man/woman, and . . . man/wife' (2003: 70). Despite these challenges to traditional models of gender and heterosexual coupling, the language of spiritualism sometimes drew on biblical accounts as a source of legitimation, as in the 1922 volume *All the Spiritualism of the Christian Bible and the Scripture Directly Opposing It*.

Rising levels of secularism and new modes of belief would subtend social trends and challenges to familial structures that would alarm more conservative sensibilities in the early decades of the twentieth century. What Betty A. DeBerg terms the 'divinized home' – the domestic space endowed with sacredness founded on the doctrine of separate spheres – would become increasingly contested in debates concerning divorce. Rising divorce rates in America would spur a fundamentalist campaign to reinforce what were seen as biblically prescribed norms dating back to Genesis; the conversation reached its height between 1900 and 1920 (2000: 68).

As with the nineteenth century, however, the twentieth century witnessed the Bible speak polyvocally, in the service not only of separate spheres of essentialism but also of playful and provocative expressions of sexuality. Charles Bryant's 1923 silent film version of *Salome*, for instance, styles the titular character – played by bisexual actor Alla Nazimova (also the film's producer) – as an androgynous flapper, features many male characters in drag, and has been called a film 'full of flagrant homosexuality' (Slide 1996: 128). In a further homage to the transgressive original, the set and costume design overtly reference Beardsley's seductive and suggestive Art Nouveau illustrations.

Nineteenth-century defenders of constrictive social, legal and sexual codes – of the kind that would drive Sue Bridehead to tears – would turn to their Bibles for support. Yet, at the same time, those pursuing more flexible gender expression, women's legal and political status and sexual diversity would also turn to Scripture, not only to challenge its authority but also to instrumentalize it in the service of new possibilities. In this sense, the words on the page become meaningful by virtue of their readers. If Jn 1.16 declares that 'the Word was made flesh', the roiling variety of meanings imparted to the Bible over the course of the century denote the many ways in which the flesh – the bodies, genders and sexualities of a changing readership – also made the Word.

REFERENCES

Barker, J. (1855), *Origin and Authority of the Bible: Report of a Public Discussion between Joseph Barker, Esq., and the Rev. Brewin Grant*, Glasgow: Robert Stark.

Barton, S. C. (2009), '"Male and Female He Created Them" (Genesis 1:27): Interpreting Gender after Darwin', in *Reading Genesis after Darwin*, ed. S. C. Barton and D. Wilkinson, 181–202. Oxford: Oxford University Press.

Besant, A. (1882), *Marriage, As It Was, As It Is, and As It Should Be*, 2nd edn, London: Freethought Publishing Company.

Christian Manliness: A Book of Examples and Principles for Young Men (1866), London: Religious Tract Society.

DeBerg, B. A. (2000), *Ungodly Women: Gender and the First Wave of American Fundamentalism*, Macon: Mercer University Press.

Dorsey, B. (2015), '"Making Men What They Should Be": Male Same-Sex Intimacy and Evangelical Religion in Early Nineteenth-Century New England', *Journal of the History of Sexuality*, 24(3): 345–77.

Drysdale, G. (1861), *The Elements of Social Science: Or, Physical, Sexual and Natural Religion*, 4th edn, London: E. Truelove.

DuBois, E. C. and R. C. Smith, eds. (2007), *Elizabeth Cady Stanton, Feminist as Thinker: A Reader in Documents and Essays*, New York: New York University Press.

Duffey, E. B. (1889), *The Relations of the Sexes*. 1876, New York: M. L. Holbrook & Company.

Ellis, S. (1843), *The Wives of England*, London: Fisher, Son & Co.

Foucault, M. (1978), *The History of Sexuality*, Vol. 1, trans. R. Hurley, New York: Pantheon.

Fuchs, E. (2008), 'Reclaiming the Hebrew Bible for Women: The Neoliberal Turn in Contemporary Feminist Scholarship', *Journal of Feminist Studies in Religion*, 24(2): 45–65.

Grimké, S. M. (1838), *Letters on the Equality of the Sexes, and the Condition of Woman*, Boston: Isaac Knapp.

Hale, S. J. (1853), *Woman's Record; or, Sketches of All Distinguished Women from 'The Beginning' Till A.D. 1850*, New York: Harper & Brothers.

Hardy, T. (1999), *Jude the Obscure*, ed. N. Page, New York: Norton.

Hughes, T. (1880), *The Manliness of Christ*. 1879, Boston: Houghton, Osgood and Company.

Humez, J. M., ed. (1981), *Gifts of Power: The Writings of Rebecca Jackson, Black Visionary, Shaker Eldress*, Boston: University of Massachusetts Press.

Illustrated Girl's Own Treasury (1861), London: Ward and Lock.

Jowett, B. (1860), 'On the Interpretation of Scripture', in *Essays and Reviews*, 330–433, London: John W. Parker and Son.

Keary, E. (1874), *Little Seal-Skin and Other Poems*, London: George Bell and Sons.

Kirton, J. W. (1882), *Cheerful Homes, How to Get and Keep Them; or, Counsels to Those about to Marry*, London: Ward, Lock, and Co.

Landels, W. (1859), *Woman's Sphere and Work, Considered in the Light of Scripture: A Book for Young Women*, London: J. Nisbet.

LaPorte, C. (2011), *Victorian Poets and the Changing Bible*, Charlottesville: University of Virginia Press.

Laqueur, T. W. (1992), *Making Sex: Body and Gender from the Greeks to Freud*, Cambridge, MA: Harvard University Press.

Larsen, T. (2009), 'Christina Rossetti, the Decalogue, and Biblical Interpretation', *Journal for the History of Modern Theology*, 16(1): 21–36.

Larsen, T. (2011), *A People of One Book: The Bible and the Victorians*, Oxford: Oxford University Press.

Marcus, S. (2007), *Between Women: Friendship, Desire, and Marriage in Victorian England*, Princeton: Princeton University Press.

Mill, J. S. (1869), *The Subjection of Women*, London: Longmans, Green, Reader, and Dyer.

Morgan, T. (1996), 'Perverse Male Bodies: Simeon Solomon and Algernon Charles Swinburne', in *Outlooks: Lesbian and Gay Sexualities and Victorian Culture*, ed. P. Horne and R. Lewis, 61–85, London: Routledge.

Mott, L. (1850), *Discourse on Woman*, Philadelphia: T.B. Peterson.

Nye, R. A. (1998), *Masculinity and Male Codes of Honor in Modern France*, Berkeley: University of California Press.

Patmore, C. (1863), *The Angel in the House*, 2 vols, London: Macmillan.

Paxton, A. (2018), *Willful Submission: Sado-Erotics and Heavenly Marriage in Victorian Religious Poetry*, Charlottesville: University of Virginia Press.

Priest, R. D. (2014), 'Reading, Writing, and Religion in Nineteenth-Century France: The Popular Reception of Renan's Life of Jesus', *Journal of Modern History*, 86(2): 258–94.

Roden, F. S. (2002), *Same-Sex Desire in Victorian Religious Culture*, New York: Palgrave.

Rossetti, C. (1883), *Letter and Spirit: Notes on the Commandments*, London: Society for Promoting Christian Knowledge.

Rossetti, C. (1997–2004), *Letters of Christina Rossetti*, 4 vols, ed. Anthony H. Harrison, Charlottesville: University of Virginia Press.

Ruskin, J. (1882), *Sesame and Lilies: Three Lectures. 1865*, New York: John Wiley & Sons.

Schroeder, J. A. (2014), *Deborah's Daughters: Gender Politics and Biblical Interpretation*, Oxford: Oxford University Press.

Shanley, M. L. (1993), *Feminism, Marriage, and the Law in Victorian England*, Princeton: Princeton University Press.

Slide, A. (1996), *The Silent Feminists: America's First Women Directors*, Lanham: Scarecrow Press.

Sprague, E. W. (1922), *All the Spiritualism of the Christian Bible and the Scripture Directly Opposing It*, Detroit: E. W. Sprague.

Stanton, E. C. (1898), *The Woman's Bible*, New York: European Publishing Company.

Swinburne, A. (2000), *Poems and Ballads & Atalanta in Calydon*, ed. K. Haynes, Harmondsworth: Penguin.

Taylor, B. (1983), *Eve and the New Jerusalem: Socialism and Feminism in the Nineteenth Century*, London: Virago Press.

Tharu, S. and K. Lalita, eds. (1991), *Women Writing in India: 600 B.C. to the Early Twentieth Century*, New York: Feminist Press at CUNY.

Tosh, J. (2007), *A Man's Place: Masculinity and the Middle-class Home in Victorian England*, New Haven: Yale University Press.

Townsend, J. (2008), 'Staking Salome: The Literary Forefathers and Choreographic Daughters of Oscar Wilde's "Hysterical and Perverted Creature"', in *Oscar Wilde and Modern Culture: The Making of a Legend*, ed. J. Bristow, 154–79, Athens: Ohio University Press.

Tromp, M. (2003), 'Spirited Sexuality: Sex, Marriage, and Victorian Spiritualism', *Victorian Literature and Culture*, 31(1): 67–81.

Vance, N. (2013), *Bible and Novel: Narrative Authority and the Death of God*, Oxford: Oxford University Press.

Wade-Gayles, G., ed. (1995), *My Soul Is a Witness: African-American Women's Spirituality*, Boston: Beacon Press.

Wolosky, S. (2002), 'Women's Bibles: Biblical Interpretation in Nineteenth-Century American Women's Poetry', *Feminist Studies*, 28(1): 191–211.

Woolf, V. (2008), *A Room of One's Own*, ed. Morag Schiach, Oxford: Oxford University Press.

Yacovazzi, C. L. (2013), '"Are You Allowed to Read the Bible in a Convent?": Protestant Perspectives on the Catholic Approach to Scripture in Convent Narratives, 1830–1860', *US Catholic Historian*, 31(3): 23–46.

Zemka, S. (1995), 'The Holy Books of Empire', in *Macropolitics of Nineteenth-Century Literature: Nationalism, Exoticism, Imperialism*, ed. J. Arac and H. Ritvo, 102–37, Durham: Duke University Press.

CHAPTER 8

Popular Culture

SCOTT McLAREN

The sound of gunshots jarred Wadic Shachity from sleep in the early hours of that July morning. As soon as he opened his eyes, he knew something was very wrong. The smell of smoke was unmistakeable. One look out of the window was all it took to confirm his worst fears. Jerusalem was in flames and the lives of all those within its walls were suddenly in grave danger. Pandemonium reigned as hundreds of people – shouting to one another in Arabic, Hebrew and a dozen other languages – rushed into the streets in an effort to escape the blaze. As they did, trunks and other belongings rained down on them as these and other objects were thrown from the open windows above. One such trunk struck Shachity violently on the head, fracturing his skull, just as he was bolting past the Central Hotel ('Fire Panic' 1904: 10). As he fell to the ground and the world darkened around him, he might well have wondered if all this was really happening – and could it be at last God's final judgement on the Old City?

Undoubtedly the fire had been real. No less real were Shachity's grievous injuries. What was not real – or not quite real – was Old Jerusalem itself. Although it certainly looked real and was inhabited by genuine citizens of Jerusalem, the city in which Shachity had fled for his life was a 1:1 scale model of the Old City of Jerusalem that had been constructed by the Jerusalem Exhibit Company for the St. Louis World's Fair in 1904. Occupying an astonishing eleven acres, this New Jerusalem, as the company called it, comprised three hundred separate buildings including the Dome of the Rock, the Wailing Wall, the Church of the Holy Sepulchre and the Tower of David. Fairgoers willing to pay the admission fee of 50 cents were permitted to explore all of the buildings and attractions – the cyclorama of the Crucifixion, the Temple of Solomon, the Bethlehem manger, and the Tomb of Christ – without further charge. All of this was intended not only, in the words of President Theodore Roosevelt, 'to secure prominence to the *religious side* of the world's development in connection with this World's Fair', but also to rake in what the company promised its investors would be 'assured Large Profits' earned from the sale of admission tickets as well as separate food stalls, restaurants and souvenir shops inside the walls (Shamir 2012).

The Jerusalem Exhibit is a towering example of the ways in which the Bible could transform – and be transformed by – nineteenth-century popular culture. Intended to reach a massive audience, the Jerusalem Exhibit complicated the relationship between pilgrim, tourist and fairgoer. Situated in the centre of the fair and directly behind buildings devoted to advances in machinery, electricity, cinema and the automobile, it also subverted the notion that the triumphalist and imperialist nature of world fairs were solely about the future and modernization. At the same time, its spiritual message was thoroughly commercialized by the fair's wider capitalist agenda. Just as importantly, the

Jerusalem Exhibit was a highly curated and sanitized version of the ancient city. Like an expurgated Bible, it not only drew explicit attention to Jerusalem's Christian sites, but also interpreted those sites in ways that were unquestionably Protestant in nature. Meanwhile, the presence of other religions, though not effaced, was largely relegated to the background (Long 2003: 47–70).

By the close of the nineteenth century, thanks in large part to the titanic distribution efforts of the British and Foreign Bible Society (BFBS), the Bible was, by a very wide margin, the most popular book in the world (Howsam and McLaren 2015). But the complex relationship between the Bible and Victorian popular culture had to do with more than simply the number of copies that had been produced and distributed across the globe. In Britain itself, as Timothy Larsen argues, the Bible was more than just a dominant thread in everyday thought and culture – its presence was an inescapable constant in every aspect of Victorian life for believers and unbelievers alike (2012). Across the Atlantic, countless thousands, including many from outside the United States, were drawn to tour the streets of the Jerusalem Exhibit in Missouri by an irresistible desire to see the Bible stir to life before their very eyes. In this there was a kind of nostalgic yearning not only to revisit a faraway land so often read about but also to experience a Jerusalem that no longer – and perhaps never did – really exist: the imagined Jerusalem of the remote past. And yet Victorian popular culture, including those aspects firmly grounded in the Bible and therefore chiefly oriented towards the past, would have been impossible absent the vast and forward-looking changes that had taken place as a result of the industrial and technological innovations that helped create the modern world. Marvels like the Jerusalem Exhibit simply could not have been constructed, nor could the multitudes of fairgoers attended, without access to the latest in railroads, steamships and other new modes of transport and communication. But bringing the Bible to life wasn't cheap. To pay for everything, the Jerusalem Exhibit offered not just a religious experience but a *commodified* religious experience that could be measured in dollars and cents. It cost money to visit. And it cost money to purchase souvenirs. Oh, but how wonderful to own that precious bauble and to later hold it and remember the transformative experience of visiting the New Jerusalem – even after its cardboard and plaster walls had long since been dismantled (Figure 8.1).

Popular culture, at least as we understand it today, is largely an invention of the Victorians. As John Storey argues, while popular culture certainly existed before the nineteenth century, the enormous changes that took place over the course of that century – industrialization, modernization and urbanization – combined to make the production of new forms of culture possible. In the eighteenth century, popular culture, such as it was, revolved chiefly around practices that were communal and local in nature such as theatregoing, public drinking and cockfighting. By contrast, studies of popular culture in the nineteenth century tend to foreground the production and distribution of commodities and commodified forms of culture sometimes described as 'rational recreations' (2016: 2). A significant majority of these 'recreations' were often tied to some aspect of Victorian print culture. This is unsurprising. As the nineteenth century progressed, reading became steadily more commonplace for many reasons: a growing number of people *could* read; advances in printing technologies meant books, periodicals, newspapers and printed ephemera were becoming steadily less expensive; and real wages were on the rise.

None of this is to suggest that drinking, theatregoing and other activities ceased in the nineteenth century, or that people did not write, publish and read books in the eighteenth century. But the emphasis of popular culture underwent a decided shift, first but not only in Britain and America, as new industries and methods of manufacturing took root, populations

FIGURE 8.1: Jerusalem Exhibit, St. Louis World's Fair, 1904. Walls of Jerusalem and the Ferris wheel looking from west restaurant pavilion, Louisiana Purchase Exposition, St. Louis, U.S.A. © Library of Congress.

grew and became more concentrated in urban centres, and a startling array of innovations in the production of print proliferated. And although these innovations did not all come at once – stereotyping, steam and cylinder presses, typesetting machines, the widespread use of manufactured paper, binding machines, the advent chromolithography and photography – their effect on the readers in the market was powerful because it was cumulative. Nor, in the case of the Bible, were these developments seen as accidental. Indeed, as far as the founders of the BFBS were concerned, the advent of stereotyping technologies at just the moment the Society came into existence was nothing short of providential (Howsam and McLaren 2015: 54). In that same spirit, those who believed that the Bible was in danger of becoming marginalized and forgotten as the Victorian media landscape broadened with almost inconceivable rapidity, took every opportunity, leveraged every economy and exploited every technological advance, to place the Bible at the heart of daily life.

Innovations in printing methods and technologies affected not only the Bible but also almost every aspect of Victorian popular culture. The idea of childhood, for example, was reinforced not only by the passage of child labor laws in response to industrialization but also by an explosion of literature – typified by periodicals like *The Boy's Own Magazine* – aimed specifically at this segment of the market. In this way, though Victorians did not invent childhood, they were undoubtedly behind its commodification in ways that continue to be with us today. It is no coincidence that, as childhood became steadily more commodified in the form of books and other products such as children's clothing, children's furniture and children's toys, that publishers of religious literature took note. In response to the emergence of these new markets, a steady stream of new subgenres of biblical literature began to appear including curated and expurgated family bibles, sleek and attractive youth bibles, as well as illustrated and inexpensive thumb bibles. Similarly, although Victorians did not invent the concept of travel, the rise and spread of a tourism industry – and all the ancillary products that come along with that such as travel clothing, luggage and guidebooks – thoroughly commodified that experience as well. This led not only to a rise in trips to the seaside but also to more ambitious peregrinations in the form of pilgrimages and tours to the Holy Land. Tourism of this kind was driven by advances in biblical archaeology and became so popular that Hilton Obenzinger describes it as a kind of 'Holy Land Mania' 1999: 14) – of which the Jerusalem Exhibit itself is an excellent example. Just as importantly, those who could not travel themselves also participated in this rising 'Mania' by purchasing increasingly lavish illustrated tour and guidebooks designed as mementos and proxies for such travel. Indeed, even science itself, particularly those scientific discoveries about the age of the Earth and the origins of humanity that sit at the centre of our historical awareness, did not escape commodification in popular culture. Popular lectures and popular magazines aimed not at scientists, but at the wider reading public, proliferated on all sides of the debate. As this debate raged, moreover, a new generation of agnostics and atheists – the so-called 'Bible Smashers' – brought the fight to the Bible itself as they exploited the same communications technologies to desacralize it and to strip it of its exalted cultural associations, and even its Shakespearean language, in order to bring it down to the level of mere literature. From there, they reasoned, it was just a small step to reimagining the stories in the Bible as little more than fables or fairy tales.

As a book, then, the Bible's place in popular culture was determined not only by religious and cultural beliefs, not only by economic and social conditions, but also by new communications technologies used to convey it as a narrative, to manufacture it as a commodity, and to promote it as a product. The remainder of this chapter will explore how the titanic energy with which Victorians sought to commodify the Bible and the biblical experience helped to make the Bible ever more popular, ever more accessible, and ever more vital to readers and consumers – all at a time when its cultural and religious authority was under siege in unprecedented and discomfiting ways. It was a struggle fought across the pages of countless niche bibles and other publications directly related to the Bible: carefully expurgated family and youth bibles for communal reading in Victorian households, guidebooks and tour books promising to make the Bible and its geography more immediate and vital, as well as comics and penny papers promiscuously distributed in the hope of toppling the Bible from its high pedestal and rendering it merely one book among countless others. What follows below is a consideration of the complex and often reciprocal relationship the Bible bore to wider Victorian popular culture with an emphasis on its mass production and distribution, childhood and family life, travel and tourism and emergent forms of mass media.

MASS PRODUCTION AND DISTRIBUTION

In the year 1800, a destitute girl named Mary Jones embarked barefoot on a twenty-five-mile journey to the town of Bala in Wales to purchase a copy of the Bible in her native Welsh language. Converted to Methodism at the age of eight, Mary Jones had saved her meagre earnings for six years before setting out to make the purchase. But upon her arrival, she discovered that all the copies had already been sold, leaving her devastated and empty-handed. Over the years, the story of Mary and her Bible would be told again and again to an entire generation of children in evangelical households. To this day, it is still credited with inspiring Reverend Thomas Charles, a Calvinist Methodist minister and onetime member of the Society for the Promotion of Christian Knowledge, with establishing the BFBS in 1804. 'I have seen some of them overcome with joy', he wrote in a letter to Joseph Tarn, the assistant secretary of the newly formed BFBS in 1804, 'and burst into tears of thankfulness, on their obtaining possession of a Bible as their own property and for their own use. Young females, in service, have walked over thirty miles to me with only the bare hope of obtaining a Bible each; and returned with more joy and thanksgiving than if they had obtained great spoils' (Jenkins 1908: 2: 518). Although Charles's reference to 'young females' suggests that there may have been many girls in a similar plight, it was after hearing Mary's story that one of Charles's associates, Joseph Hughes, is said to have exclaimed, 'Surely a Society might be formed for the purpose; and if for Wales, why not also for the Empire and the world?' (Howsam 1991: 3). Charles and Hughes were joined by the prominent Anglican abolitionists William Wilberforce and Granville Sharp and together they laid the foundations of a society dedicated to distributing inexpensive copies of the Bible 'without note or comment' in the hope of avoiding doctrinal controversies and encouraging cooperation across denominational lines. And, although their insistence on the Authorized Version (or the King James Version) meant they were obliged to use one of the three presses permitted to print the Bible in England, never before had so many technological affordances been available to make its universal distribution possible (Howsam 1991: 6).

In addition to harnessing the power of the steam engine to run printing presses, perhaps the most useful invention – at least as far as the BFBS founders were concerned – to appear in the earliest years of the nineteenth century was stereotyping. A method pioneered by Johann Muller in Leiden in the early eighteenth century for printing a Bible in Dutch, the technique was not widely deployed until the early nineteenth century when Andrew Wilson set up a foundry in 1802 for the express purpose of creating and supplying printers with stereotype plates. The process involved the creation of a plaster-of-paris mould taken from composed type locked into a forme. A thin layer of lead was then poured into the mould to make a single solid plate. The result was a plate that could be used repeatedly to mass produce identical (or near-identical) copies. And because these plates could be stored between use, it meant that printers were able to avoid time-consuming and costly manual typesetting should a second or subsequent impression be needed. This was especially important for printers and publishers engaged in publishing long books that were composed of stable content: books exactly like the Bible. Another transformative innovation to gain traction in the early years of the nineteenth century was the mechanized production of paper. Prior to the nineteenth century, paper was predominantly produced in individual sheets by hand. The Fourdrinier machine, patented in 1806, revolutionized the papermaking industry by automating the process and producing a continuous sheet of paper. That these remarkable innovations – steam printing, stereotyping and machine-made paper – all appeared at just around the time that Mary Jones was looking for a copy of the Bible in Welsh struck Charles and the other founders of the BFBS as nothing short of divinely ordained (Howsam 1991: 79; Mosley 2009: 185, 191–3, 197–8).

Advances in printing technology during the nineteenth century, however providential they may have seemed to Thomas Charles, impacted more than just the production and dissemination of bibles. These innovations fuelled a wider explosion of print, paving the way for the emergence and proliferation of new forms of cheap literature, revolutionizing the production of religious literature, educational texts, children's books, novels, periodicals and newspapers. Among the most worrying changes in the market, at least as far as those interested in Bible distribution were concerned, was the sudden and huge popularity of cheap serials that, though previously known as 'penny parts', by the middle decades of the nineteenth century were disparagingly referred to as 'penny dreadfuls', 'bloods', and 'shilling shockers' (Brantlinger 1998: 10). These publications, driven solely by a profit motive, sensationalized crime, horror and depravity of all kinds by, at least in the views of some, preying on the public's appetite for titillation and scandal (Brantlinger 2012: 35). Typically eight to sixteen pages long, 'penny dreadfuls' featured eye-catching illustrations and bold headlines designed to capture the attention of potential readers. Sold in markets, railway stations and by street vendors, they were easily accessible to the working class and were often passed around or exchanged among friends. Not only were they ubiquitous; they were also addictive. Often published as running serials with continuous storylines, once hooked, readers were known to eagerly await each new instalment. These were soon followed by 'sensation novels' in the 1860s aimed at, in the censorious words of William Thomson, Archbishop of York, 'exciting in the mind some deep feeling of overwrought interest by the means of some terrible passion or crime' (Ward 2014: 62). Although they anticipated the modern mass-market thriller popular today, reviewers in the nineteenth century deplored them using metaphors of moral corruption, disease and poison. Thus as the nineteenth century progressed, the Victorian reader was menaced by a proliferating number of texts that, far from providing spiritual edification, were, to paraphrase literary critic Patrick Brantlinger, purveyors of filth and excrement, polluters of the minds of the reading public, and befoulers of the national culture (2012: 143). And yet, if Christians hoped to turn people away from these inexpensive forms of exciting and sensationalist literature, they had to do more than merely condemn. They had to provide engaging and inexpensive alternatives.

Despite the fact that the BFBS was responsible for producing what can only be described as a previously unimaginable cataract of bibles – and thus by far the most 'popular' bibles of the Victorian era – the BFBS had a reputation for producing bibles that were cheap and therefore plain. Indeed, when the Society began producing more luxurious editions in the mid-nineteenth century, such as the roan gilt-edged Pearl Bible, there was serious concern that the Society was beginning to *appear* too commercial in its orientation. In a report written for private circulation in 1867, the Reverend J. P. Hewlett, fretted, 'In earlier days the *charitable* nature of our operations was constantly kept before the public. There was an urgent necessity to be met, and it *was* met, sometimes in the way of *direct gift*, more commonly in that of handing over a plain, cheap Bible'. But lately, he lamented, the Society had became more intent on competing with other publishers, allowing percentages, establishing depots and producing 'gilt-edged and clasped Bibles' (Howsam 1991: 197). Founded on the principle of distributing bibles 'without note or comment', the inclusion of introductory materials, notes, or commentaries, to say nothing of elaborate artwork, engravings or other visual embellishments, were all out of the question. This, together with its abiding reluctance to compete directly with others in the trade, meant that, despite its enormous capacity, the BFBS was never going to be able to counter the rising popularity of penny dreadfuls and sensationalist novels. That task would fall to other publishers: publishers who in fact did operate purely commercial houses who were keenly interested in developing new markets while at the same time avoiding the prevailing restrictions on the publication of the Authorized or King James Version of the Bible.

Restrictions concerning who might print the Bible in England extended back to the sixteenth century when, in 1577, Queen Elizabeth granted Christopher Barker an exclusive right to print 'all and singular Bibles and New Testaments whatsoever, in the English tongue or in any other tongue whatsoever, and any translation with or without notes'. It was an extraordinarily broad and exclusive right that was soon extended to also included the presses at the universities of Cambridge and Oxford, as well as selected printers in Wales and Scotland. Although intended to ensure the integrity and accuracy of the text, these patents also conferred on printers an enormous opportunity to make money (Campbell 2011: 148*ff.*). Indeed, that was one of the complaints made against the patent by readers: that it drove up the cost of bibles unreasonably. In part because it was both so broad and so lucrative, the patent was often infringed by other printers, and by the beginning of the nineteenth century even the patent holders had given up on exercising any control over the publication of anything other than the Authorized or King James Version. And yet because earlier translations of the Bible by that time has fallen into almost complete disuse, rival publishers needed to find ways to publish the Authorized translation without flagrantly infringing the patent. One of the earliest strategies developed was to produce illustrated bibles under titles such as 'History of the Bible', or to include vast commentaries along with the biblical text that allowed these printers to argue that they were printing what amounted to something more than or other than simply the Bible (Perry 2018: 25–6; Carpenter 2003: xvi). These strategies helped lay the groundwork for the emergence in the eighteenth century – and its enormous growth in popularity throughout the nineteenth – of what became a true centrepiece of Victorian culture: the family Bible. The family Bible was also a part of a wider trend that witnessed an increasing emphasis on the production of lavish illustrated bibles, and bibles with extensive commentaries, all directed at middle-class readers and a growing number of middle-class families. For publishers, these bibles were especially important, not only because they allowed them to largely sidestep the royal patent, but also because they opened a new way for them to compete with the more attractive, illustrated and enticing, literary texts proliferating on all sides.

The tradition of publishing illustrated bibles in Europe extended as far back as the late fifteenth century when Lucantonio Giunta published an illustrated Italian Bible in Venice in 1490. Throughout the sixteenth century, bibles like this, containing hundreds of narrative woodcuts, were regularly published by printers in Italy, France and Germany. But it was not until the nineteenth century that a series of new techniques for reproducing illustrations, including color illustrations, less expensively and in more detail emerged with such force that some historians have come to call what occurred in that era of printing history an 'illustration revolution' (Twyman 2009). These techniques, some new and others improved, involved the use of woodcuts, copper and steel engravings, lithography, chromolithography and photogravure, and all contributed to a significant progression in the affordability and quality of illustrated books, periodicals and bibles. Woodcuts for printing illustrations continued to be a particularly popular and durable method for producing printed illustrations throughout the century largely because it was relatively inexpensive, the woodblocks were more durable than type, and individual woodcuts could be locked inside the forme alongside type, thus allowing for the easy juxtaposition of images and text on a single page. At the same time, metal engravings became a popular means for reproducing maps and portraits. Steel engraving, which eventually supplanted copper engraving, offered more durability and finer details in the printed image. Lithography, invented by Bavarian playwright Alois Senefelder in 1796, allowed for the production of high-quality images in a remarkably cost-effective manner by drawing an image on a flat stone with a greasy crayon. The ink would only stick where the crayon had been used, allowing the whole stone to be inked and used to print both text and image from a perfectly flat surface. Chromolithography, a colour printing technique that emerged in the 1830s, used the same technique but involved the use of multiple stones each inked in a different color. Finally, photogravure, a photomechanical process invented in the 1850s, enabled the mass reproduction of photographic images with impressive detail and tonal range – a technique that was particularly useful for the production of guidebooks. Collectively, these technologies marked a transformative era in the history of printing, as they led to the production of higher-quality illustrations at increasingly affordable costs.

Although all of these techniques would eventually be used in the production of illustrated bibles, woodcuts remained the most common means for illustrating bibles throughout the whole of the Victorian period. *The Pictorial Bible* was one of the most popular and relatively inexpensive illustrated bibles to appear in the nineteenth century. Published in the 1830s in parts for six pence by Charles Knight, the completed Bible contained hundreds of woodcuts depicting 'historical events' and 'natural history, costume, and antiquities'. The editor, John Kitto, had made two missionary trips to the Middle East and would go on to become one of the century's great popularizers of bible geography. Charles Knight, on the other hand, though also the publisher of the ideologically secular Society for the Diffusion of Useful Knowledge's (SDUK) *Penny Magazine,* decided to pursue this project with Kitto when it was clear the SDUK had no interest in the project. The *Pictorial Bible* was a success and Charles and Kitto also collaborated on the 1839 *The Pictorial History of Palestine* as well as the 1845 *The Pictorial Sunday Book* (Bar-Yosef 2005: 112–13). A few years later, across the Atlantic, one of the century's most famous and luxurious illustrated bibles, the *Illuminated Bible*, was published by Harper and Brothers in New York. Appearing in fifty-four parts between 1843 and 1846, Harper and Brothers decided on an astonishing press run of 50,000 copies per instalment. When complete, the *Illuminated Bible* featured over 1,600 woodcut illustrations by J. A. Adams and J. B. Chapman and set such a high standard for illustrated bibles that some critics even wondered if the illustrations might not distract readers from the biblical text itself (Noll 2022: 314–15). In a testament to its popularity, Harper and Brothers immediately ran another edition of 25,000 copies in 1846 as well as further editions in 1859 and 1866 (Gutjahr 1999: 71). Undoubtedly, however, the artist whose images received the most critical acclaim and the widest dissemination in the nineteenth century is Gustave Doré. Doré's illustrations were first published in France in 1865. Just four years later, the Doré Gallery opened in London and drew some 2.5 million visitors over the next twenty-five years. Doré's illustrations were published in a grand two-volume folio edition by Alfred Mame et fis in France (Schaefer 2021: 1–2). Almost immediately, a large folio edition published by Cassell, Petter and Galpin appeared in sixty-four parts in London between 1866 and 1870 at four shillings each. Both the French and English editions demonstrated just how much atmospheric detail could be captured using wood. Indeed, the ubiquity of Doré's illustrations meant that his depictions became almost synonymous with very idea of illustrated bibles and his influence can be clearly found in the later work of James Tissot, John August Knapp and Barry Moser.

CHILDHOOD AND FAMILY LIFE

But adding illustrations to bibles, however compelling, was of necessity only a part of a wider strategy on the part of publishers to situate the Bible at the heart of Victorian culture and consciousness. The nineteenth century also saw the vast expansion in the market for children's literature as well as bibles aimed specifically at families and women. The increasingly discrete nature of these emergent markets, tied to wider changes in Victorian commerce, technology and culture, became at least as important in helping publishers and religious organizations popularize and commodify the Bible at all levels of society. None of this would have been possible had not the Victorian era witnessed significant transformations in how childhood and families were perceived and understood. Indeed, the emergence of the concept of the 'modern child', one characterized by innocence and a need for protection and guidance from adults, emerged as an integral part of Victorian popular culture largely through the widespread embrace of books and periodicals aimed specifically at young readers (Petzold 2016: 80–2). Rapid industrialization and urbanization in the nineteenth century also played a significant role in shaping the Victorian conception of childhood. The plight of child laborers in factories and mines, exposed by social reformers like Charles Dickens and Elizabeth Barrett Browning, fueled public concern for the welfare of children and led to the introduction of child labor laws and mandatory education. The overall trend in Victorian Britain across the whole of the nineteenth century witnessed a progressive improvement in child labor conditions and education access. Early legislation, such as the Health and Morals of Apprentices Act of 1802 and the Cotton Mills and Factories Act of 1819, focused on limiting working hours and setting age restrictions for child workers in specific industries. Over time, a series of Factory Acts passed in 1833, 1844, 1874 and 1878 progressively covered more industries and workshops, while steadily reducing working hours for children and improving educational provisions. And the advent of compulsory education through the Elementary Education Act (Forster's Education Act) of 1870 and the Free Education Act of 1891 aimed to ensure widespread access to primary education for all children, while subsequent acts raised the school leaving age (Frost 2009: 55–75). A concurrent expansion of the middle class and a growing emphasis on domesticity and the nuclear family helped to situate both the child and the mother as the central figures in family life. Children were increasingly seen as the bedrock upon which family values rested and a source of emotional fulfilment for their parents – a view both reflected and reinforced in popular literature, novels, poetry and bibles produced expressly for children.

Although the origin of children's literature is often traced to the work of John Newbery in the eighteenth century, some of the earliest books designed specifically for children were 'thumb bibles' – bibles in radically abridged form, often with illustrations, and printed in diminutive formats to be held by small hands. Indeed, the earliest such Bible was a versification of selected stories from the Bible by John Weever and printed in London under the title *An Agnus Dei* in 1601. The tradition developed throughout the eighteenth century, a notable example being Elizabeth Newbery's *The Bible In Miniature, or a Concise History of the Old and New Testaments* published in 1780. But the term 'thumb bible' was not finally coined until 1849, by Longman and Co. of London. By that time, the genre has developed considerably, moving beyond the provision of summaries as these bibles sought to inculcate moral lessons couched in engaging narratives drawn from the Scriptures. The emphasis on the innocence and vulnerability of these young readers helped to entrench the growing Victorian understanding of childhood as a distinct phase of life deserving of special attention and care. Stories were specifically selected and framed by writers and publishers to instil a strong sense of religious and moral values in young readers while imparting specific lessons about honesty, obedience, charity and other virtues deemed essential to their social development. Such bibles became the foundation for the most common type of religious educational resources in Britain and America, the locus where many Victorians received their first impression of the Bible, and, as abridged, simplified and illustrated texts, such bibles open a window on evolving Victorian views about religion, pedagogy, the Bible and childhood itself (Dalton 2015).

Undoubtedly – and despite the cataract of bibles pouring forth from the presses of the BFBS, together with the proliferating number of bibles published specifically for children – it is the family Bible that sat at the very centre of Victorian consciousness and that constituted most profoundly the commodification and popularization of the Bible in the nineteenth century. As recent scholars have argued, such bibles were not only read by families: they also read the families that owned them. In other words, just as these bibles were marketed at the Victorian family, they also constructed those families through their uses of notes, illustrations, paratexts, and advertisements. In this way such bibles became a kind of icon of the English, British, and, later, the imperial family. To own a family Bible and to display it in one's home, even before it had been opened, conveyed a message about both the religious and the political loyalties of those belonging to the household. In the process, Victorian men, women and children became national religious consumers whose cultural identities as believers were not only Christian, Protestant or even Anglican – but also, in the words of Mary Carpenter, participants in 'a burgeoning mass market of commercial religious publication and other religious "goods"' (Carpenter 2002: xvi).

Perhaps somewhat paradoxically, the direct forerunner of Victorian 'family' bibles first emerged in the eighteenth century as a distinct new genre aimed not at entire families, but rather exclusively at the paterfamilias or male head of the household. Such bibles were advertised as comprehensive repositories of knowledge, designed to facilitate the acquisition or reinforcement of the owner's status as a gentleman and a respected member of society. Accordingly, the content of these bibles extended beyond purely religious or scholarly material, strategically incorporating illustrations that piqued the interests of the intended male audience. Most intriguing is the fact that these same bibles typically included detailed engravings of women who were notably voluptuous and occasionally even provocative, strongly hinting that the appeal of these texts transcended what were their ostensibly erudite or genteel purpose. As the nineteenth century dawned, however, family bibles underwent a significant transformation as publishers shifted their marketing strategies to target female consumers instead (Carpenter 2002: 6–8). This shift was ultimately rooted in steadily rising rates of female literacy and education as the century progressed but also in the central role women assumed in Victorian families. As women became increasingly literate, they also became more involved in their families' religious education. At the same time, Coventry Patmore's 'Angel of the House' ideal, popularized in his 1854 poem of the same name, gained widespread traction, reinforcing Victorian gender norms that valued women who were submissive, self-sacrificing and devoted to the needs of husbands and children.

Recognizing that Victorian women were assuming primary responsibility for cultivating piety in the home, publishers began to adapt the content and design of their family bibles to cater to female consumers (Figure 8.2). For example, they foregrounded passages focusing on female biblical figures, incorporated moral lessons and included sections for recording family genealogies. Family bibles also helped to construct a dichotomy between the idyllic portrayal of British families – shaped by prevailing imperial and Victorian values – and families that existed beyond the purview of both Christianity and the British Empire. The characterization of British household leaders as benevolent yet firm was starkly contrasted with the portrayal of their foreign counterparts, who were depicted as despotic rulers. Similarly, the depictions of British women and mothers were framed to indicate a higher degree of contentment within their domestic spheres when compared to the allegedly debased women residing in regions beyond the reach of British cultural influence. Publishers also redesigned the bibles to be more visually appealing and elegant, offering attractive bindings and decorative elements that would appeal to what they believed was a uniquely female aesthetic. At the same time, advertising campaigns started to emphasize the role of women as spiritual caretakers, responsible for the religious education of their families. By thus promoting family bibles as essential tools for nurturing family values and religious devotion, publishers effectively tapped into the aspirations of the growing female market, leading to a more prominent role for women in the consumption and use of these texts.

And yet there remained the thorny problem that not all Bible's narratives seemed calculated to shore up Victorian family values. What to do about stories like the ones describing Noah's intoxication after the Flood (Gen. 9.20-27), Lot's incestuous relations with his two daughters (Gen. 19.1-29), the rape, murder and dismemberment of the Levite's concubine (Judges 19), Amnon's rape of his half-sister Tamar (2 Sam. 12.1-22), David's adulterous affair with Bathsheba (2 Sam. 11.1-27), among many others? Of course, none of these stories were included in children's bibles. But in family bibles this became somewhat more challenging, particularly in view of the eighteenth-century tradition that such bibles were comprehensive repositories of knowledge. In response to shifting demographics and the emphasis on female consumers, publishers no longer advertised family bibles as 'repositories of universal knowledge', but instead offered bibles that differentiated the text, so that certain passages liable to cause 'modesty to blush' or that might raise 'any unpleasant and unhallowed thoughts', were printed in smaller type or marked as being appropriate only for the male heads of households to read 'in the closet'. These 'closeted' or 'disciplined' bibles thus disciplined not only the text of the Authorized version but also disciplined the families that owned and read them (Carpenter 2002: 33). The widespread appeal of these bibles, commencing in the nineteenth century, signified a successful segmentation of the Bible into distinct components: sections that could be considered universal, and those that recounted prohibited or deviant behaviors that could potentially incite curiosity among individuals with naïve, feminine, or youthful dispositions – that is, sections suitable for family reading and those reserved exclusively for the perusal of male household heads in private spaces (Carpenter 2002: 35; Brown 2004: 119–20).

The first 'expurgated' or 'disciplined' family Bible published in Britain appeared in 1818 and was edited by Benjamin Boothroyd. Born in Pudsey, Yorkshire, Boothroyd began his career as a weaver, later becoming a minister to a congregation of dissenters. A genuine scholar, he published a two-volume Hebrew Bible between 1810 and 1813 before publishing his expurgated family Bible. Though it marked a turning point for the publication of such bibles, moving away from the idea of a repository of 'universal knowledge' to providing a sacred text intended to be appropriate for all members of the family, it was not universally welcomed. Some critics argued that the removal or alteration of certain passages compromised the integrity of the biblical text and the authority of Scripture. Others voiced concerns that by censoring the Bible, readers might develop a skewed or incomplete understanding of its teachings. Still, Boothroyd's edition gained widespread positive attention and prepared the ground for more of the same. Thomas Williams's *Cottage Bible and Family Expositor*, published in the mid-1820s, is another notable example of a family Bible. Williams went further than Boothroyd, however, separating lengthy genealogies, enumerations of tribes and detailed descriptions of laws

– which he considered 'matters particular to the Jews' – from the main text deemed appropriate for all (Carpenter 2002: 33–4). In his introduction, Williams explained his editorial approach and motivations for expurgation. He aimed to produce a Bible that was less embarrassing for women and children, while also eliminating parts that might provoke boredom or distraction among readers and listeners. By doing so, Williams sought to encourage family Bible reading and religious education while emphasizing the important role women played in moral instruction. And though it, too, provoked some opposition by a few who argued that expurgation on any grounds amounted to meddling with Holy Writ, Williams's *Cottage Bible* found a welcome reception among families across Britain.

TRAVEL AND TOURISM

The ubiquity of the Bible in Victorian society – entire bibles, portions of Scripture, serialized bibles, children's bibles and family bibles – tells only part of the story about its place in nineteenth-century popular culture. As the beginning of this chapter makes clear, the Bible's influence could be felt in virtually all the commodities and commodified forms of popular culture that emerged in the nineteenth century and that were enabled, at least in part, by the technological advances that accompanied the Industrial Revolution. And while the application of steam power, together with innovations in papermaking and stereotyping, undoubtedly transformed the world of communication, so too did the application of steam power to modes of transportation on land and sea transform the popular understanding of work, recreation and travel abroad. Before the advent of the steamship and the locomotive, travel was often only undertaken reluctantly – for business, military service or religious pilgrimages. As travel became steadily less dangerous, less time consuming and less expensive, a distinct new form of travel emerged: tourism. No longer was one limited simply to listening to stories and reading about faraway places. Now, at least for members of the emergent middle class, it was possible to see distant lands with one's own eyes. But to undertake such a journey, even under these more favorable conditions, one had to be sufficiently motivated by what the potential experience might bring. And for a people as steeped in the narratives of the Bible as the Victorians were, there was one place that called to them like no other: the Holy Land.

A deep-seated fascination with the Holy Land among believers and unbelievers alike in the Victorian era did not grow out of exposure to the Bible alone, but also from a vibrant and rapidly expanding publishing enterprise that sought to bring the Holy Land to life on the pages of both books and periodicals aimed at all classes of society. James Silk Buckingham's *Travels in Palestine* (1821), and George Robinson's *Three Years in the East: Being the Substance of a Journal Written during a Tour and Residence in Greece, Egypt, Palestine, Syria, and Turkey, in 1829, 1830, and 1831* are representative examples among a wide variety of popular travelogues that appeared in the first half of the nineteenth century. Unlike Edward Robinson's 1841 influential *Biblical Researches in Palestine, Mount Sinai and Arabia Petraea*, a book that laid the foundations of modern biblical archaeology, the books penned by Buckingham and Robinson were aimed not at scholars but at everyday readers. Both offered vivid descriptions of the region's natural beauty, biblical history and contemporary society couched within engaging and even adventurous narratives. Buckingham in particular was keenly aware that many books of this sort already existed but that Palestine was an inexhaustible source of interest for many reasons, chief among them that it was 'the cradle of our religion, and the scene of all that is venerable in Holy Writ' (1821: vi). Accordingly, Buckingham devoted a considerable portion of his narrative to the description of biblical sites and included a number of 'vignettes' or small woodcut illustrations of the Tomb of Rachel, the Cistern of Solomon, the Holy Sepulchre, Jerusalem as a whole and several others (1821: 212, 224, 246, 259). Robinson's narrative covers much of the same ground in a more desultory fashion, giving the appearance that the author itinerated across these lands almost at happenstance without fear for either 'his person or his purse'. And, in even more detail than Buckingham, Robinson proffered meticulous descriptions (though no woodcuts) of a host of biblical sites in and around Jerusalem (1837: vi, 38–82).

These works and the many others like them helped prepare the ground for more ambitious and costly publishing projects, particularly David Roberts's monumental *The Holy Land, Syria, Idumea, Arabia, Egypt, and Nubia*, a groundbreaking work that captivated the imagination of Victorian Britain by offering an unprecedented visual tour of the sacred sites and landscapes of the Middle East. Published in twenty parts and offered at pricing from a guinea (with cheap covers) to more than £2 for color lithographic plates mounted as originals. Issued between 1842 and 1849, the work counted 634 subscribers – Queen Victorian among them. The monumental publication featured over 120 lithographs based on Roberts's own sketches, which he created during his travels in the region beginning in 1838. Although only a dozen or so of the plates depict actual holy places, those that did achieved an almost iconic status for the remarkable window they opened into the architecture and landscapes of the Middle East. 'Jerusalem from the Mount of Olives', for example, offers a panoramic view of the city of Jerusalem as it existed in the Victorian era, depicting the city's distinctive architecture including the Dome of the Rock and the Church of the Holy Sepulchre, all set against a small collection of human figures in the foreground. Rendered in meticulous detail, this image and others like it allowed the viewer to situate themselves, like those figures, within the sacred landscape and translate abstract biblical texts into a kind of visual guidebook. In another image, 'The Departure of the Israelites', Roberts depicted a large-scale, horizontal composition that captured a dramatic moment with great attention to detail, as a multitude of men, women and children, along with livestock and other belongings set out from the city. Roberts masterfully utilized perspective to convey the vastness of the scene, with the Egyptian city and pyramids in the background, adding a sense of grandeur and historical context to the image. This image not only showcases the artist's technical skill but also highlights the Victorian interest in the geography and topography of the biblical world. Images like these allowed Victorians not only to connect biblical narratives with recognizable landscapes, but also contributed to an emergent genre of Orientalist art which simultaneously romanticized and exoticized the region, often with an emphasis on its biblical significance. As a result, the publication of *The Holy Land, Syria, Idumea, Arabia, Egypt, and Nubia* had a profound impact on Victorian society because it allowed individuals who could not or had not yet travelled to the region a chance to vicariously experience these locales in terms that were at once both visually concrete and tantalizingly exotic. In the process, books like these, even those decidedly humbler and more affordable, all combined to stimulate the Victorian reading public's fascination with Holy Land, a fascination that in time would contribute significantly to Britain's nascent tourism industry (Figure 8.2) (Bar-Yosef 2005: 70, 78, 94–5).

The expansion of the railway network in the mid-nineteenth century played a pivotal role in the development of tourism, allowing for faster, more affordable, and more comfortable travel options. At the same time, the advent of steam-powered ships enabled an emergent industry for international travel, including visits to European countries and the Middle East. The convergence of these transportation innovations created entirely

FIGURE 8.2: Mother and Children Reading the Bible, Library of Congress, 1877. This illustration was published in Philadelphia by Joseph Hoover (1830–1913) as a single chromolithograph sheet in 1877.

new opportunities for travel experiences and fostered a burgeoning interest in both domestic and international exploration. One of the first people to take advantages of these new affordances, not only for himself but for others, was Thomas Cook. A former cabinet maker, Baptist missionary and temperance campaigner, Cook organized his first excursion by special train to transport nearly five-hundred fellow teetotallers from Leicester to Loughborough for a temperance rally in the summer of 1841. One of the primary appeals of Thomas Cook's offerings was the relatively affordable cost of his tours, which made them accessible to a broader segment of the population, including the middle and working classes (Wharton 2006: 181). Initially, Cook's travel business relied on the rapidly expanding railway network in Britain, utilizing steam locomotives to transport passengers to various destinations. But by the 1850s, he was organizing tours to popular European cities such as Paris, as well as Switzerland and Italy, and by the late 1860s, he had even begun to offer tours to the Middle East. Advertising, of course, played a crucial role in the success of Thomas Cook's travel business. The company utilized an array of marketing techniques, including the publication of guidebooks, brochures, posters and newspaper advertisements to promote its tours and services. But, thanks in large part to the widespread distribution of the Bible, as well as a growing number of travelogues like those published by Buckingham, Robinson, Roberts and others, there was already an appetite for the travel to the Holy Land. All Cook needed to do was take advantage of it.

In 1869, shortly after the opening of the Suez Canal, Thomas Cook embarked on his first organized tour to the Holy Land, a Victorian milestone in the popularization of religious tourism. This inaugural journey began with a departure from London, crossing the Channel to France, and then proceeded by train to Marseilles. From there, the group of intrepid travellers boarded a steamer to Alexandria, Egypt, and continued to Jaffa by sea, where they commenced their overland journey through the Holy Land. Over the course of several weeks, Cook's tour covered key religious sites such as Jerusalem, Bethlehem, Nazareth and the Sea of Galilee, providing pilgrims with a putatively unique and immersive experience of the biblical world. Throughout the trip, Cook and his team attended to the practical aspects of the journey, ensuring comfortable accommodations, transportation and safety for the travellers. And yet there was an element of disappointment in all this for at least some travellers. The Jerusalem of the nineteenth century was not the Jerusalem many expected to encounter: the Jerusalem of their imaginings, the celestial city that years of poring over the Bible and even the travelogues had nurtured and sustained. Charles Dudley Warner, for example, noted the strange experience of a 'shoemaker pilgrim' who, before having taken one of Cook's tours, 'gave his Sunday and evenings to a most diligent study of the Bible; and at length extended his reading to other books, commentaries and travels, which bore upon his favourite object'. Completely devoted to the study of both the Bible and the Holy Land, the determined shoemaker saved for some thirty years before finding himself 'in possession of the sum that he could spare for the purchase of a Cook's ticket to the Holy Land'. Alas, it was not as he imagined it would be. But, as Warner remarked, 'the imagination is stronger than the memory' and he foresaw that same shoemaker seated as his bench years later, entirely forgetful of what he had seen with his own eyes, beholding instead 'the kingdoms' of Israel and Judah, 'and not those that Mr. Cook showed him for an hundred pounds' (Figure 8.3) (Warner 1876: 209, 210).

NEW FORMS OF MASS MEDIA

Not everyone had the determination of the 'pilgrim shoemaker' to diligently save money for decades on end. Although Thomas Cook was known for his attempts to make religious tourism as affordable as possible, there were many who could afford neither the time nor the money to make the journey. For those who could not, attempts were soon made to bring the spectacle of the Holy Land to them in the form of panoramas and dioramas. Such attractions, moreover, had one great advantage over the Holy Land itself: these were curated experiences that could be made to satisfy the religious and aesthetic appetites of those who saw them without the trouble of navigating a rush of inconvenient and sometimes jarring changes that had occurred in Palestine across many centuries of intervening history. Ostensibly, this was in the service of faith. But, like publishing and tourism, panoramas and the like were expected to make money (Wharton 2006: 165–7). Fashioned for paying customers who came to them with certain expectations, panoramas were designed to allow viewers to feel as though they were witnessing events firsthand and in such a way that biblical narratives were largely reinforced rather than subverted. In essence, panoramas were enormous cylindrical paintings that depicted an immersive 360-degree view of a landscape or historical event. These were often displayed in purpose-built circular buildings and viewed by walking around a central platform. Sometimes, the paintings were also accompanied by sound effects, music, and narration to enhance the experience. In 1819, after returning from the Middle East, Pierre Prévost opened one of the first panoramas of Jerusalem in Paris. Dioramas, a direct forerunner of the cinema,

FIGURE 8.3: The Thomas Cook office in Jerusalem located just inside the Jaffa gate (*c.* 1890). This poster was published as a color lithograph by John, Riddle, and Couchman & Co., of London, circa 1901.

were also used to bring biblical scenes to life. Composed of painted perspective scenes that were enhanced with lighting and other technical effects, their origins can be traced back to late eighteenth-century London. The Regent Park Diorama, designed and built in the summer of 1823, is one of the first examples from the nineteenth century to demonstrate how such technology could be used. An audience of up to 200 were seated some 30 feet from canvases in a dark circular room. The room itself was built on wheels that allowed the room to be rotated. As the room containing the audience rotated, one of two 'picture rooms' would come into view where lighting was used to create the illusion of depth. While the second room was hidden, the images it contained could be changed. David Roberts's stunning images of the Holy Land, discussed earlier, were among the first to be used in such exhibitions. Interestingly, however, though the immersive dioramas created using Roberts's work were undoubtedly successful from a commercial perspective, it is not clear that Roberts himself was directly involved or that he received any form of compensation for the use of his work (Giebelhausen 2017).

Although panoramas and dioramas were as popular in the United States as they were in Britain, it was in America that things were taken yet one step further. This chapter began with a description of the Jerusalem Exhibit – a life-size recreation of the ancient city – that was part of the St Louis World's Fair. Covering some 11 acres, the Jerusalem Exhibit was carefully designed to provide visitors with a realistic experience of walking through the streets of Jerusalem through the use of careful measurements, scholarship and genuine artefacts. At the same time, the exhibit served a patriotic purpose as well. As Burke Long has noted, 'The elaborate fantasy of Jerusalem as Holy Land . . . lent moral and religious authority . . . to a particular vision of America and her limitless future' (2003: 49). Once inside the city walls, paying customers could tour familiar sites including the Towers of David, the Wailing Wall and the Via Dolorosa. There were also dramatizations of biblical stories, a diorama of the Mount of Olives, and most impressively, a cyclorama made up of narrative murals and wax figures, of the Crucifixion. Souvenirs were also readily available, including an official Souvenir Album that, like the Exhibit itself, embodied a decidedly Protestant approach to the Old City. Accordingly, though visible as part of the Exhibit, the Dome of the Rock and Islam were confined to roles that were purely ornamental. In the same spirit, Catholic shrines cluttered with holy objects were also conspicuous by their absence. And, though the Jerusalem Exhibit was the most elaborate and largest construction of its kind, it was preceded by many other similar exhibits and reconductions on a smaller scale in the nineteenth century. Among the most notable of these was 'Palestine Park', a smaller scale model of Jerusalem and its surroundings constructed in 1874 around Lake Chautauqua – a body of water that conveniently assumed the role of the Mediterranean Sea. Later expanded and reconstructed, children could sail toy boats on the Sea of Galilee while photographers sold stereographs of the miniature landscapes and buildings. The park attracted thousands of visitors each year, and its success led to the creation of similar attractions at other Chautauqua locations across the United States (Long 2003: 28–47). Remarkably, Palestine Park continues to exist today as part of the Chautauqua Institution Historic District.

With a strong appetite to experience visually – either firsthand or through technological proxy – the lands and peoples described in the Bible on both sides of the Atlantic, it is perhaps not surprising that some of the earliest forms of cinema set out to capture these same themes. Cinema also grew in large part out of the public's fascination other forms of immersive entertainment including panoramas, dioramas, cycloramas, peep shows, exhibits and even theatre. Not surprisingly, people were as willing to pay to experience the Bible through film as they were to buy books and reserve tickets to see a play. The first motion picture adaptation of the medieval *Passion Play*, produced in France in 1897, was soon followed by a 1903 production of *Samson and Delilah*. Similar films appeared at a steady rate across Europe for years, especially between 1909 and 1911, until Cecil B. DeMille's silent film *The Ten Commandments*, released in 1923, set a new standard for its sprawling narrative and groundbreaking visual effects. Interestingly, the film straddles

FIGURE 8.4: *The Ten Commandments*, DeMille, 1923 movie poster.

two worlds, juxtaposing the biblical story of Moses and the Ten Commandments with two brothers, Dany and John McTavish, living in 1920s America. In the second half of the film, Dany prospers by living according to the Mosaic law, while John experiences financial and personal ruin as a direct result of his dishonesty and infidelity. John does find redemption in the end, but it comes at the cost of his own life. Today the film's moral tones seem heavy-handed, but DeMille's contemporary audiences were far too enthralled by the visual spectacle to worry overmuch about that. Indeed, DeMille's film was so successful that it set the stage for countless film adaptations of this and other biblical stories in the decades that followed (Figure 8.4).

* * *

The story of the Bible in Victorian popular culture is one marked by an unremitting tension between past and present, faith and commerce, tradition and innovation. The many ways in which the Bible intruded upon, informed and circumscribed the daily lives of Victorians was, as Timothy Larsen notes, inescapable. The BFBS's tireless efforts to translate and distribute the Bible across the world; the emergence and proliferation of niche bibles for children and families; and the commodification of the biblical experience through tourism, panoramas, exhibits and early cinema, all exemplify the many ways in which the Bible affected and was affected by the Victorian era's rapidly changing economic, cultural and technological landscapes. In its own way, the Jerusalem Exhibit at the 1904 St. Louis World's Fair serves as a kind of distillation of this complex interplay between the Bible, technology, consumerism and popular culture on both sides of the Atlantic. On the one hand, the Exhibit appealed to a sense of nostalgia and spiritual longing by recreating the biblical past through an immersive, large-scale representation of the Old City of Jerusalem. On the other hand, it would have been impossible even to imagine had the entrepreneurs behind it not willingly embraced the countless technological advancements needed to bring this imagined and decidedly sanitized version of the biblical past to life. Seen from a distance, the very idea of popular culture, something defined by ephemeral infatuations with disposable products and entertainments, could hardly be further away from a storied and sacred text often thought of as fixed and eternal. And yet, taken together, they reveal in striking ways that perennial human need to anchor ourselves in something that feels enduring while also and paradoxically yearning for novelty and change.

REFERENCES

Bar-Yosef, E. (2005), *The Holy Land in English Culture, 1799–1917*, Oxford: Oxford University Press.

Brantlinger, P. (1998), *The Reading Lesson: The Threat of Mass Literacy in Nineteenth-Century British Fiction*, Indiana: Indiana University Press.

Brown, C. G. (2004). *The Word in the World :Evangelical Writing, Publishing, and Reading in America, 1789–1880*, Chapel Hill, NC: University of North Carolina Press.

Buckingham, J. S. (1821), *Travels in Palestine, Through the Countries of Bashan and Gilead, East of the River Jordan: Including a Visit to the Cities of Geraza and Gamala, in the Decapolis*, London: Longman.

Campbell, G. (2011), *The Bible: The Story of the King James Version*, Oxford: Oxford University Press.
Carpenter, M. W. (2003), *Imperial Bibles, Domestic Bodies : Women, Sexuality, and Religion in the Victorian Market*, Athens, OH: Ohio University Press.
Dalton, R. (2015), *Children's Bibles in America: A Reception History of the Story of Noah's Ark in US Children's Bibles*, New York: Bloomsbury Publishing.
. 'Fire Panic at the World's Fair' (1904), *New York Times*, July 6, 10.
Frost, G. (2009), *Victorian Childhoods*, London: Praeger.
Giebelhausen, M. (2017), *Painting the Bible: Representation of Belief in Mid-Victorian Britain*, Taylor & Francis.
Gutjahr, P. (1999), *An American Bible: A History of the Good Book in the United States, 1777–1880*, Stanford University Press.
Howsam, L. (1991), *Cheap Bibles: Nineteenth-Century Publishing and the British and Foreign Bible Society*, Cambridge: Cambridge University Press.
Howsam, L. and S. McLaren (2015), 'Producing the Text: Production and Distribution of Popular Editions of the Bible', in *New Cambridge History of the Bible. Volume 4: Modernity, Colonialism, and their Successors*, ed. J. Riches, 49–82, Cambridge: Cambridge University Press.
Jenkins, D. (1908), *The Life of the Rev. Thomas Charles, B.A. of Bala*, 3 vols, Denbigh: Llewelyn Jenkins.
Larsen, T. (2012), *A People of the Book: The Bible and the Victorians*, Oxford: Oxford University Press.
Long, B. (2003), *Imagining the Holy Land: Maps, Models, and Fantasy Travels*, Bloomington: Indiana University Press.
Mosley, J. (2009), 'The Technologies of Printing', in *The Cambridge History of the Book in Britain. Volume 5: 1695-1830*, ed. M. F. Suarez and M. L. Turner, 163–99, Cambridge: Cambridge University Press.
Noll, M. (2022), *America's Book: The Rise and Decline of a Bible Civilization, 1794–1911*, Oxford: Oxford University Press.
Obenzinger, H. (1999), *American Palestine: Melville, Twain, and the Holy Land Mania*, Princeton: Princeton University Press.
Perry, S. (2018), *Bible Culture & Authority in the Early United States*, Princeton University Press.
Petzold, J. (2016), 'Inventing the Victorian Boy: S.O. Beeton's The Boy's Own Magazine', in *The Making of English Popular Culture*, ed. J. Storey, 76–89, London: Routledge.
Robinson, G. (1837), *Three Years in the East: Being the Substance of a Journal Written during a Tour and Residence in Greece, Egypt, Palestine, Syria, and Turkey in 1829–1830, 1831, and 1832*, London: Henry Colburn.
Schaefer, S. (2021), *Gustave Doré and the Modern Biblical Imagination*, Oxford: Oxford University Press.
Shamir, M. (2012), 'Back to the Future: The Jerusalem Exhibit at the 1904 St. Louis World's Fair', *Journal of Levantine Studies*, 2(1): 93–113.
Storey, J., ed. (2016), *The Making of English Popular Culture*, London: Routledge.
Turner, W. (1820), *Journal of a Tour in the Levant*, 3 vols, London: John Murray.
Twyman, M. (2009), 'The Illustration Revolution', in *The Cambridge History of the Book in Britain. Volume 6: 1830-1914*, ed. D. McKitterick, 117–43, Cambridge: Cambridge University Press.
Ward, I. (2014), *Sex, Crime and Literature in Victorian England*, Bloomsbury Publishing.
Wharton, A. J. (2006), *Selling Jerusalem: Relics, Replicas, Theme Parks*, Chicago: University of Chicago University Press.

INDEX

abolitionist(s)   38, 44–6, 123, 136–7, 151
Abraham (biblical)   19, 44
Adam (biblical)   38, 46–7, 117, 122–3
Adams, Henry   34
Adams, John Quincy   34
adultery   129, 133, 157
advertising   160–2
Africa   1, 35, 96, 100
African Methodist Episcopal Church   94–7, 105
Agassiz, Louis   113
agnostic(s)   116
agnosticism   116–17, 150
Ahab (biblical)   46
alcoholism   48
Alfred Mame et fils   76, 79, 81, 154
Allen, Richard   95–6
America
    and art   79, 81–4, 88
    and denominationalism   92, 93, 100–1, 103–4
    and entertainment   163–4
    and literature   47–48, 53
    and politics   36–40, 133, 142
    and race   94–7, 123
American Bible Society   37, 76, 100
American Civil War   35, 37, 39, 94, 100–1, 123
American(s), *see also* Black Americans
    feminists   132, 136
    politicians   34
    publishers   154
    theologians   15, 27, 100, 103–4
    writers   45–7, 53
Angelico, Fra (Guido di Pietro)   70, 71
Angels   36, 85
Anglican(s)   8, 14–16, 26, 31, 52, 110, 112–13
Anglicanism   31–2, 137
Anglo-Catholic(s)   23, 57, 133
Anglo-Catholicism   15, 31, 47
Anthony, Susan   3

Anti-Catholicism   37, 102–4, 163
Anti-Christian   117
anti-semitism   137
apocrypha   102
Arnold, Matthew   16, 57–8
atheism   13, 52, 54, 113, 115, 142
atheist(s)   30, 31, 54
atonement   14
Australia   48
autobiography   45
avant-garde   64–5, 84–8

Babylonian Exile   9, 16
Balaam (biblical)   45–6
Balzac, Honoré de   53
Baptist(s)   39, 101, 131, 138, 160
Barker, Thomas Jones   1, 3
Barry, Charles   76
Barth, Karl   19–20
Baudelaire, Charles   57
Baur, Ferdinand Christian   10–11, 14, 17
Beardsley, Aubrey Vincent   142
Beecher, Layman   7
Besant, Annie   133
Bible
    and education   36–40, 45, 94, 103, 155–6
    as literature   16–17, 31, 45, 54, 58, 60, 149–50
    and politics   29–30, 32, 34–40
    production and distribution   2, 75, 100, 103–4, 148, 150–6
    translation   26–7, 35, 92, 100, 103–4, 130, 136
Biblical archaeology   12, 43, 73–6, 150, 158–9
Biblical criticism   5–19, 30, 49, 91, 97–100, 110–12, 120, 129–30, *see also* Higher criticism
    German   8–11, 15, 18, 24–7, 39–40, 43, 53–4, 93, 110
Biblical inerrancy   2, 6–7, 93–4, 100–1, 104–5, 119

Biblical inspiration   6–7, 12–13, 16–17, 27, 53, 54, 99, 116, 137
Biblical typology   44–9, 53, 70–1
Biblicism   2–3, 6–8, 92, 95, 98–100, 103
Bibliolatry   39
Bida, Alexandre   79
Black Americans   45–6, 84, 94–7, 105, 136
Blake, William   66–8
Book of Common Prayer   131
Bradlaugh, Charles   52
Brazil   36
Bridgewater Treatises   113
Briggs, Charles Augustus   100–1
British and Foreign Bible Society   2, 76, 134, 148–9, 151–2, 156
British Association for the Advancement of Science   117
British Museum   73
British Royal Academy   65–8
Broad Church   31–2, 138
Brontë, Charlotte   2, 58, 60
Brown, Ford Maddox   71, 78
Browning, Elizabeth Barrett   47, 155
Bryan, William Jennings   119
Buckingham, James Silk   158–9
Buckland, William   111–13
Burwash, Nathaniel   27, 33
Butler, Josephine   45

Cain (biblical)   57
Caird, Edward   18
Calvinism   16, 57, 97–8, 119–20, 122
Cambridge University   111–12, 153
Canada   27, 33, 35–6, 102, 123
Carlyle, Thomas   45, 47
Carpenter, J. Estlin   91, 104
Cassell & Co.   76, 82, 154
Catholic Church   33, 92, 101–5, 117–18
Catholicism   18, 33, 37, 45, 69, 84, 141
Catholics   12, 17, 23, 28, 36–7, 92, 101–4
Channing, William Ellerty   97–100
Chateaubriand, François-René de   69
Chautauqua Institute   82, 163
Chesnut, Mary   39
childhood   149–50, 155–6
children
    and family life   34, 131, 135, 154–8, 160
    and schools   38, 103
    and labor   2, 155
    and literacy   82
    and literature   51
    and play   163
    and social reform   45, 155
Christ, *see* Jesus Christ
Christendom   19, 33, 35
Christian faith   2, 6–7, 11, 24–5, 28, 99, 113
Christian Social Union   15
Christian socialism   138
Christianity
    early   10–11, 14, 101–3
    and ethics   17–18, 122
    and gender   136–9
    and historicism   28, 58, 91, 116
    and missions   35, 96, 100
    and revelation   13, 91, 97, 99–100, 104–5
Christology   7, 10–11, 19–20, 44
Church and State   30–3, 64
Church, Frederick   84
Church of England   13, 31–2, 137
Church of Jesus Christ of Latter-day Saints   92
Church of Scotland   12, 33
Cinema   163–5
Cole, Thomas   84
Colenso, John William   26, 32–3, 35
Coleridge, Samuel Taylor   93
Collins, Wilkie   47
colonialism   1, 3–4, 23, 35, 44, 48, 73, 134, 135
Congregationalism   97, 100
Conrad, Joseph   48
Conselheiro, Antonio   36
Conversionism, evangelical   43, 95–6, 136
Cook, Thomas   160–2
copyright   82
Corelli, Marie   52
Corinthians, biblical books of 1 and 2   37
Council of Trent   101–2
Courbet, Gustave   65, 84
Cranach, Lucas   70
creation (biblical)   110, 116–17, 123, 130–1
Cuvier, Georges   109

Dalziel Brothers   78–9
Daniel (biblical)   73
Daniel, biblical book of   73, 82–3
Dante   69, 76
Darwin, Charles   2, 31–2, 110, 115–19, 121
Darwinism   27, 93–4, 115–16, 119–20
David (biblical)   9, 44, 139–40, 157
David, Jacques-Louis   69

INDEX

De Wette, Wilhelm Martin Leberecht   9–10, 98
death   40, 58, 65, 112
Deborah (biblical)   46
deism   5, 24, 116
Delacroix, Eugène   69, 76
DeMille, Cecil B.   76, 88, 163–5
denominationalism   92–3
Dickens, Charles   3, 43, 47, 51, 60, 155
Dickinson, Emily   46
Disraeli, Behjamin   44
Dissenters   26, 157
divorce   129, 133, 142
Doré, Gustave   50, 76–7, 154
Dostoyevsky, Fyodor   44, 54
Douglass, Federick   95–6
Driver, Samuel   122
Duffey, Eliza   131
Durand, Godefroy   79–80
Dürer, Albrecht   70–1
Dutch Reformed Church   63

Eakins, Thomas   84
East India Company   134
ecclesiology   18
Eden, Garden of   48, 122, 132
Edersheim, Alfred   51
education   23, 99, 103, 133, 135, 155–6
Egypt   73
Eliot, George (Mary Anne Evans)   31, 47–8
Elizabeth I, Queen   153
Ellis, Sarah Stickney   132
Emerson, Ralph Waldo   16, 98–9
enlightenment   8–10, 65, 85, 92, 131
Ephesians, biblical book of   94, 131
eschatology   18–19, 24, 36, 40
Eucharist   47
Evangelicalism   95, 100, 111–12, 130, 135
Evangelicals   17, 19, 112, 133, 141, 151
Eve (biblical)
   in art   70
   and gender   130–2
   in literature   46–7
   and Original Sin   122, 135–6
   and race   123
Exodus, biblical book of   68–9, 94
exoticism   74, 141, 159
Eyck, Jan van   72

fall (biblical), *see* original sin
Farrar, Frederic William   51

Feminism   46, 95–6
First Vatican Council   102
Flandrin, Hippolyte   69, 71
Flaubert, Gustave   51, 53
flood (biblical)   110–11, 113, 123, 157
France   65, 69–70, 133
France, Anatole   52–3
Francis of Assisi   44
Free Church of Scotland   14
freethinker(s)   133–4
Frei, Hans   5–6
French Realism   84–7
French Revolution   8, 66
Frith, Francis   74
fundamentalism   123, 125, 142
Fuseli, Henry   69–70

Gaskell, Elizabeth   44, 47
Gauguin, Paul   85, 87
Gaussen, Louis   7
Geikie, John Cunningham   51
gender   130–4, 137, 139–42, 156–7
Genesis, biblical book of
   and evolution   122–3
   and fossils   110–11
   and gender   130, 134–7, 142
   and morality   125
   and race   123
   and time   93
Geneva   7
George III, King   66
Germany   8–14, 27, 39–40, 54, 110
Gethsemane, garden of   138
Gibbon, Edward   8
Gillray, James   66
Giotto di Bondone   71
Gladstone, William   43
Gogh, Vincent van   63–4
Goncharova, Natalia   86–8
Gospel   44
Gospels   11, 14–19, 24–30, 49, 52–4, 98–9
Gosse, Edmund   45
Great War   20, 23, 39–40, 87
Greek   14
Grimké, Sarah Moore   136, 138

Hale, Sarah Joseph   134–5
Hardy, Thomas   48, 129, 137
Harper and Brothers   154
Harvard University   98–9
Hawthorne, Nathanial   46–7
Hebrew   9, 15–16

Hegel, Georg Wilhelm Friedrich   9–11, 25, 29–30, 39
Heresy   31, 33, 100, 110
Herod (biblical)   141
higher criticism   2, 24–9, 39, 93, 136–7, 142
Historical Jesus   10–11, 24–34, 49–54, 73, 79
historicism   5–20, 23–34, 53–4, 73–5, 104–5, 109–12
Hodge, Charles   101
Holy Land   12, 73–6, 79, 82, 84, 150, 158–63
Holy Spirit (or Ghost)   7, 15, 98
homosexuality   139–42
Hopkins, Gerard Manley   57
Hort, Fenton John Anthony   14
Hughes, Thomas   138–9
Hugo, Victor   44
Huxley, Thomas Henry   117

iconoclasm   82
idolatry   15–16
Ignatius of Antioch   14
Impressionism   63, 84–5
incest   133, 157
India   35, 54, 57, 100, 134, 135
indigenous peoples   3–4, 36
Industrial Revolution   2, 158
Ingres, Jean-Auguste-Dominique   69–71
Isaiah (biblical)   63
Isaiah, biblical book of   16–17, 63
Ishmael (biblical)   46
Islam   163
Israel   45
Israelites   15–16, 45, 73

Jacob (biblical)   85
Jameson, Anna   47
Jerusalem   71, 75, 148, 159, 161–2
Jerusalem Exhibit   82, 147–50, 161, 163, 165
Jesus Christ, *see also* Historical Jesus
  biographical treatment   28–9, 49–57
  Crucifixion   69, 79, 138, 163
  and divinity   15
  and gender   138–9
  and humanity   14, 54, 79
  incarnation   14–15, 54, 58, 143
  as Jewish   11
  as messiah   10, 19
  and race   73, 97
  resurrection   24, 58, 96
  teachings of   13, 53–4
  and typology   44–9
Jews   7, 92, 120, 122, 134, 139, 158
Joachim of Fiore   15
Job (biblical)   39, 57
Job, biblical book of   16, 39, 66–7
John, biblical Gospel of   6, 11, 14–15, 47, 143
John the Baptist (biblical)   140–2
Jowett, Benjamin   26, 31, 58, 129–30
Joyce, James   48
Judaism   49, 58, 117, 120, 122–3, 130, 137

Kabbalah   120, 125
Kandinsky, Vassily   87–8
Kingsley, Charles   44, 138
Knight, Charles   154

labor rights   3
Laplace, Pierre-Simon   115
Laqueur Thomas   131
Latin   102–4
Lee, Jarena   95–6
Leighton, Frederic   78
Leo XIII, pope   12
Leviticus, biblical book of   3
liberalism, theological   98
liberals, theological   7–8, 18–20, 98–100, 110–11, 125
Lightfoot, Joseph Barber   14
Lincoln, Abraham   37
literacy   2, 82, 94–7, 99, 136, 148–9, 156, 160
lithography   76, 151, 153–4
Loisy, Alfred   18
London   7, 35, 76, 79, 154, 162
Longman and Co.   155
Luke, biblical Gospel of   36, 47
Luther, Martin   12, 92
Lutheranism   16, 18
Lyell, Charles   130

magic lantern   75, 82–3, 88
Manet, Édouard   63, 84–5
Mark, biblical Gospel of   141
marriage.   46, 129, 131–4, 139
Martin, John   73
Martineau, Harriet   52
Marx, Karl   25

INDEX

Marxism 53
Mary Magdalene (biblical) 57
Mary, mother of Jesus (biblical)
    and femininity 71–2, 84, 135,
      140–1
    and motherhood 3, 47–8, 72
    and sentimentalism 28–9
    and typology 44, 47–8
masturbation 139
materialism 13, 115, 120
Matthew, Biblical Gospel of 13, 36, 37, 44, 95, 141
Maurice, Frederick Denison 138
Melchizedek (biblical) 28
Melville, Herman 46
Methodism 31, 33, 94–7, 100
methodist(s) 26–7, 33, 94–7, 111–12, 151, 153–4
Mill, John Stuart 45, 136–7
Millais, John Everett 3, 48, 71, 78
millennialism 8, 18–19, 36, 40, 82
Millerites 36, 82
Milton, John 69, 110–11
miracles 24–5, 27, 33, 53, 79, 99, 117
Monet, Jean-Baptiste Pierre Antoine de, chevalier de Lamarck 125
More, Hannah 47
Moreau, Gustave 141
Mosaic Law 16, 36, 137
Moses (biblical) 9, 12, 26, 44–6, 73, 97, 138
Motherhood 47, 57, 72, 131–2, 135, 137, 154–7
Mott, Lucretia 134–5
Muscular Christianity 137–9
myth 9–10, 26, 52, 54, 65

Napoleon, Bonaparte 73
Napoleon III 28, 33
Natural law 113, 115
Natural theology 110, 113, 115–17, 120, 122
Nazarenes (Brotherhood of St Luke) 70–1, 77–8, 84
Neander, August 12–13, 15
Nebuchadnezzar (biblical) 73
Neoclassicism 69, 70
Nevin, John Williamson 15
New Testament 9–11, 14–16, 44–5, 79
New York City 12, 37, 84
New Zeland 112

Newbery, Elizabeth 155
Newman, John Henry 17, 45
Nietzsche, Friedrich 20, 27–8
Nightingale, Florence 45, 47
Noah (biblical) 37, 122, 157
Norton, Andrews 98–100
Notovitch, Nicholas 54, 57
Numbers, biblical book of 45, 123

Old Testament 7, 9–10, 15–16, 26, 44–5
Origen 140
Original Sin 119–22, 131, 135, 136, 141
Orsel, Victor 69–70
Orthodox Church 57
Overbeck, Friedrich 70–1, 76
Oxford Movement 7, 47
Oxford University 13, 111–12, 153

Palestine 49
panoramas 82, 84, 161–3
papal infallibility 102–3, 105
parables (biblical) 12–13
Paris 63, 69, 84, 141, 160, 161
Parker, Theodore 27, 33, 37, 99
Parkes, Joseph 31, 51
Parousia (Second Coming) 8, 40
Patmore, Coventry 131, 135, 156
Paul (biblical) 14, 19, 39, 110, 131, 136–7
Payne, Daniel Alexander 97
Penny Dreadfuls 150, 151–2
Pentateuch 9, 15, 26
Peter (biblical) 57
Pfleiderer, Otto 16
Pforr, Franz 71–2
Philadelphia 37
Philo of Alexandria 130
photography 12, 73–4, 82
photogravure 153–4
picturesque 74
Pietism 7
Plagues of Egypt (biblical) 68–9, 73
Plato 13, 130
Polycarp, bishop 14
polygenesis 123
Pontius Pilate 53
Preadamists 123–4
Pre-Raphaelite Brotherhood 71–2, 78, 84, 140
Presbyterian(s) 7, 8, 26–7
Presbyterianism 33, 100–1
Price, George McCready 123, 125
Princeton Theological Seminary 16, 101

prostitution 52, 139
Protestantism 37, 82, 92–3, 99
Psalms, biblical book of 16, 35, 40, 57, 96
Pugh, Samuel Sargent 138
Pusey, Edward Bouverie 7, 16

Quakers 136

railways 159–61
rape 47, 157
Raphael (Raffaello Sanzio da Urbino) 69, 75
reformation 30
Reimarus, Hermann Samuel 24–5
Religious Tract Society 112
renaissance 5, 9, 63, 69–71, 79, 153
Renan, Ernest 13, 28–9, 33–4, 49–51, 57, 79
Revelation, biblical book of 36, 65, 69, 82–3, 87–8
revivalism 95, 100
revivalism, evangelical 6–8, 13, 15, 95, 135
Riel, Louis 36
Ritschl, Albrecht 17–19
Roberts, David 73–4, 76, 159–60, 163
Robinson, Edward 12, 158–9
Roman Catholic, *see* Catholic
Romans, biblical book of 3, 19, 110
Romanticism 66, 69–70, 72–3, 85, 93, 112
Roosevelt, Theodore 147
Rossetti, Christina 47, 57, 133–5
Rossetti, Dante Gabriel 71
Ruskin, John 45, 135
Russia 44, 54, 57, 86–8
Rydberg, Viktor 13

sadism 140–1
Saïd, Edward 73
Sallman, Walter 79
Salzmann, Auguste 74–5
Satan 39, 40, 57, 67
scepticism 64, 74–5, 116, 129, 142
Schaff, Philip 15, 17
Schelling, Friedrich Wilhelm Joseph 9, 15
Schleiermacher, Friedrich 9–12, 17
Schnorr von Carlsfeld, Julius 77–9, 82
Schweitzer, Albert 19–20, 25, 28–9, 33–4, 79
Scopes trial 119
Scottish Common Sense Realism 93, 101
secularism 18, 35–6, 43–5, 142
Seeley, John Robert 26, 32, 51

Sermon on the Mount 11
Seventh-Day Adventists 82, 123
sexuality 47, 58, 130, 132, 135, 139–43
Shakespeare, William 69
Sheldon, Charles Monroe 53
Shelley, Mary 47
slavery 37–9, 44–6, 94–5, 101, 123, 133, 136
Slavery Abolition Act 1
Smith, Joseph 92
Smith, William Robertson 14
Society for the Conversion of Negro Slaves 94
Society for the Diffusion of Useful Knowledge 154
Society for the Promotion of Christian Knowledge 151
Sojourner Truth 136
Sola Scriptura 92, 101, 129
Solomon (biblical) 9, 140
Song of Solomon (Song of Songs), biblical book of 46, 140
South Africa 32, 35
Sparks, Jared 97
spiritualism 142
St. Louis World's Fair 82, 147–9, 163
Stanley, Arthur Penrhyn 16
Stanton, Elizabeth Cady 3, 137
Stowe, Harriet Beecher 44, 46
Strachey, Lytton 23
Strauss, David Friedrich 10–11, 24–34, 49–50, 57, 79
sublime 68–9
Suez Canal 161
suffrage, women's 46, 133, 135, 137
sunday schools 49, 82
supernaturalism 7–10, 12–14, 27, 66, 99
Swinburne, Algernon Charles 140–1

Tanner, Henry Ossawa 84
temperance 133, 160
Tennyson, Alfred 57
Thailand 100
thermodynamics 119–20
Thessalonians, biblical books of 1 and 2
Thomson, William 119
Thumb bibles 155–6
Timothy, biblical books of 1 and 2 3 39, 131
Tissot, James 51, 79–80, 82, 154
Titian (Tiziano Vecellio) 69
Tolstoy, Leo 44
Torah 92, 120, 122
tourism 74, 150, 158–61

INDEX

Tractarianism 7, 47
Transcendental Unitarians 99
transcendentalism 97
Trinity 7
Tübingen Stift 10, 16, 17, 25, 29
Turner, Joseph 68–9, 76
Twain, Mark (Samuel Clemens) 46

Union Theological Seminary 15
Unitarian(s) 27, 33, 91, 104
Unitarianism 33, 97–100

Victoria, Queen 1, 35, 159
von Harnak, Adolf 18
Vulgate 102–3, 105

Wallace, Alfred Russel 116
Wallace, Lee 52

Ward, Mary Augusta 43, 52–3, 58
Wellhausen, Julius 15–16
Wesleyan(s) 27
West Africa Squadron 1
West, Benjamin 65–6
Westcott, Brooke Foss 14
Westminster Confession of Faith 27
Whewell, William 113
Wilberforce, Samuel 117
Wilberforce, William 151
Wilde, Oscar 51–2, 140–2
Women's Rights 3, 45–7, 95–6, 129–37, 142–3
Woolf, Virginia 129

Zola, Émile 63
Zurich 30–1
Zwingli, Huldrych 30

www.ingramcontent.com/pod-product-compliance
Lightning Source LLC
Chambersburg PA
CBHW081821300426
44116CB00014B/2436